BURT FRANKLIN: RESEARCH & SOURCE WORKS SERIES 595
American Classics in History & Social Science 157

THE CORRESPONDENCE AND PUBLIC PAPERS

OF

JOHN JAY

VOL. I.

1763–1781

THE CORRESPONDENCE AND PUBLIC PAPERS

OF

JOHN JAY

FIRST CHIEF-JUSTICE OF THE UNITED STATES, MEMBER AND PRESIDENT OF THE
CONTINENTAL CONGRESS, MINISTER TO SPAIN, MEMBER OF COMMISSION
TO NEGOTIATE TREATY OF INDEPENDENCE, ENVOY TO GREAT
BRITAIN, GOVERNOR OF NEW YORK, ETC.

1763-1781

EDITED BY

HENRY P. JOHNSTON, A.M.

VOL. I.

BURT FRANKLIN
NEW YORK

308
卐331C
v.1

Published by LENOX HILL Pub. & Dist. Co. (Burt Franklin)
235 East 44th St., New York, N.Y. 10017
Originally Published: 1890
Reprinted: 1970
Printed in the U.S.A.

S.B.N.: 8337-18479
Library of Congress Card Catalog No.: 73-140983
Burt Franklin: Research and Source Works Series 595
American Classics in History and Social Science 157

Reprinted from the original edition in the University of Illinois
Library at Urbana.

PREFACE.

JOHN JAY's public services extended over and beyond the formative period of our national life—from 1774 to 1801. During those twenty-seven years he devoted himself to varied important duties with a zeal, fidelity, ability, and success that from the beginning of his career entitled him to rank with the distinguished fathers of the Republic and framers of its Constitutional system. The several official positions he occupied called out his talents and energies in four directions. First, he promoted the general interests of the Colonies during the early years of the Revolutionary struggle, in serving at intervals from 1774 to 1779 as delegate in the Continental Congress. Again, as Minister or Envoy, at different periods, to Spain, France, and Great Britain, he rendered perhaps his most conspicuous service to the country. Again, as Chief-Justice, both of his own State and of the United States, he impressed grand juries and all concerned with the necessity of encouraging a profound respect for law and constitutions in the new order of things, and at the outset, through his own personal dignity and integrity, gave character to our highest courts since traditionally preserved. And again, in his native

v

State of New York, he proved himself invaluable as a member of Provincial bodies and committees in providing the sinews of war, in suppressing conspiracies, in drafting laws, in organizing the machinery of the new State, in urging, through the "Federalist" and in the New York Convention, the adoption of our common Constitution, and finally, in twice filling the office of Governor. As Congressman, diplomatist, jurist, and State leader, seeking in each sphere of action to secure substantial results without display or effect, he was pre-eminently a man for his times. Perhaps, also, as nearly as any one in our civil history, he filled the ideal of a public servant.

The first "Life" of Jay was published in 1833. This work, issued in two volumes, one of which was devoted to sections from his correspondence, was edited by William Jay, son of John Jay, and ranks as a standard contribution to our historical literature. For many years, however, it has been out of print, and practically inaccessible except in libraries. Other biographies have since appeared, the latest of which, published in the current year, and edited by Mr. George Pellew, is a re-study from the Jay papers and other authoritative sources.

To meet the need of a purely documentary edition the present set of four volumes has been prepared upon the plan of the writings of Washington, Franklin, Jefferson, Adams, Hamilton, and others. This change and expansion provides for the addition of numerous letters and documents from the Jay correspondence not published in the volumes of 1833.

Jay's papers were voluminous, and the greater portion have been carefully preserved by his immediate descendants and in public and private collections. What can be said of but few of his contemporaries, he retained with his own drafts most of the personal or semi-official letters written to him during a period of nearly half a century, many of which, received from eminent and observing men, throw those side-lights upon affairs and social and political life in general so much sought and prized by students of American history to-day. As the correspondence of this description supplements and explains much that Jay himself wrote, a considerable number of new selections have been introduced into, and constitute a feature of, the present edition. The principal space is allotted, necessarily, to Jay's own writings.

By courtesy of the Hon. John Jay, the fine collection of Jay papers in his possession has been placed in the hands of the publishers and editor for the preparation of this work. It should also be said that the labor of examination and selection has been greatly relieved by an exhaustive and critical index and analysis of the papers arranged by Miss Ruth Putnam.

Some selections have been made from other manuscript sources and from printed works.

HENRY P. JOHNSTON.

NEW YORK CITY, *June*, 1890.

CONTENTS OF VOLUME I.

CORRESPONDENCE AND PUBLIC PAPERS

OF

JOHN JAY.

TO JAY FROM HIS FATHER.

DEAR JOHNNY:

Your observation on yᵉ Study of yᵉ Law, I believe, is very just, and as its your inclination to be of that Profession, I hope you 'll closely attend to it with a firm resolution that no difficulties in prosecuting that Study shall discourage you from applying very close to it, and if possible, from taking a delight in it.—The dictionary you 've bought is doubtless necessary for you, but as to other Books, I suppose you have them in yᵉ College, or doubtless on application to your uncle or Aunt Chambers, they would let you have yᵉ reading of such of his Books as you may want. It 's paying very dear for them to buy them at York. I 'm glad you 've wrote to Doctʳ: Johnson. We all remember our love to you & I always am

Dear Johnny

Yʳ. affec. Father

PETER JAY.[1]

Augᵗ· 23ᵈ, 1763.
[Rye, N. Y.]

---

[1] This letter, indicating the time when Jay made choice of the legal profession, is the earliest of any special personal interest found among his papers. He was then in his nineteenth year, a student in the Senior Class at King's, now Columbia, College, where he graduated with the highest honors in 1764. His father, Peter Jay, member of a well-known Huguenot family in New York City and a successful merchant there, appears to have followed his youthful course with keen interest and at a later date sympathized with and encouraged him in his public attitude. The Jay homestead was, at this time, at Rye, N. Y., the family having removed from the city in 1746.

TO JAY FROM HIS FATHER.

DEAR JOHNNY: RYE, 16 January, 1764.

.   .   .   .

Seal the inclosed before you deliv^r: it to Mr. Kissam and you may conclude an agreem^t. with him vizt : [1]

To pay him £200 when the time of your being with him commences, that is, immediately after your passing your Degrees at College in May next, tho' perhaps he will not require y^e whole sum to be then paid, & be satisfied to have it in two paym$^{ts.}$; but leave that to himself to do therein as he chuses.

To engage for 5 years if his agreem^t: with y^e Lawyers don't allow less, but that you shall be at Liberty to apply the two last to y^e study of y^e Law and attend y^e office occasionally so as to be no hindrance to your study and to which I believe M^r· Kissam can have no objection, considering ye sum he requires.

If you should immediately proceed to articles of agreem^t: it will be necessary to have it inserted that if either of you should dye before the time of your being with him commences, that in that case the whole agreem^t: shall be void, as it would not be reasonable that ye money should be paid.

On the whole you must agree in ye best manner you can, but I would observe that in case ye Lawyers do soon come to another agreem^t: (in consequence of some not approvg: ye last made by Mr. Kissam & others) whereby a less sum than £200 is to be required, it will then be reasonable that Mr. Kissam do lower his demand accordingly. . . .

I am, Dear Johnny Y^r· affect^e· Father

PETER JAY.

---

[1] Upon graduation in May, of this year, Jay entered the law office of Benjamin Kissam, Esq., a prominent member of the bar at New York, and was himself admitted to practice in 1768. John Adams, as he passed through the city on his way to Philadelphia in August, 1774, wrote in his diary, commenting on men and measures : "Mr. Jay is a young gentleman of about twenty-six ; Mr. Scott says, a hard student and a good speaker."

BENJAMIN KISSAM TO JAY.

DEAR JAY :[1]

I have been strongly sollicited to take a Jaunt with Mr. Inglis to Philadelphia, and he proposes to set off on Tuesday next. I have consented to go provided my horse is well, and news of the Repeal of the Stamp Act should not arrive in the mean time.

Will you then be good enough to send my Horse down by a careful hand, if he is fit to go the Journey. As upon the Repeal of the Stamp Act, we shall doubtless have a Luxuriant Harvest of Law, I would not willingly, after the long Famine we have had, miss reaping my part of the crop. Should this news arrive in my absence, I shall upon hearing it, immediately return, and as soon as it reaches you I beg you 'll come down and be ready to secure all Business that offers. Mr. Hicks will give you any assistance you may want, in case any thing difficult should turn up.[2] Make my Compl[ts]: to Mr. & Mrs. Jay & all the Family—

I am your affectionate
B : KISSAM.

25 April, 1766.

To Mr. John Jay
near Rye

---

[1] See preceding letter and note.

[2] On the following day, April 26th, Kissam wrote again to Jay : " We were last night strangely deluded with a mistaken account of the Repeal of the Stamp Act, and all the Bells have been ringing since Break of Day. Upon inquiry we find that the intelligence amounts to no more than that the Bill had passed the House of Commons on the 28 of Feb.[y] and was to be sent up to the Lords on the 3[d] March. There is indeed a Letter dated at Falmouth on the 5th of March which says the Stamp Act is repealed, but this can be no more than its having passed the House of Commons, which we find they commonly call a Repeal."

JAY TO BENJAMIN KISSAM.

NEW-YORK, 12th August, 1766.

DEAR SIR :[1]

To tell you that I often find myself at a loss for something to say, would be telling you nothing new ; but to inform you that whenever I sit down to write, my invention makes a point of quarrelling with my pen, will doubtless be to account for the . . . in my letters. In writing to those who, I know, prefer honest hearts to clear heads, I turn thought out of doors, and set down the first ideas that turn up in the whirl of imagination. You desire me " to give you some account of the business of the office : " whether my apprehension is more dull than common, or whether I have slept too late this morning and the drowsy god is still hovering over my senses, or from what other cause, matter, or thing I know not ; but I really do not well understand what you would have me do. You surely do not mean that I should send you a list of *new* causes on your docket ; for I imagine 't is perfectly indifferent whether you receive a fee in the cause A. *vs.* B., or B. *vs.* A. : the number of them, indeed, may (as the New-England lawyers' phrase is) be a matter of *some speculation*. And, therefore, to remove every hook and loop whereon to hang a doubt, I won't acquaint you that there are a *good many ;* for *you* and I may annex different ideas to these words—but that you have ———— new ones in the Supreme, and ———— in the Mayor's Court.

---

[1] This and the letter following were exchanged between Jay and Kissam while the latter was temporarily absent from New York on professional business.

If by wanting to know how matters go on in the office, you intend I shall tell you how often your clerks go into it; give me leave to remind you of the old law maxim, that a man's own evidence is not to be admitted in his own cause. Why? Because 't is ten to one he does violence to his conscience. If I should tell you that I am all day in the office, and as attentive to your interests as I would be to my own, I suspect you would think it such an impeachment of my modesty as would not operate very powerfully in favour of my veracity. And if, on the other hand, I should tell you that I make hay while the sun shines, and say unto my soul,—" Soul, take thy rest, thy lord is journeying to a far country;" I should be much mistaken, if you did not think the confession looked too honest to be true.

When people in the city write to their friends in the country, I know, it is expected that their letters should contain the news of the town. For my part, I make it a rule never to frustrate the expectations of my correspondents in this particular, if I can help it; and that as much for my own sake as for theirs: for it not only saves one's invention a good deal of fatigue, but fills up blank paper very agreeably. Things remain here, if I may speak in your own language, pretty much in *statu quo.* Some, with reluctance, shuffling off this mortal coil; and others solacing themselves in the arms of mortality. The ways of men, you know, are as circular as the orbit through which our planet moves, and the centre to which they gravitate is *self:* round this we move in mystic measures, dancing to every tune that is loudest played by heaven or hell. Some, indeed, that happen to be jostled out of place, may fly off in tangents like wandering stars, and either lose themselves in a trackless void, or find another way to happiness ; but for the most part, we continue to frolic till we are out of breath ; then the music ceases, and we fall asleep. It is said you want more soldiers. I suspect Mr. Morris was lately inspired by some tutelar deity. If I remember right, he carried a great many *flints* with him. Good Lord deliver you from battle, murder, and from sudden death.

Pray, how do all these insignia of war and bloodshed sit upon Sam Jones's lay stomach. I wonder how he can bear to see Justice leaning on an officer's arm, without getting a fit of the spleen ; or behold the forum surrounded with guards, without suffering his indignation to trespass on his stoicism. I dare say he is not much pleased with such unusual pomp of justice, such unprecedented array of terror ; and would rather see the court hop lamely along upon her own legs, than walk tolerably well with the assistance of such crutches. God bless him. I wish there were many such men among us ; they would reduce things to just principles.

I have just read over what I have written, and find it free enough in all conscience. Some folks, I know, would think it too free, considering the relation we stand in to each other.

If I were writing to some folks, prudence would tell me to be more straight-laced : but I know upon what ground I stand; and professional pride shall give me no uneasiness, while you continue to turn it, with Satan behind your back.

Yours, truly,
JOHN JAY.

BENJAMIN KISSAM TO JAY.

DEAR SIR:

I just now received your long letter of the 12th inst., and am not a little pleased with the humour and freedom of sentiment which characterize it. It would give me pain if I thought you could even suspect me capable of wishing to impose any restraint upon you, in this high and inestimable privilege of friendship. Because I can see no reason why the rights of one relation in life should destroy those of another, I detest that forbidding pride which, with formal ceremony, can stalk over the social rights of others, and elevate the soul in a vain conceit of its own dignity and importance; founded merely in some adventitious circumstance of relative superiority. Take this, therefore, if you please, as a *nolli prosequi* for the heinous crime of writing a free and familiar letter to me; with this further, that whenever you transgress in the other extreme, you must not expect to meet with the same mercy.

I really believe, Jay, your pen was directed by the rapid whirl of imagination; nay, I am convinced that this whirl was begun, continued, and ended with a strong tide. I can't help conceiving it under the idea of a mill-tide, which keeps the wheels in a quick rotation, save only with this difference, that the motion of that is uniform, yours irregular—an irregularity, however, that bespeaks the grandeur, not the meanness of the intellectual source from whence the current flows. . . .

I will now explain to you what I meant by asking how business went in the office. And first, *negatively*, I did not want a list or the number of the new causes ; neither was I anxious to know how often you visited the office. But, as a regard to your modesty on the one hand, and your veracity on the other, has induced you to evade an answer to the last, I will, nevertheless, solve the dilemma for you by saying, that I believe you have too much veracity to assume a false modesty, and that you are too honest to declare an untruth. And, as you have left me between two extremes, I shall take the middle way ; and do suppose that, upon the whole, you attend the office as much as you ought to do ; so that you see I save both your modesty and veracity, and answer the question as you state it into the bargain.

But, *affirmatively*, I am to tell you, that I did mean to ask in general, whether my business decreased much by my absence ; and whether my returns at the last term were pretty good ; and whether care has been taken to put that business forward as much as possible. I conclude, however, that though you did not take me, as the Irishman said, yet these things have been properly attended to.

Here we are, and are likely to be so, I am afraid, these ten days. There are no less than forty-seven persons charged, all upon three several indictments, with the murder of those persons who lost their lives in the affray with the sheriff. Four or five of them are in jail, and will be tried this day : what their fate will be, God only knows ; it is terrible to think that so many lives should be at stake upon the principles of a constructive murder : for I suppose that the immediate agency of but a very few of the party can be proved. . . .

I am, your affectionate friend,

BENJAMIN KISSAM.

ALBANY, the 25th of August, 1766.

BENJAMIN KISSAM TO JAY.

DEAR JACK:

When you consider that all the causes you have hitherto tried have been by a kind of inspiration, you will need only a small degree of enthusiasm to be persuaded that my lameness is a providential mercy to you, by calling you to *action* again. If it was not for you, or some other such apostolic lawyer, my clients would be left in the lurch this court, as I am afraid I cannot attend myself. But, sir, you have now a call to go forth into my vineyard; and this you must do, too, upon an evangelical principle—that the master may receive the fruits of it. All I can tell you about the causes is little more than to give you a list of their titles; but this is quite enough for you. One is about a horse-race, in which I suppose there is some cheat; another is about an eloped wife; another of them also appertains unto horse-flesh. These are short hints; they may serve for briefs. If you admire conciseness, here you have it. There is one writ of inquiry.

As to the cause about Captain's island, this, tell Mr. Morris, must go off. Because, as you are concerned against me, I can't tell where to find another into whose head the cause can be infused in the miraculous way of inspiration; and without this it would rather be too intricate for any one to manage from my short hints. There will probably be some of my old friends, who may inquire after me, and perhaps some new ones will want to employ me: will you be kind enough to let them know that you will take care of any business for me. I ask these favours from you, John, with great freedom. I wish you good success with my consignments, and hope they'll come to a good market. If they don't, I am sure it will not be the *factor's* fault; and if my clients' *wares* are bad, let them bear the loss.

You will see my docket, with memoranda to direct what is to be done. If my leg is better, perhaps I may see you on

Wednesday; but it is very uncertain. Where Mr. Morris is not *against* me, I am sure he will be *with* me; and you may call on him for that purpose with as much freedom as if I had a perfect right to command his service. I know the goodness of his heart; and his friendship for me will make him embrace every opportunity to serve me with pleasure.

I am, your humble Servant,

BENJ. KISSAM.

NEW YORK, 6th Nov., 1769.

JAY TO DOCTOR KISSAM.[1]

DEAR KISSAM:

The manner in which you tell your brother that you expected a letter from me contains a reproof which gives me pain. I confess appearances have been against me, and my conduct even to you, my friend, must have appeared exceptionable. My last letter I hope will apologize for seeming omissions; you have doubtless received it before this. Neglect of friends is a species of littleness to which I think I am a stranger.—No, my dear Sam, your former attachment to my happiness has made too deep an impression ever to be erased by absence—an absence which when I suffer my feelings to be influenced by regard to my own pleasure I most sincerely regret. I assure you few incidents can happen so

---

[1] Dr. Samuel Kissam, then at Paramaribo, South America, where, as he wrote to Jay in 1771, he found business prospects flattering.

conducive to my satisfaction as the return of those happy days when our mutual confidence created mutual happiness and reciprocal good offices promised permanence to friendship. The duplicity and disengenuousness which shades the characters of many about me daily remind me of the openness and sincerity of my absent friend, and I think I know the value of these amiable qualifications too well to be remiss in cultivating his esteem. These are the genuine effusions of my heart ; rest satisfied of their reality and remember that the confidence characteristic of friendship disdains the fetters of distrust and suspicion. Be not surprised at this remark. I do not mention it because I think your behaviour would otherwise be uninfluenced by it. No ! my dear Sam, the generosity of your temper excludes such a thought. I mention it with no other view than that you may the more readily mark the consistency of this sentiment with the general tenor of my conduct.

You may remember that my last was interrupted by a call to Rye. I found my mother extremely [ill], but she is now better. From thence I went to Fairfield to try two causes, and returned to New York the day before yesterday. I have much news, but as your brother sends you the papers I shall not trouble you with repeating it. I suppose he has informed you of Miss Scots having gone off with and married to Litchfield. I am glad you correspond with Fady [Jay's brother Frederick]. I am sure it will afford him no less improvement than pleasure. Our old friends are well. Let me hear from you by every opportunity and

believe me to be
Your friend
JOHN JAY.

1st March, 1770.

PETER JAY TO WILLIAM LIVINGSTON.

RYE, the 31st January, 1774.

SIR :

My son having informed me of his Inclination of being connected in your Family, and your favourable reception of his application, I take the earliest opportunity of acquainting you with our concurrence.

Tho' we have not the pleasure of knowing the young Lady, yet the confidence we have in our son's Prudence, satisfies us of the Propriety of his choice. Give me leave, Sir, to assure you that I will always readily adopt every measure that may conduce to their happiness, and tend to render the Connection between our Familys agreeable to both.

Be pleased to present our Compliments to Mrs. Livingston and the young Lady.[1]

I am,
Sir, your very humble servant
PETER JAY.

To William Livingston, Esq.
　　at Elizabethtown.

---

[1] The "young Lady" in question, whom Jay married, April 28, 1774, was Sarah Van Brugh Livingston, daughter of William Livingston, subsequently Governor of New Jersey, etc. See Miss Philipse's letter to Mrs. Jay, July 1, 1774. A portrait and sketch of Mrs. Jay appear in Mrs. Ellett's "Queens of American Society."

LETTER TO THE COMMITTEE OF CORRESPONDENCE, BOSTON.[1]

NEW YORK, May 23, 1774.

GENTLEMEN :

The alarming measures of the British Parliament relative to your ancient and respectable town, which

---

[1] Jay's public career begins with his participation in the meetings held by citizens of New York during the alarm and excitement consequent on the passage of the Boston Port Bill, March 31, 1774. At the first meeting, May 16, 1774, a committee of fifty, with Isaac Low as chairman, was nominated to correspond with the other colonies " upon all matters of moment," and on the 19th "a great concourse of the inhabitants " assembled at the Coffee House and confirmed the nominations. Of this committee, known as the Committee of Correspondence, Jay was a member. On the 23d it met in the forenoon and appointed a sub-committee, consisting of Messrs. McDougall, Low, Duane, and Jay, to report " at 8 o'clock P.M." the draft of an answer to a communication from the Boston Committee of Correspondence. The citizens of Boston had held a meeting May 13th, and voted " That it is the opinion of this town that if the other Colonies come into a joint resolution to .op all importations from Great Britain, and exportations to Great Britain, and every part of the West Indies, till the Act for blocking up this harbour be repealed, the same will prove the salvation of North America and her liberties." The answer from New York appears above, it being the draft of the sub-committee, of which Jay, as stated, was a member. Its historical importance lies in the fact that while suggestions for holding a general congress of the colonies to consult on common rights had previously been made in Rhode Island, Pennsylvania, and elsewhere, the proposition to the same effect from New York was framed in such pointed terms as to hasten action in the matter and, with a similar call from Virginia, to lead to the assemblage of the famous Congress in September following. This New York draft was possibly from Jay's own pen.

Jay took an active part in the proceedings of the General Committee. At the meeting of July 19th, for example, he moved, " That a committee be appointed to take the distresses of the poor of the town of Boston, and ways and means for their relief, into consideration, and make their report with all convenient speed." Such a committee was named with Jay as a member, and donations for Boston secured. The Committee of Correspondence was succeeded, November 22d, by another composed of sixty members, called the Committee of Inspection, which in turn was succeeded, May 1, 1775, by still another General Committee of one hundred. Jay was elected to both, but, as appears from the succeeding note, p. 17, he was to be preoccupied much of the time with the duties of a more important station.

has so long been the seat of freedom, fill the inhabitants of this city with inexpressible concern. As a sister colony, suffering in defence of the rights of America, we consider your injuries as a common cause, to the redress of which it is equally our duty, and our interest to contribute. But what ought to be done in a situation so truly critical, while it employs the anxious thoughts of every generous mind, is very hard to be determined.

Our citizens have thought it necessary to appoint a large Committee, consisting of fifty-one persons to correspond with our sister Colonies on this and every other matter of public moment, and at ten o'clock this forenoon, we were first assembled. Your letter enclosing the vote of the town of Boston and the letter of your Committee of Correspondence were immediately taken into consideration.

While we think you justly entitled to the thanks of your sister Colonies for asking their advice on a case of such extensive consequences, we lament our inability to relieve your anxiety by a decisive opinion. The cause is general, and concerns a whole continent who are equally interested with you and us ; and we foresee that no remedy can be of avail unless it proceeds from the joint act and approbation of all. From a virtuous and spirited union much may be expected, while the feeble efforts of a few will only be attended with mischief and disappointment to themselves and triumph to the adversaries of liberty.

Upon these reasons we conclude, that a Congress of Deputies from the colonies in general is of the utmost moment; that it ought to be assembled with-out delay, and some unanimous resolutions formed in this fatal emergency, not only respecting your de-plorable circumstances, but for the security of our common rights. Such being our sentiments, it must be premature to pronounce any judgment on the ex-pedient which you have suggested. We beg, how-ever, that you will do us the justice to believe that we shall continue to act with a firm and becoming regard to American freedom, and to co-operate with our sister colonies in every measure that shall be thought salutary and conducive to the public good.

We have nothing to add, but that we sincerely con-dole with you in your unexampled distress, and to request your speedy opinion of the proposed Con-gress, that if it should meet with your approbation, we may exert our utmost endeavours to carry it into execution.

[ALEXANDER McDOUGALL,
ISAAC LOW,
JAMES DUANE,
JOHN JAY.
Com. on Draft of Letter.]

MISS PHILIPSE TO MRS. JAY.

YONKERS, July 1st [1774].

You will I hope, my dear and amiable friend, excuse my not writing to you before. I have several times been pre-vented from doing myself that Pleasure; but as it is not yet too late, accept of my Congratulations on an event that has contributed so much to the felicity of my dear Mrs Jay, and my ardent wishes for the long continuance of the Happiness you enjoy.[1] The fan and gloves I received, and beg my thanks. It was no small mortification to me in not having it in my power to accept of your kind invitation by Cousin Kitty Livingston of being one of the Bridesmaids. In town I own that I had flattered myself with the pleasing expectation of being one of the number. Had it not been for my Papa (who thought the weather too warm for me to be in town) I should have reallized all those pleasures of which I had formed such a delightful idea. The being with my dear Mrs. Jay would have been my principal inducement, and spending with her some hours as agreeable as those I enjoyed at Elizabethtown. But apropos—Mama and I were a little Jealous at your stopping twice at Collo. Cortlandts and not once at Philipsborough, you being such a prodigious favorite. However, we all hope soon to be favored with a visit from you and Mr. Jay. Papa and Mama beg their compts: to you and Mr. Jay with Congratulations.

Cousin Kitty Van Horne has spent three weeks with me and proposes staying a week longer. But, my dear Sally, do not you intend to favor me with a letter. Remember you are a long one in my debt, and that I cannot think of losing my correspondent. It would not indeed be generous in you in depriving me of so great an opportunity of improvement. If at Elizabethtown, please to give my love to Cousin Livingstons, and to Cousin Susan and Kitty, and believe me to be sincerely

Your truly affectionate Friend
MARIA ELIZA PHILIPS.

Do not omit my Compts:
to Mr. Jay & congratulations.

---

[1] See letter, *ante*, from Peter Jay to Wm. Livingston, January 31, 1774.

ADDRESS TO THE PEOPLE OF GREAT BRITAIN.[1]

From the Delegates appointed by the several English Colonies of New-Hampshire, Massachusetts Bay, Rhode Island and Providence Plantations, Connecticut, New-York, New-Jersey, Pennsylvania, the Lower Counties on the Delaware, Maryland, Virginia, North Carolina, and South Carolina, to consider their grievances in General Congress, at Philadelphia, September 5th, 1774.

FRIENDS AND FELLOW-SUBJECTS :

When a nation, led to greatness by the hand of liberty, and possessed of all the glory that heroism, munificence, and humanity can bestow, descends to

---

[1] During the spring and summer of 1774 the several Colonies, through their Assemblies or Committees of Correspondence, resolved upon holding a General Congress of Delegates to take common action against the alarming encroachment of Parliamentary authority. The Boston Port Bill, like the Stamp Act, had aroused indignation and distrust, and a crisis threatened. Delegates being elected to the proposed Congress, that body met at Philadelphia, September 5, 1774, and on October 20th adopted the well-known Articles of " Association " interdicting all trade with Great Britain, that were to be followed later by still stronger bonds of union. Important addresses were also issued. The delegates representing New York City and County were Messrs. Philip Livingston, John Alsop, Isaac Low, James Duane, and John Jay. They were unanimously elected by the freeholders, freemen, and other taxpayers of the city, July 28th, upon the platform of a " non-importation agreement," as the most efficacious means of compelling a redress of grievances. See note p. 13.

It was during the session of this Congress that Jay first became known beyond the limits of his own constituency as a writer of marked ability. He was the author of the above " Address " to the people of England, which Jefferson, among others, admired and praised. Lee, of Virginia, and Livingston, of New Jersey, were his colleagues on the committee appointed to prepare the document. See " Life of Jay," vol. i., p. 30, and vol. ii., pp. 380–84. Jay also served on the committees " to state the rights of the colonies," to prepare a letter to the Colony Agents in London, etc.

the ungrateful task of forging chains for her friends and children ; and instead of giving support to freedom, turns advocate for slavery and oppression, there is reason to suspect she has either ceased to be virtuous, or been extremely negligent in the appointment of her rulers.

In almost every age, in repeated conflicts, in long and bloody wars, as well civil as foreign, against many and powerful nations, against the open assaults of enemies and the more dangerous treachery of friends, have the inhabitants of your island, your great and glorious ancestors, maintained their inde pendence, and transmitted the rights of men and the blessings of liberty to you, their posterity.

Be not surprised, therefore, that we, who are descended from the same common ancestors ; that we, whose forefathers participated in all the rights, the liberties, and the constitution you so justly boast of, and who have carefully conveyed the same fair inheritance to us, guarantied by the plighted faith of government, and the most solemn compacts with British sovereigns, should refuse to surrender them to men who found their claims on no principles of reason, and who prosecute them with a design that, by having *our* lives and property in their power, they may with the greater facility enslave *you*.

The cause of America is now the object of universal attention : it has at length become very serious. This unhappy country has not only been oppressed, but abused and misrepresented ; and the duty we owe to ourselves and posterity, to your interest, and the general welfare of the British empire, leads us to address you on this very important subject.

KNOW THEN, That we consider ourselves, and do insist that we are and ought to be, as free as our fellow-subjects in Britain, and that no power on earth has a right to take our property from us without our consent.

That we claim all the benefits secured to the subject by the English constitution, and particularly that inestimable one of trial by jury.

That we hold it essential to English liberty, that no man be condemned unheard, or punished for supposed offences without having an opportunity of making his defence.

That we think the Legislature of Great Britain is not authorized by the constitution to establish a religion fraught with sanguinary and impious tenets, or to erect an arbitrary form of government in any quarter of the globe. These rights we, as well as you, deem sacred. And yet, sacred as they are, they have, with many others, been repeatedly and flagrantly violated.

Are not the proprietors of the soil of Great Britain lords of their own property? Can it be taken from them without their consent? Will they yield it to the arbitrary disposal of any man, or number of men whatever? You know they will not.

Why then are the proprietors of the soil of America less lords of their property than you are of yours? or why should they submit it to the disposal of your parliament, or any other parliament or council in the world, not of their election? Can the intervention of the sea that divides us cause disparity in rights? or can any reason be given why English subjects, who live three thousand miles from the royal palace, should enjoy less liberty than those who are three hundred miles distant from it?

Reason looks with indignation on such distinctions, and freemen can never perceive their propriety. And yet, however chimerical and unjust such discriminations are, the parliament assert, that they have a right to bind us in all cases without exception, whether we consent or not; that they may take and use our property when and in what manner they please; that we are pensioners on their bounty for all that we possess; and can hold it no longer than they vouchsafe to permit. Such declarations we consider as heresies in English politics, and which can no more operate to deprive us of our property, than the interdicts of the pope can divest kings of sceptres, which the laws of the land, and the voice of the people have placed in their hands.

At the conclusion of the late war—a war rendered glorious by the abilities and integrity of a minister, to whose efforts the British empire owes its safety and its fame: at the conclusion of this war, which was succeeded by an inglorious peace, formed under the auspices of a minister, of principles, and of a family unfriendly to the Protestant cause, and inimical to liberty; we say, at this period, and under the influence of that man, a plan for enslaving your fellow-subjects in America was concerted, and has ever since been pertinaciously carrying into execution.

Prior to this era, you were content with drawing from us the wealth produced by our commerce. You restrained our trade in every way that could conduce to your emolument. You exercised unbounded sovereignty over the sea. You named the ports and nations to which alone our merchandise should be carried, and with whom alone we should trade; and though some of these restrictions were grievous, we nevertheless did not complain : we looked up to you as to our parent state, to which we were bound by the strongest ties; and were happy in being instrumental to your prosperity and grandeur.

We call upon you yourselves to witness our loyalty and attachment to the common interest of the whole empire: Did we not, in the last war, add all the strength of this vast continent to the force which repelled our common enemy? Did we not leave our native shores, and meet disease and death, to promote the success of British arms in foreign climates? Did you not thank us for our zeal, and even reimburse us large sums of money, which, you confessed, we had advanced beyond our proportion, and far beyond our abilities? You did.

To what causes, then, are we to attribute the sudden changes of treatment, and that system of slavery which was prepared for us at the restoration of peace?

Before we had recovered from the distresses which ever attend war, an attempt was made to drain this country of all its money, by the oppressive stamp act. Paint, glass, and other commodities which you would not permit us to purchase of other nations, were taxed ; nay, although no wine is made in any country subject to the British state, you prohibited our procuring it of foreigners without paying a tax, imposed by your parliament, on all we imported. These and many other impositions were laid upon us most unjustly and unconstitutionally, for the express purpose of raising a revenue. In order to silence complaint, it was indeed provided, that this revenue should be expended in America for its protection and defence. These exactions, however, can receive no justification from a pretended necessity of protecting and defending us. They are lavishly squandered on court favourites and ministerial dependants, generally avowed enemies to America, and employing themselves by partial representations to traduce and embroil the colonies. For the necessary support of government here, we ever were and ever shall be ready to provide. And whenever the exigences of the state may require it, we shall, as we have heretofore done, cheerfully contribute our full proportion of men and money. To enforce this unconstitutional and unjust scheme of taxation, every fence that the wisdom of our British ancestors had carefully erected against arbitrary power has been violently thrown down in America, and the inestimable right of trial by jury taken away in cases that touch life and property. It was ordained, that whenever offences should be committed in the colonies against particular acts imposing various duties and restrictions upon trade, the prosecutor might bring his action for the penalties in the courts of Admiralty : by which means

had in a great measure been rendered abortive by our
ceasing to import that commodity, a scheme was concerted by the ministry with the East India Company,
and an act passed enabling and encouraging them to
transport and vend it in the colonies.   Aware of the
danger of giving success to this insidious manœuvre,
and of permitting a precedent of taxation thus to be
established among us, various methods were adopted
to elude the stroke.   The people of Boston, then
ruled by a governor, whom, as well as his predecessor
Sir Francis Bernard, all America considers as her
enemy, were exceedingly embarrassed.   The ships
which had arrived with the tea were by his management prevented from returning.   The duties would
have been paid, the cargoes landed and exposed to
sale ; a governor's influence would have procured and
protected many purchasers.   While the town was
suspended by deliberations on this important subject,
the tea was destroyed.   Even supposing a trespass
was thereby committed, and the proprietors of the
tea entitled to damages, the courts of law were open,
and judges appointed by the crown presided in them.
The East India Company, however, did not think
proper to commence any suits, nor did they even de
mand satisfaction either from individuals, or from the
community in general.   The ministry, it seems,
officiously made the case their own, and the great
council of the nation descended to intermeddle with
a dispute about private property.   Divers papers,
letters, and other unauthenticated *ex parte* evidence
were laid before them ; neither the persons who

destroyed the tea, nor the people of Boston, were called upon to answer the complaint. The ministry, incensed by being disappointed in a favourite scheme, were determined to recur from the little arts of finesse, to open force and unmanly violence. The port of Boston was blocked up by a fleet, and an army placed in the town. Their trade was to be suspended, and thousands reduced to the necessity of gaining subsistence from charity, till they should submit to pass under the yoke, and consent to become slaves, by confessing the omnipotence of parliament, and acquiescing in whatever disposition they might think proper to make of their lives and property.

Let justice and humanity cease to be the boast of your nation! Consult your history, examine your records of former transactions, nay, turn to the annals of the many arbitrary states and kingdoms that surround you, and show us a single instance of men being condemned to suffer for imputed crimes, unheard, unquestioned, and without even the specious formality of a trial; and that too by laws made expressly for the purpose, and which had no existence at the time of the fact committed. If it be difficult to reconcile these proceedings to the genius and temper of your laws and constitution, the task will become more arduous, when we call upon our ministerial enemies to justify, not only condemning men untried and by hearsay, but involving the innocent in one common punishment with the guilty, and for the act of thirty or forty, to bring poverty, distress, and calamity on thirty thousand souls, and those not your enemies, but your friends, brethren, and fellow-subjects.

It would be some consolation to us if the catalogue of American oppressions ended here. It gives us pain to be reduced to the necessity of reminding you, that under the confidence reposed in the faith of government, pledged in a royal charter from a British sovereign, the forefathers of the present inhabitants of the Massachusetts Bay left their former habitations, and established that great, flourishing, and loyal colony. Without incurring, or being charged with a forfeiture of their rights, without being heard, without being tried, without law, and without justice, by an act of parliament their charter is destroyed, their liberties violated, their constitution and form of government changed : and all this upon no better pretence, than because in one of their towns a trespass was committed on some merchandise, said to belong to one of the companies, and because the ministry were of opinion, that such high political regulations were necessary to compel due subordination and obedience to their mandates.

Nor are these the only capital grievances under which we labour. We might tell of dissolute, weak, and wicked governors having been set over us; of legislatures being suspended for asserting the rights of British subjects ; of needy and ignorant dependants on great men advanced to the seats of justice, and to other places of trust and importance ; of hard restrictions on commerce, and a great variety of lesser evils, the recollection of which is almost lost under the weight and pressure of greater and more poignant calamities.

Now mark the progression of the ministerial plan for enslaving us. Well aware that such hardy attempts to take our property from us, to deprive us of the valuable right of trial by jury, to seize our persons and carry us for trial to Great Britain, to blockade our ports, to destroy our charters, and change our forms of government, would occasion, and had already occasioned, great discontent in the colonies, which might produce opposition to these measures ; an act was passed to protect, indemnify, and screen from punishment, such as might be guilty even of murder, in endeavouring to carry their oppressive edicts into execution ; and by another act the dominion of Canada is to be so extended, modelled, and governed, as that by being disunited from us, detached from our interests by civil as well as religious prejudices, that by their numbers daily swelling with Catholic emigrants from Europe, and by their devotion to an administration so friendly to their religion, they might become formidable to us, and on occasion, be fit instruments in the hands of power to reduce the ancient, free Protestant colonies to the same state of slavery with themselves.

This was evidently the object of the act : and in this view, being extremely dangerous to our liberty and quiet, we cannot forbear complaining of it, as hostile to British America. Superadded to these considerations, we cannot help deploring the unhappy condition to which it has reduced the many English settlers who, encouraged by the royal proclamation, promising the enjoyment of all their rights, have purchased estates in that country. They are now the subjects of an arbitrary government, deprived of trial by jury, and when imprisoned, cannot claim the benefit of the *habeas corpus* act, that great bulwark and palladium of English liberty. Nor can we suppress our astonishment that a British Parliament should ever consent to establish in that country a religion that has deluged your island in blood, and dispersed impiety, bigotry, persecution, murder, and rebellion, through every part of the world.

This being a state of facts, let us beseech you to consider to what end they lead. Admit that the ministry, by the powers of Britain, and the aid of our Roman Catholic neighbours, should be able to carry the point of taxation, and reduce us to a state of perfect humiliation and slavery: such an enterprise would doubtless make some addition to your national debt, which already presses down your liberties, and fills you with pensioners and placemen. We presume, also, that your commerce will somewhat be diminished. However, suppose you should prove victorious, in what condition will you then be? what advantages or what laurels will you reap from such a conquest? May not a ministry, with the same armies enslave you? it may be said, you will cease to pay them; but remember, the taxes from America, the wealth, and we may add the men, and particularly the Roman Catholics of this vast continent, will then be in the power of your enemies; nor will you have any reason to expect, that after making slaves of us, many among us should refuse to assist in reducing you to the same abject state.

Do not treat this as chimerical. Know that in less than half a century, the quit-rents reserved to the crown from the numberless grants of this vast continent, will pour large streams of wealth into the royal coffers. And if to this be added the power of taxing America at pleasure, the crown will be rendered independent of you for supplies, and will possess more treasure than may be necessary to purchase the remains of liberty in your island. In a word, take care that you do not fall into the pit that is preparing for us.

We believe there is yet much virtue, much justice, and much public spirit in the English nation. To that justice we now appeal. You have been told that we are seditious, impatient of government, and desirous of independence. Be assured that these are not facts, but calumnies. Permit us to be as free as yourselves, and we shall ever esteem a union with you to be our greatest glory, and our greatest happiness; we shall ever be ready to contribute all in our power to the welfare of the empire; we shall consider your enemies as our enemies, and your interest as our own.

But if you are determined that your ministers shall wantonly sport with the rights of mankind : if neither the voice of justice, the dictates of the law, the principles of the constitution, or the suggestions of humanity can restrain your hands from shedding human blood in such an impious cause, we must then tell you, that we will never submit to be hewers of wood or drawers of water for any ministry or nation in the world.

Place us in the same situation that we were at the close of the last war, and our former harmony will be restored.

But lest the same supineness, and the same inattention to our common interest, which you have for several years shown, should continue, we think it prudent to anticipate the consequences.

By the destruction of the trade of Boston the ministry have endeavoured to induce submission to their measures.   The like fate may befall us all.   We will endeavour, therefore, to live without trade, and recur for subsistence to the fertility and bounty of our native soil, which affords us all the necessaries, and some of the conveniences of life.   We have suspended our importation from Great Britain and Ireland ; and in less than a year's time, unless our grievances should be redressed, shall discontinue our exports to those kingdoms, and the West Indies.

It is with the utmost regret, however, that we find ourselves compelled, by the overruling principles of self-preservation, to adopt measures detrimental in their consequences to numbers of our fellow-subjects in Great Britain and Ireland.   But we hope that the magnanimity and justice of the British nation will furnish a parliament of such wisdom, independence, and public spirit as may save the violated rights of the whole empire from the devices of wicked ministers and evil counsellors, whether in or out of office ; and thereby restore that harmony, friendship, and fraternal affection, between all the inhabitants of his majesty's kingdoms and territories, so ardently wished for by every true and honest American.

LETTER TO THE COMMITTEE OF MECHANICS, NEW YORK.[1]

GENTLEMEN :

The polite and respectful terms in which you are pleased to communicate your approbation of our conduct, in an important office, demand our most sincere and grateful acknowledgments.

Honoured by the united suffrages of our fellow-citizens, and animated by a sense of duty, and the most cordial affection for our oppressed country, however unequal to the delicate and arduous task, we undertook it with cheerfulness, and have discharged it with fidelity.

While, from abundant experience, we bear testimony to the unshaken zeal for constitutional liberty, which has ever distinguished the worthy inhabitants of this metropolis, and is nobly exerted at the present alarming crisis, your anxious solicitude for the restoration of that harmony and mutual confidence between the parent state and America, on which the glory and stability of the British Empire so absolutely depend, cannot fail of recommending you to the esteem of all good men, and of holding you up as an example worthy of imitation and applause.

[1] Letter in answer to an " Address from the Committee of Mechanicks of New York, presented to the Delegates who represented the City at the General Congress." Printed in Force's " American Archives."

To soften the rigour of the calamities to which, in this tempestuous season, we may be exposed, let us all, with one heart and voice, endeavour to cultivate and cherish a spirit of unanimity and mutual benevolence, and to promote that internal tranquillity which can alone give weight to our laudable efforts for the preservation of our freedom, and crown them with success.

We are, gentlemen, with the most affectionate regard, your obliged and very humble servants,

PHILIP LIVINGSTON,   JAMES DUANE,
JOHN ALSOP,   JOHN JAY.
ISAAC LOW,

To Mr. Daniel Dunscomb, Chairman, and the Committee of Mechanicks in the City of New York. [November 18 (?), 1774.]

LETTER FROM CONGRESS TO THE "OPPRESSED INHABITANTS OF CANADA."[1]

FRIENDS AND COUNTRYMEN:

Alarmed by the designs of an arbitrary Ministry to extirpate the rights and liberties of all *America*, a sense of common danger conspired with the dictates

---

[1] Before its adjournment the Congress of 1774, referred to in note, p. 17, made provision for the meeting of another similar body on May 10, 1775. In New York a Provincial Convention was called for the special purpose of electing delegates to the new Congress, and on April 22, 1775, Mr. Jay was again chosen, with Messrs. Philip Livingston, James Duane, John Alsop, Simon Boerum, William Floyd, Henry Wisner, Philip Schuyler, George Clinton, Lewis Morris, Francis Lewis, and Robert R. Livingston, Jr., representing the different counties of the Province, as his colleagues. This Congress of 1775, which met, as before, at Philadelphia, became the continuous body known as

of humanity is urging us to call your attention, by our late address, to this very important object.

Since the conclusion of the late war, we have been happy in considering you as fellow-subjects ; and from the commencement of the present plan for subjugating the continent, we have viewed you as fellow-sufferers with us. As we were both entitled by the bounty of an indulgent Creator to freedom, and being both devoted by the cruel edicts of a despotic Administration, to common ruin, we perceived the fate of the Protestant and Catholic colonies to be strongly linked together, and therefore invited you to join with us in resolving to be free, and in rejecting, with disdain, the fetters of slavery, however artfully polished.

We most sincerely condole with you on the arrival of that day, in the course of which the sun could not shine on a single freeman in all your extensive dominion. Be assured that your unmerited degradation has engaged the most unfeigned pity of your sister

the Continental Congress of the Revolution, the individual members changing from time to time. Jay's first connection with it lasted until May 25, 1776, a little over a year. During that time he was closely absorbed with his public duties and served on many important committees, as the published proceedings of the Congress show. On May 26th he was appointed with Samuel Adams and Silas Deane, to prepare and report a letter to the people of Canada, which was approved, on the 29th, in the form given above. Jay's biographer credits him with its authorship (vol. i., p. 34), as he does with the authorship of the " Address to the People of Ireland," a document similar in style and having the same object as that to the Canadians. It appears in Force's " American Archives." Jay was also one of the committee to prepare the declaration issued by Congress July 6th, " setting forth the causes and necessity " of taking up arms against the mother country. Two days later the " Petition to the King " was signed by the delegates, the document being drawn up by Mr. Dickenson ; the measure, however, originated with Jay, and was successfully urged by him against strong opposition. In regard to this, see " Life," etc., vol. i., p. 36.

colonies ; and we flatter ourselves you will not, by tamely bearing the yoke, suffer that pity to be supplanted by contempt.

When hardy attempts are made to deprive men of rights bestowed by the Almighty ; when avenues are cut through the most solemn compacts for the admission of despotism ; when the plighted faith of government ceases to give security to dutiful subjects ; and when the insidious stratagems and manœuvres of peace become more terrible than the sanguinary operations of war, it is high time for them to assert those rights, and with honest indignation oppose the torrent of oppression rushing in upon them.

By the introduction of your present form of government, or rather present form of tyranny, you and your wives and your children are made slaves. You have nothing that you can call your own, and all the fruits of your labour and industry may be taken from you whenever an avaricious governor and a rapacious council may incline to demand them. You are liable by their edicts to be transported into foreign countries, to fight battles in which you have no interest, and to spill your blood in conflicts from which neither honour nor emolument can be derived. Nay, the enjoyment of your very religion, on the present system, depends on a legislature in which you have no share, and over which you have no control ; and your priests are exposed to expulsion, banishment, and ruin, whenever their wealth and possessions furnish sufficient temptation. They cannot be sure that a virtuous prince will always fill the throne ; and should a wicked or careless king concur with a wicked ministry in exacting the treasure and strength of your country, it is impossible to conceive to what variety and to what extremes of wretchedness you may, under the present establishment, be reduced.

We are informed you have already been called upon to waste your lives in a contest with us. Should you, by complying in this instance, assent to your new establishment, and war break out with *France*, your wealth and your sons may be sent to perish in expeditions against their islands in the West Indies.

It cannot be presumed that these considerations will have no weight with you, or that you are so lost to all sense of honour. We can never believe that the present race of Canadians are so degenerated as to possess neither the spirit, the gallantry, nor the courage of their ancestors. You certainly will not permit the infamy and disgrace of such pusillanimity to rest on your own heads, and the consequences of it on your children forever.

We, for our parts, are determined to live free, or not at all ; and we are resolved that posterity shall never reproach us with having brought slaves into the world.

Permit us again to repeat that we are your friends, not your enemies, and be not imposed upon by others who may endeavour to create animosities. The taking of the fort and military stores at *Ticonderoga* and *Crown Point*, and the armed vessels on the lake, was dictated by the great law of self-preservation. They were intended to annoy us, and to cut off that friendly intercourse and communication, which has hitherto subsisted between you and us. We hope it has given you no uneasiness, and you may rely on our assurances that these colonies will pursue no measures whatever, but such as friendship and a regard for our mutual safety and interest may suggest.

As our concern for your welfare entitles us to your friendship, we presume you will not, by doing us an injury, reduce us to the disagreeable necessity of treating you as enemies.

We yet entertain hopes of your uniting with us in the defence of our common liberty, and there is yet reason to believe, that should we join in imploring the attention of our sovereign, to the unmerited and un-paralleled oppression of his American subjects, he will at length be undeceived, and forbid a licentious min-istry any longer to riot in the ruins of the rights of mankind.

JAY TO MRS. JAY.

My Dear Sally:

My last to you was by Mrs. Graham which I hope you have received. It would give me pleasure to have an opportunity of acknowledging the receipt of one from you. I sometimes fear you are indisposed and that your silence proceeds from a desire of concealing it.

Your Papa is hearty and well. The Congress spent yesterday in festivity. The Committee of Safety [of Philadelphia] were so polite as to invite them to make a little voyage in their gondolas as far as the fort which is about twelve miles from the city. Each galley had its company and each company entertained with variety of music, etc., etc. We proceeded six or eight miles down the river when the tide being spent and the wind unfavourable, we backed about and with a fine breeze returned, passed the city and landed six miles above the town at a pretty little place called Parr's Villa. It appears to have been the property of a gentleman of some taste—a garden, a walk, a summer house, etc, much out of order and partly in ruins. I wished you and a few select friends had been with me. This idea, tho' amidst much noise and mirth, made me much alone.

Adieu, my beloved,

I am most sincerely yours,

JOHN JAY.

PHILADELPHIA, 29 September, 1775.

JAY TO COLONEL WOODHULL, PRESIDENT NEW YORK PROVINCIAL CONGRESS.

PHILADELPHIA, November 26, 1775.

SIR :

I have the honour of transmitting to you the enclosed resolutions of Congress relative to the island of Bermuda.

We have not yet had the pleasure of hearing that you had made a House, and are not without some anxiety on that head. In a few days we shall write you collectively, and should be glad frequently to be informed of the state of the Province.

The New England exploit [1] is much talked of, and conjectures are numerous as to the part the Convention will take relative to it. Some consider it as an ill compliment to the government of the Province, and prophesy that you have too much Christian meekness to take any notice of it. For my own part, I do not approve of the feat, and think it neither argues much wisdom nor much bravery ; at any rate, if it was to have been done, I wish our own people, and not strangers, had taken the liberty of doing it. I confess I am not a little jealous of the honour of the Province, and am persuaded that its reputation cannot be maintained without some little spirit being mingled with its prudence.

I am, sir, with respect and esteem, your most obedient servant,

JOHN JAY.

To Colonel Nathaniel Woodhull,
at New York.

JAY TO MRS. JAY.

MY DEAR WIFE :

I have now the pleasure of informing you that the New York Convention has at length made some provision for their delegates, vizt., four dollars per day for their attendance on the last and this Congress, so that I shall not be so great a sufferer as I once appre-

---

[1] The reference here is to the destruction, November 23, 1775, of the Tory Rivington's press in New York by a party of light horsemen from Connecticut under Captain Sears. The party also seized Bishop Seabury, " Lord " Underhill, Mayor of Westchester borough, and Judge Fowler, who had protested against the proceedings of the Continental Congress, and carried them off, with a portion of Rivington's type, to New Haven.

hended. The allowance indeed does by no means equal the loss I have sustained by the appointment, but the Convention I suppose consider the honour as an equivalent for the residue.

The Congress this day refused to give me leave of absence for next week. There are but five New York delegates here, Col. Morris and Mr. Lewis being absent, so that should either of us leave the town, the Province would be unrepresented. We expect, however, soon to adjourn, and your Papa has engaged Mr. Hooper to accompany him to Elizabethtown, where I hope we shall soon be all very happy. My horses were new shod, wheels greased, cloaths put up, and every thing ready to set off early in the morning, when on going to Congress this morning all my pleasing expectations of seeing you on Christmas Day were disappointed. Don't you pity me, my dear Sally? It is, however, some consolation that should the Congress not adjourn in less than ten days, I am determined to stay with you till ——, and depend upon it nothing but actual imprisonment will be able to keep me from you.

At present I find the objections of the Congress so reasonable that I am sure you would blame me were I to attempt leaving them without permission . . . To-morrow or on Tuesday next the Congress will I believe determine the time of adjournment, so that it is probable I shall have the happiness of wishing you a happy New Year.

Adieu, my beloved,
Your affectionate
JOHN JAY.

PHILADELPHIA, 23 December, 1775.

JAY TO COLONEL McDOUGALL.[1]

DEAR SIR :

Since writing my last to you I find the Congress will not adjourn even for the holidays. They have not indeed so determined, but that seems to be the opinion of the members.

Where does Mr. Alsop stay? Should any thing happen to one of us the colony would be unrepresented. For my part I wish some of the absent gentlemen would return ; we but just make a quorum. Did not this circumstance forbid my leaving the Congress I would pay you a short visit during the session of the Convention. What has become of Queens and Richmond? Rival governments or governors are solecisms in politics.

It appears to be prudent that you should begin to impose light taxes rather with a view to *precedent* than profit. Suppose saltpetre, wool, or yarn should be received in payment ; I think such a measure would tend to encourage manufactures. They are essential to the support of the poor and care should be taken to increase materials for them. The people of this place are amazingly attentive to this object. It keeps people easy and quiet ; by being employed they gain bread, and when our fellow mortals are busy and well fed they forget to complain. I hope your Convention will leave a Committee of Safety.

Adieu—yours most sincerely,

JOHN JAY.

PHILADELPHIA, 23 December, 1775.

---

[1] Alexander McDougall, of New York City, at this date colonel of the First New York Continental Regiment and later brigadier and major-general in the army.

ALEXANDER HAMILTON TO JAY.

N. York, Decem^r. 31st, 1775.

DEAR SIR :

It is hardly necessary to inform you that I received your favour in answer to my letter on the subject of Capt. Sear's expedition, and that I shall be at all times ready to comply with your request of information concerning the state of the province, or any matters of importance that may arise. Any thing that may conduce to the public service or may serve as a testimony of my respect to you will be always gladly embraced by me.

I have much reason to suspect that the tories have it in contemplation to steal a march upon us, if they can, in respect of a new Assembly. I believe the governor will shortly dissolve the old and issue writs for a new one. The motives for it, at this time, are probably these— It is hoped the attention of the people being engaged in their new institutions, Congresses, and the like, they will think the Assembly of little importance, and will not exert themselves as they ought to do, whereby the tories will have an opportunity to elect their own creatures, or at least it is expected the people may be thrown into divisions and ferments, injurious to present measures.

The tories will be no doubt very artful and intriguing, and it behooves us to be very vigilant and cautious. I have thrown out a hand bill or two to give the necessary alarm, and shall second them by others.

It appears to me that as the best way to keep the attention of the people united and fixed to the same point, it would be expedient that four of our Continental delegates should be candidates for this city and county,—Mr. Livingston, Mr. Alsop, Mr. Lewis, and Mr. Jay. The minds of all our friends will naturally tend to these, and the opposition will of course be weak and contemptible, for the whigs I doubt not constitute a large majority of the people. If you approve the hint I should wish for your presence here, Absence you know is not very favorable to the influence of any person however great. I shall give you farther notice as I see the scheme advance to execution. I am Dr. Sir

Your very humb. servant,

A. HAMILTON.[1]

JAY TO ROBERT R. LIVINGSTON.[2]

PHILADELPHIA, 6th January, 1776.

DEAR ROBERT :

Amid the various sources of consolation in seasons of poignant distress, which the wise have long amused themselves and the world with, the little share of observation and experience which has fallen to my lot convinces me that resignation to the dispensations of a benevolent as well as omnipotent Being can alone administer relief. The sensations which the first paragraph of your letter has occasioned mock the force of philosophy, and I confess have rendered me the sport of feelings which you can more easily conceive than I express. Grief, if a weakness, is nevertheless on certain occasions amiable, and recommends itself by being in the train of passions which follow virtue. But remember, my friend, that your country bleeds and calls for your exertions. The fate of those very friends whose misfortunes so justly afflict you, is linked with the common cause, and cannot have a separate issue. Rouse, therefore, and after vigorously

[1] "Young Hamilton," as Jay speaks of him at this date, then in his nineteenth year.

[2] Delegate from New York in Continental Congress; subsequently Chancellor, etc.

discharging the duties you owe your country, return to your peaceful shades, and supply the place of your former joys, by the reflection that they are only removed to a more kindred soil, like flowers from a thorny wilderness by a friendly florist, under whose care they will flourish and bloom, and court your embraces for ever. Accept my warmest thanks for the ardour with which you wish a continuance and increase of that friendship to which I have long been much indebted. Be assured that its duration will always be among the first objects of my care. Let us unite in proving by our example that the rule which declares juvenile friendships, like vernal flowers, to be of short continuance, is not without exceptions, even in our degenerate days. Mr. Deane has this moment come in, so that I must conclude, as I hope to conclude every letter to you, with an assurance that I am

Your affectionate friend,

JOHN JAY.

P. S.—Fifty tons of saltpetre arrived this day.

JAY TO ROBERT R. LIVINGSTON.

PHILADELPHIA, 4th March, 1776.

MY DEAR FRIEND:

Fame says you are still much indisposed. I pray God she may on this, as she does on many other occasions, prove a liar. I wrote you last week from Elizabethtown. Tell me whether you have received that, and which other of my letters. I was in hopes of finding a letter from you here for me ; and the disappointment is the greater, as the state of your health for some time past has given me much anxiety. The prospect of being soon deprived of a father, and probably a mother, whom you know I tenderly love, the unhappy situation of my family, added to the distress I feel for the late misfortunes and sickness of my friend, have occasioned more gloomy ideas in my mind than it has ever before been the subject of : despondency, however, ill becomes a man. I hope I shall meet every severe stroke of fate with firmness and resignation, though not with sullen indifference. It gives me consolation to reflect that the human race are immortal, that my parents and friends will be divided from me only by a curtain which will soon be drawn up, and that our great and benevolent Creator will (if I please) be my guide through this vale of tears to our eternal and blessed habitation.

Notwithstanding your letter, I shall expect that your disorder is to be ascribed more to your solicitude than constitution. I well remember that though to appearance not robust, you could endure great fatigue, and few of our contemporaries have enjoyed more health than yourself. I have a kind of *confidence* that exercise, temperance, and cheerfulness would be as friendly to you as they were to old CORNARO. I wish you could get away from home and pursue no other objects. Try, if it be only for a month or two, and give up all kind of business of what nature soever. Don't permit anybody to say a word to you about your causes, your rents, your farm

—nay, for the present avoid even politics, defer join-ing the Congress, the Assembly, or any other body of men whose object is business. Suppose, when the season becomes more mild, you were to take lodgings at Bristol? The waters would probably be useful to you, you would see as much and as little company as you pleased, and I promise to go to church with you every Sunday. Tell Mrs. Livingston I beg she will join her persuasion to mine. Such a little journey would be useful to you both, and I should think the middle of April would not be too early for it.

The Committee for Canada was appointed before I reached this place. It consists of Dr. Franklin, Mr. Chase, and a Mr. Carrol from Maryland. Had I been here I should have proposed you, though I must confess I think you can employ your time more to the advantage of your health in many other ways. Your country has no demands upon you till that be re-established. Let me entreat you, therefore, to confine your attention to it. Twenty-seven tons of powder, some saltpetre, and three hundred arms ar-rived here yesterday, and we hear from good authority that five tons of powder have arrived safe at North Carolina.

This is all the news I have heard since I have been in town. As to politics, you know the letters of Con-gress people should be silent on that subject in these times, when letters often miscarry, etc. God bless you and give you health.

I am yours, etc.,

JOHN JAY.

COLONEL McDOUGALL TO JAY.

HEAD QUARTERS, 7ᵗʰ March, 1776.

DEAR SIR:

While I am waiting for General Lee, just at the Point of his departure, I am induced to put a few incoherent thoughts together. I fear the Confederacy will suffer by altering General Lee's destination, from Canada. The officer who is to command there should speak French, if such an officer can be procured; a Frenchman's eyes sparkle when he is addressed in that Language; many reasons might be urged in favor of his taking that command. The confidence the well affected Canadians would have in his experience, as well as our Troops loudly proclaim him to be the man. The advantages of his acquaintance with the manners of the people of that nation is among the many motives that designate him for that Colony. The object of the Enemy there will be more fixed than in Virginia, which renders it more necessary the officer should be a man of experience. In Virginia the attacks of the Enemy must from the nature of the Country be irregular, and may therefore be more easily repulsed by an officer of less experience than those made on Quebec, in the Spring. For you may rest assured the ministry will pay particular attention to the relief of that Town & Colony, for there they have some prospect with a tolerable force to secure the Province, not only from the Confederacy, but to gain some strength by awing the inhabitants to take up arms in their favour. Such an event would greatly increase our embarassment. If these reasons have any weight pray reconsider the expediency of sending the General to the Southard. The sloop we are fitting out is ready, but waits to know from Congress what pay you allow the officers and saylors on board the Smalest Continental Vessels, and the description of the Continental Colours. *I beg you to furnish me with a Copy of these with-*

out delay as the Public Service suffers, without regarding at whose expense the armament is to be. Send me also a sample of the Pikes made at Phil[a].

     I am in great Haste
        Your affectionate
           ALEX[R]. MCDOUGALL.

FREDERICK JAY [1] TO JAY.

          NEW YORK, 16th March, 1776.

DEAR JACK:

  Yours of the 10th Inst., I have now before me. I received a letter from Papa yesterday, by which I find that he is better—tho' very weak. You may depend that if he does grow worse I shall acquaint you of it. I should have returned to Rye long ere this, but receiving a cargoe from Curacao, was obliged to stay. Have sold all off & put £200 in my Pocket; the first cost was £288—10—6—good business—but times are such at present as deters me from orderg. any thing more. This Day all our militia turned out with great spirit. They are throwing up entrenchments at the Hospital, Bayard's Mount, at the Furnace, Peck's slip, Beekman's slip, Ten Eyck's wharf, Back of the Governor's House, & several other Places. Never did People in the world act with more Spirit & Resolution than the New Yorkers do at this present time.

       Your affec. Brother
          F. JAY.

---

[1] John Jay's next younger brother, who had been with him on the N. Y. Committee of One Hundred in 1775, and who was associated with the local committee in Westchester Co. in 1776; afterwards member of the N. Y. Assembly to the close of the war.

ROBERT R. LIVINGSTON TO JAY.

CLAREMOUNT, 20th March, 1776.

DEAR JOHN:

Your letters of 26th Jan., 25th Feb., and 4th inst., are all before me.[1] They are written with so much friendship and affection as to afford me great consolation, and convince me, notwithstanding my heavy losses, that in you I have more left than falls to the lot of most of my fellow-mortals. May the blessing be continued to me, and I know how to value it.

I sympathize most sincerely with you in your melancholy apprehensions about your parents. I know and I can feel such a loss; but you draw your consolation from a never-failing source, which will enable you to bear this misfortune whenever it shall happen, with that resignation to the will of Heaven which becomes one who is satisfied both of its wisdom and goodness. If we could shake off human frailty in the hour of affliction, we should certainly think it less reasonable to lament the death of a good man than to complain of the absence of a friend, who by that absence infinitely increases his happiness; to wish them back is selfish

---

[1] In a letter of the 25th February, Jay writes to Livingston:

"Your letter of the 15th inst. informs me that you continue indisposed and that you are nursing yourself at home. I am sorry for both. The first alarms me on account of your health and the second forbodes your being long sick. Amusement and exercise ought to be your objects; at home you can have little of either. Domestic concerns, variety of business, and twenty things going wrong for want of that care and attention which a sick man should not think of, agitate your mind and prevent that even flow of spirits and that calm throughout the whole man so necessary to invite the return of health. This would be my case were I in your situation. If it be yours get rid of it. The spring advances fast and as soon as the roads will permit you, go to the camp, to Philadelphia, in short anywhere, so that you are but moving. You must, however, leave off riding post—no more sixty or seventy miles a day. Travel like a citizen of the world who thinks himself at home at every inn, and leaves it as you would your house when you are about to take an airing. If I can with any tolerable propriety leave the Congress I will accompany you, and as I have often done, save your horse from many a sweat."

and unworthy of true friendship, and yet we may, we must grieve when we are not permitted to take leave. It is, I am sensible, a weakness, but I cannot help suffering myself to be afflicted at this circumstance. I know the pleasure that the best of fathers always took in my company and conversation ; and when I indulge the thought, I am unhappy that by my absence I lessened any of his enjoyments. But where am I running. God bless you—farewell.

Your friend,
Robert R. Livingston.

JAY TO COLONEL McDOUGALL.

Philadelphia, March 23^d, 1776.

Dear Colonel:

When the clerk of the Congress gave me the printed papers which I enclosed you, he told me they contained the navy establishment. Whatever deficiencies there may be in them as to that matter, will I hope be supplied by the extract now enclosed.

As to continental colours, the Congress have made no order as yet concerning them, and I believe the captains of their armed vessels have in that particular been directed by their own fancies and inclinations. I remember to have seen a flag designed for one of them, on which was extremely well painted a large rattlesnake, rearing his crest and shaking his rattles, with this motto, "*Don't tread on me,*" but whether this device was generally adopted by the fleet, I am not able to say,—I rather think it was not.

I am by no means without my apprehensions of danger from that licentiousness which in your situa-

tion is not uncommon ; nothing will contribute more
to its suppression than a vigorous exertion of the
powers vested in your Convention and Committee of
Safety, at least till more regular forms can be introduced. The tenderness shown to some wild people
on account of their supposed attachment to the cause,
has been of disservice. Their eccentric behaviour,
by passing unreproved, has gained countenance, and
has lessened your authority, and diminished that dignity so essential and necessary to give weight and
respect to your ordinances. Some of your own people are daily instigated (if not employed) to calumniate
and abuse the whole province, and misrepresent all
their actions and intentions. One in particular has
had the impudence to intimate to certain persons that
your battalions last campaign were not half full, and
that Schaick's regiment had more officers than pri-
vates ; others report that you have all along supplied
the men-of-war with whatever they pleased to have,
and through them our enemies in Boston. By tales
like these they pay their court to people who have
more ostensible consequence than real honesty, and
more cunning than wisdom.

I am happy to find that our intermeddling in the
affair of the test is agreeable to you. For God's sake
resist all such attempts for the future.

Your own discernment has pointed out to you the
principle of Lord Stirling's advancement ; had the
age of a colonel's commission been a proper rule, it
would have determined in favour of some colonel at
Cambridge, many of whose commissions are prior in

date to any in New-York.   The spirit you betray on this occasion becomes a soldier.

The enclosed copy of a resolve of Congress will, I hope, settle all doubts relative to rank, which may arise from your new commission.   The consequence you drew from that circumstance was more ingenious than solid, for I can assure you that the Congress were not disposed to do any thing wrong or uncivil; and I can also add, that your not having joined your regiment last summer has been explained to their satisfaction, as far as I am able to judge; with respect to this, however, as well as some other matters, I shall defer particulars till we meet.   In a word, with some men in these as in other times, a man must either be their tool and be despised, or act a firm disinterested part and be abused.   The latter has in one or two matters been your fate, as well as that of many other good men.   Adieu.   I am, dear sir,

Your friend

JOHN JAY.

JAY TO COMMITTEE OF SAFETY, NEW YORK.

PHILADELPHIA, April 7, 1776.

GENTLEMEN :

The Congress having been informed of a very extraordinary oath, ordered by Gov. Tryon to be administered to passengers in the late packet, whereby they bound themselves not to disclose anything relative to American affairs except to the ministry have appointed a Committee (of which I am one) to ascertain this fact.

I must therefore request of you, gentlemen, to appoint proper persons to examine into this matter, and if possible ascertain the truth of the report, by affidavits taken before the mayor or one of the judges of the supreme court.

> I have the honour to be, gentlemen,
> Your most obedt. servt.
> JOHN JAY.

To the Honble. the Committee of Safety
for the Colony of New York.

CONGRESS AND INDEPENDENCE.[1]

It has long been the art of the enemies of America to sow the seeds of Dissensions among us and thereby weaken that union on which our salvation from tyranny depends. For this purpose jealousies have been endeavoured to be executed, and false reports, wicked slanders and insidious misrepresentations industriously formed and propagated.

Well knowing that while the people reposed confidence in the Congress the designs of the ministry

[1] In the early stages of the discussion on the expediency of formally separating from the mother country, Jay, with the majority of his colleagues in Congress and the leaders of the day, took a conservative position. The above paper was doubtless intended, with many others printed at the time, to forestall precipitate action on so vital a question. Whether it was published in the form here given does not appear, but a longer communication signed " Seek Truth," following the same line of argument and containing the same or like extracts from the records of Congress, is to be found in Force's " American Archives," 4th Ser., vol. v., p. 1011, suggesting the possibility that it may have been Jay's own elaboration of this first draft preserved among his papers. As the situation changed and a Declaration of Independence became the one necessary and saving step, few men labored more zealously to make it an accomplished fact than Jay. See his resolutions in N. Y. Convention, July 9, 1776.

would probably be frustrated, no pains have been spared to traduce that respectable assembly and misrepresent their designs and actions. Among other aspersions cast upon them, is an ungenerous and groundless charge of their aiming at Independence, or a total separation from G. Britain. Whoever will be at the trouble of reviewing their Journal will find ample testimony against this accusation, and for the sake of those who may not have either leisure or opportunity to peruse it, I have selected the following paragraphs which abundantly prove the malice and falsity of such a charge.

Page 59.—The Congress in giving orders for securing the stores taken at Crown Point and Ticonderogah direct " That an exact inventory be taken of all such cannon and stores, in order that they may be safely returned, when the Restoration of the former Harmony between Great Britain & these Colonies, so *ardently wished for by the latter*, shall render it prudent and consistent with the over-ruling Law of self Preservation."

Page 63.—The Congress after resolving that the Colonies ought to be put in a state of Defence, thus proceed—" But as *we most ardently wish for a Restoration of the Harmony* formerly subsisting between our mother country and these Colonies, the interruption of which must, at all events be exceedingly injurious to both countries, *that with a sincere Design of contributing by all the means in our Power,* (not incompatible with a just regard for the undoubted Rights and true interests of these Colonies) *to the Promotion of their most desirable Reconciliation* an humble and dutiful Petition be presented to his Majesty, Resolved *that measures be entered into for opening a negotiation, in order to accommodate the unhappy Disputes subsisting between Great Britain and these Colonies*, and that *this* be made a *Part of the Petition to the King*."

Page 64.—The Congress recommend to the Convention of New York " to persevere the more vigorously in preparing for their Defence, as it is very uncertain whether *the earnest endeavours of the Congress to accommodate the unhappy Differences between Great Britain and the Colonies, by conciliatory measures will be successful*."

Page 84.—The Congress in order to rescue the Province of Massachusetts Bay from anarchy, advise their " Assembly or Council exercise the Powers of Government *until a Governor of his Majesty's appointment will consent to govern the colony according to its charter*."

Page 87.—The Congress in their vote for a general fast recommend that we should " offer up our joint supplications to the all wise, omnipotent and merciful Disposer of all Events (among other things) *to bless our rightful Sovereign King George the third*, that *a speedy end* may be put to the *civil Discord between Great Britain and the American Colonies* without further effusion of Blood, and that all America may soon behold a gracious Interposition of Heaven for the Redress of her many Grievances, the Restoration of her invaded Rights, and *a Reconciliation with the parent State on terms constitutional and honourable to both*."

Page 149.—The Congress after declaring the Reasons which Compelled them to recur to arms, then express themselves—" Lest this Declaration should disquiet the minds of our friends and fellow subjects in any Part of the Empire, we assure them that *we mean not to dissolve that union which has so long and so happily subsisted between us*, and which we sincerely *wish* to see restored. Necessity has not yet *driven* us into that *desperate* measure, or induced us to excite any other nation to war against them. We *have not* raised armies with *ambitious Designs of separating from Great Britain*, and establishing independent States."

150.—" We most humbly implore the Divine goodness *to dispose our adversaries to Reconciliation on reasonable terms.*"

Page 155.—In the Petition to the King, every line of which breaths affection for his Majesty & Great Britain, are these remarkable sentences :

"Attached to your Majesty's Person, Family, and Government, with all the Devotion that Principle and affection can inspire, *connected with Great Britain by the strongest ties that can unite Societies, and deploring every Event* that lends in *any degree* to *weaken* them, we *solemnly assure* your Majesty, that we not only *most ardently desire* the former *Harmony* between her and these colonies may be *restored*, but that a *Concord* may be *established between them* upon so *firm a basis* as to perpetuate its blessings uninterrupted *by any future Dissentions* to succeeding Generations in both countries." " We beg leave further to assure your Majesty that notwithstanding the *sufferings* of your loyal colonists during the course of this present controversy our Breasts retain *too tender a Regard* for the *Kingdom from which we derive our origin*, to request such a Reconciliation as might in *any manner be inconsistent with her Dignity or welfare.*"

Page 163.—In the last address of the Congress to the People of Great Britain are the following Passages :

" *We are accused of aiming at Independence ;* but *how* is this accusation *supported ?* by the *allegations* of your *ministers*, not by *our actions.* Abused, insulted and contemned, *what steps have we pursued to obtain Redress ? We have carried our dutiful Petitions to the Throne ; we have applied to your justice for Relief.*"

Page 165.—" Give us leave most solemnly to assure you *that we have not yet lost sight of the object we have ever had in view, a Reconciliation with you on constitutional Principles, and a Restoration of that friendly Intercourse which to the advantage of both, we till lately maintained.*"

Page 172.—In the address of the Congress to the Lord

Mayor, Aldermen and Livery of London, there is this Paragraph, vizt :

"*North America*, my Lords, *wishes most ardently for a lasting connection with Great Britain on terms of just and equal liberty.*"

From these testimonies it appears extremely evident that to charge the Congress with aiming at a separation of these Colonies from Great Britain, is to charge them falsely and without a single spark of evidence to support the accusation. Many other passages in their Journal might be mentioned, but as that would exceed the limits of this paper, I shall reserve them for some future publication.

It is much to be wished that people would read the Proceedings of the Congress and consult their own judgments, and not suffer themselves to be *duped by men who are paid for deceiving them.*

JAY TO MARINUS WILLETT.[1]

Sir :

It is much to be regretted that all human affairs are liable to errors and imperfections, and that real as well as imaginary evils are so widely spread thro the world.

The subject of your letter deserves attention ; it is however unnecessary for me to repeat what I have already said relative to it, except again to assure you that my endeavours shall not be wanting to obtain for you an appointment equal to your merit. General

---

[1] Marinus Willett, lately captain in McDougall's regiment, and subsequently lieutenant-colonel in the New York Continental Line ; mayor of New York, 1807.

Schuyler's letter does you honor, & had it been made known to the members of Congress a few months sooner, I am confident it would have had all the influence you would have wished.

I hope care will be taken of the officers you allude to ; men who deserve well of the country are entitled to its regard, and in my opinion no opportunity of distinguishing and rewarding merit ought to be omitted.

I am glad your indisposition is removed, and hope it will not be long before an occasion of again calling you to the service of your country will present itself.

I am Sir

Your very h'ble Servt

JOHN JAY.

Phila. 27 Ap. 1776.

JAY TO COLONEL McDOUGALL.

PHILADELPHIA, 27th April, 1776.

DEAR COLONEL :

Accept my thanks for your friendly letter of the 16th instant, and its enclosures, which contain useful as well as agreeable information. I am glad to see New York doing something in the naval way, and think the encouragement given by your Convention to the manufacture of arms, powder, saltpetre, and seasalt does them honour.

Many of the reasons you allege for delaying taxation are weighty, and I confess did not occur to me. It is certainly unreasonable to impose on the city, in its present circumstances, so great a share of the public expenses.

The late election, so far as it respects yourself, has taken a turn I did not expect, and at a loss to account for, except on the principle of your holding a military office, or that mutability which from various causes often strongly marks popular opinions of men and measures in times like these. But whatever may have been the reason, I am persuaded that the zeal you have shown and the sacrifices you have made in this great cause will always afford you the most pleasing reflections, and will one day not only merit, but receive the gratitude of your fellow-citizens. Posterity you know always does justice. Let no circumstances of this kind diminish your ardour; but by persevering in a firm uniform course of conduct, silence detraction and compel approbation.

I am much obliged to you for your kind attention to my house; and be assured that I shall omit no opportunity of evincing the esteem and sincerity with which I am

Your friend and humble servant,

John Jay.

ROBERT R. LIVINGSTON TO JAY.[1]

PHILADELPHIA, 17th May, 1776.

DEAR JOHN:

I was so unfortunate as to miss the last post, by which means I was prevented from letting you hear what I had done about getting you lodgings at Bristol, & the import-

---

[1] Jay, who had been an almost constant attendant on Congress for a year, was now for many months to be associated with the public bodies and affairs of his own Province. On the third Tuesday of April, 1776, he was elected member of the New York Congress, and on May 25th he took his seat in that body. His seat in the Continental Congress was not vacated by this change, and he

ant business that had been transacted here before I arrived. I could not find a tolerable house in Bristol, the rooms that were unoccupied were all too small & hot for invalids, & there was no house that could furnish more than two so that we could not have been together, tho' had the rooms been tolerable we might have made out by taking two adjoining houses had not the landladys nose placed such an obstruction in my way as my regard for your future posterity rendered it impossible for me to get over. However I have provided three Bedrooms & a large parlour in a retired country house, about two miles from Bristol upon the banks of the [Delaware] where we shall have plentiful provisions for our horses, good fishing before the door, a tavern about ¼ of a mile from us to lodge our friends, & in short every thing that we can wish to render our situation agreeable. The lodgings are to be entered upon next Wednesday, by which time I hope to see you & Mrs. Jay there; it is absolutely necessary you shd. come to settle the arrangement of our family. And (what is much more important) to settle another arrangment which I most heartily wish we could unite in making. Mr. Duane tells me he has enclosed you a copy of the resolutions of the 15th. I make no observations on it in this place for fear of accidents. It has occa-

probably would have returned to Philadelphia but for the important matters to come before the New York Congress requiring his presence there. The recommendation of the Continental Congress to the several colonies to adopt new and constitutional forms of government especially required careful deliberation, and the New York Congress directed him not to leave them "without further orders." Jay's letters show that he was heartily in favor of a change in the provincial government, but as the House had not been instructed on this issue, it called for the election of a new body, which took the name of the New York Convention—Jay being returned as a member from New York City. The Convention met at White Plains, July 9th, and a committee subsequently appointed to report on the proposed measure. The exigencies of the campaign for that year, however, delayed action on the adoption of a new form of government, until March–April of the following year, as appears from the note to the Livingston–Morris letter of April 26, 1777. Jay, meantime, was buried in the work of important committees.

sioned a great alarm here, & the cautious folks are very fearful of its being attended with many ill consequences next week when the Assembly are to meet ; some points of the last importance are to be agitated (as we imagine) very early. I wish to God you could be here. If you do not get this length meet me at least at Bristol next week from whence you may return in a few days & send some of our delegates along as the province will otherwise be often unrepresented, since I find it inconsistant with my health to be close in my attendance in Congress. You have by this time sounded our people, I hope they are satisfied of the necessity of assumming a new form of Government ; let me hear (if you dont come yourself) in what channel it will probably run. Let me know the mode in which new powers (for the old are insufficient) are to be obtained ; if by a dissolution it will be necessary to go home. Let me also know in what sphere you yourself chuse to move. You are so necessary here, that I will consent to no law which will make the honours I wish you to possess inconsistant with your attendance on Congress. I have a thought which if carried into execution might render ours the favorite colony, & offset the absurd claims of our neighbours, which may hereafter be very troublesome, but it requires much consideration, & may perhaps be impracticable. I will reserve it (with other of my reveries) till one of those happy hours in which I permit myself to think aloud in your hearing. If you should see Benson it would not be amiss to let him know that I am a little hurt at his conduct ; it may induce him to alter it without my coming to an explanation which might possibly occasion a coolness which I wish to avoid. Farewell—may heaven bless you & put an end to these evils which break in so cruelly upon our Domestick enjoyments even, & render our reflection on past pleasures the most agreeable part of our present friendship.

Your friend &c.

R. R. Livingston.

JAMES DUANE TO JAY.

I wrote you, my dear Sir, a hasty scrawl by the post on a most important subject.[1] You know the Maryland Instructions and those of Pensylvania. I am greatly in doubt whether either of their Assemblies or Conventions will listen to a recommendation the preamble of which so openly avows independence & separation. The lower Counties will probably adhere to Pensylvania. New Jersey you can gain a good judgement of from the reception this important Resolution has met with. The orators of Virginia with Col. Henry at their head are against a Change of Government ; the body of the people, Col. Nelson, on whose authority you have this sent, thinks are for it. The late Election of Deputies for the Convention of New York sufficiently proves that those who assumed [excessive] ferver & gave laws even to the Convention & Committees were unsupported by the people. There seems therefore no reason that our Colony shou'd be too precipitate in changing the present mode of Government. I wou'd first be well assured of the opinion of the Inhabitants at large. Let them be rather followed than driven on an occasion of such moment. But, above all, let us see the conduct of the middle Colonies before we come to a decision : It cannot injure us to wait a few weeks : the advantage will be great for this trying question will clearly discover the true principles & the extent of the Union of the Colonies. This,

---

[1] Duane was one of the delegates from New York in the Continental Congress. In the first sentence of the above letter he refers to one of May 16th, in which he wrote to Jay as follows :

" Yesterday, my dear Friend, was an important day productive of the Resolutions of which I enclose you a copy. I shall not enter into particulars : the Resolution itself first passed and then a Committee was appointed to fit it with a preamble. Compare them with each other and it will probably lead you into Reflections which I dare not point out. I hope you will relieve me soon as I am impatient to visit my Friends : I look upon Business here to be in such a train that I can well be spared." The resolution referred to change of colonial governments already mentioned.

my dear Sir, is a delicate subject on which I cannot enlarge at present. If I can be [of service] I would immediately set out and give you a meeting—pray hasten the release of one of the Gentlemen. I know *you ought* to be at the Convention who are not informed of the state and temper of their neighbours, & want, at least in this Respect, some Assistance.

I am pleased with the situation M^r. Livingston has found for your Saturday's retreat on the Banks of the [Delaware] —nothing cou'd have been more convenient. Present my compliments to M^rs. Jay and

believe me to be with great Regard

D^r. Sir

your affectionate & most obd^t. Servt.

JAS. DUANE.

PHILAD., 18th May, 1776.

ROBERT R. LIVINGSTON TO JAY.

PHILADELPHIA, 21 May, 1776.

DEAR JOHN:

I am much mortified at not hearing from you. I wrote to you last week, and am just now setting out for Bristol in order to meet Mrs. Livingston. I could wish to find Mrs. Jay there also. Pray send some of our colleagues along, otherwise I must be more confined than either my health or inclination will allow. You have doubtless seen the account brought by the *Rifleman* from London, by which it appears we shall have at least 34,000 commissioners.

If your Congress have any spirit, they will at least build fourteen or fifteen light boats capable of carrying a twelve-pounder, to secure Hudson River, which is to be the chief scene of action. The carpenters employed on the frigate would build two or three a day, if they were built in the manner of batteaux, which is the true construction.

I wish you would direct Gaine to send me his paper. God bless you.

Yours, most sincerely
R. R. LIVINGSTON.

JAY TO JAMES DUANE.

DEAR SIR :

Since my last, I have had the pleasure of receiving your letter of the 25th Inst. and am obliged to you for the intelligence contained in it.[1] So great are the inconveniences resulting from the present mode of Government, that I believe our Convention will almost unanimously agree to institute a better, to continue till a peace with Great Britain may render it unnecessary.

The proceedings of Maryland will probably check the ardor of some people ; I fear that the divisions of Pennsylvania will injure the common Cause.

Mrs. Jay is so much better as to quit her room.

---

[1] In a letter of May 25th, Duane informs Jay that Maryland dissents from the recommendation of Congress to institute new governments in the colonies, and that there is division of sentiment in Pennsylvania. Respecting the latter Duane writes : "The General Assembly of Pensylvania is averse to any Change. The people of this Town [Phila.] assembled last Monday in the State house yard & agreed to a set of Resolutions in favour of a Change. Another body are signing a Remonstrance against the acts of that meeting and in support of the Assembly. The Committee for the County of Philadelphia have unanimously supported the Assembly & protested against any Change. It is supposed the other Counties will follow their example & take a part in the dispute. Is it not to be feared that this point of Dissention will spread itself into the adjoining Colonies ? But I intend to make no Reflections—the facts I have hinted at will be published." Duane adds that he is awaiting the return of one of the absent delegates from New York to visit his own family : "It is more than 9 months since I have seen my children & I have spent but about ten days in that time with Mrs. Duane."

When I shall return is uncertain, the Convention having directed me not to leave them till further order.

Be so kind as to inform M^r· Lynch that I have not yet been able to procure a horse for him. We find mares fit for riding have, in consequence of the resolve of Congress forbidding races, been put to breeding ; and I believe it will be difficult to get a handsome gelding. I shall however continue my inquiries, and should I meet with anything very clever, shall perhaps be rather lavish of his guineas. Be pleased to present my Comp$^{ts·}$ to him & M^r· Rutledge, and dont forget either Merkle or White Eyes.

I am D^r· Sir

Your most obed$^{t·}$ Serv$^{t·}$

JOHN JAY.

N. YORK, 29 May, 1776.

JAY TO ROBERT R. LIVINGSTON.

NEW YORK, 29th May, 1776.

DEAR ROBERT :

The pleasure I expected from a junction of all our families at Bristol has vanished. Dr. Bard tells me the waters there would be injurious to Mrs. Jay's complaints ; so that I shall again take a solitary ride to Philadelphia, whenever the Convention, who directed me to abide here until their further order, shall think proper to dismiss me.

Messrs. Alsop and Lewis set out next Saturday for Philadelphia. Mr. Duane informs me that he is about to return home, and considering how long he has been absent from his family, I think him entitled to that indulgence. I pray God that your health may enable you to attend constantly, at least till it may be in my power to relieve you. Is Mr. Clinton returned?

Our Convention will, I believe, institute a better government than the present, which in my opinion will no longer work any thing but mischief; and although the measure of obtaining authority by instructions may have its advocates, I have reason to think that such a resolution will be taken as will open a door to the election of new or additional members. But be the resolution what it may, you shall have the earliest advice of it. And should my conjectures prove right, I shall inform the members of Duchess of your readiness to serve, and advise them to elect you.

Don't be uneasy at receiving so few letters from me. I have been so distressed by the ill health of my wife and parents, that I have scarce written any thing.

I am, dear Robert, your affectionate friend,

JOHN JAY.

GENERAL WASHINGTON TO JAY.[1]

Gen¹. Washington presents his complim^{ts.} to Mr. Livingston & Mr. Jay—thanks them most cordially for their kind Information & Invitation; but is so exceedingly hurried

---

[1] For the proceedings against Gilbert Forbes, a gunsmith in New York, charged with conspiring against the person of the Commander-in-Chief, see "Am. Archives," 4th Series, vol. vi., p. 1178. Livingston, Jay, and G. Morris were a secret committee appointed by the Convention to ferret out the plot.

just at this time, that it is not in his power to attend the examination of G. Forbes. He begs it may go on, and will take it exceedingly kind if Forbes and the examination when taken, be sent to head Quarters at half after four o'clock, when the General will have an officer or two present to question him, & compare his answers with the information given M^r· Livingston and M^r· Jay.

HEAD QUARTERS 29th June, 1776.

EDWARD RUTLEDGE[1] TO JAY.

PHILAD$^{A·}$ June 29th, 1776.

MY DEAR JAY:

I write this for the express Purpose of requesting that if possible you will give your Attendance in Congress on Monday next. I know full well that your Presence must be . . . useful at New York, but I am sincerely convinced that it will be absolutely necessary in this City during the whole of the ensuing Week.—A Declaration of Independence, the Form of a Confederation of these

---

[1] Edward Rutledge, delegate from Charleston, S. C. In a letter of June 8th, he wrote to Jay:

" The Congress sat till 7 o'clock this evening in consequence of a motion of R. H. Lee's rendering ourselves free & independant State. The sensible part of the House opposed the Motion—they had no objection to forming a Scheme of a Treaty which they would send to France by proper Persons & uniting this Continent by a Confedracy ; they saw no Wisdom in a *Declaration* of Independence, nor any other Purpose to be enforced by it, but placing ourselves in the Power of those with whom we mean to treat, giving our Enemy Notice of our Intentions before we had taken any steps to execute them. . . . The event, however, was that the Question was postponed ; it is to be renewed on Monday when I mean to move that it should be postponed for 3 Weeks or Months. In the mean Time the plan of Confederation & the Scheme of Treaty may go on. I don't know whether I shall succeed in this Motion ; I think not, it is at least Doubtful. However I must do what is right in my own Eyes, & Consequences must take Care of themselves. I wish you had been here—the whole Argument was sustained on one side by R. Livingston, Wilson, Dickenson & myself, & by the Power of all N. England, Virginia & Georgia at the other." See note p. 52.

Colonies, and a Scheme for a treaty with foreign Powers
will be laid before the House on Monday. Whether we
shall be able effectually to oppose the first and infuse Wisdom into the others will depend in a great measure upon
the exertions of the . . . and sensible part of the Members. I trust you will contribute in a considerable degree
to effect the Business and therefore I wish you to be with
us. Recollect the manner in which your Colony is at this
time represented. Clinton has Abilities but is silent in
general and wants (when he does speak) that Influence to
which he is intitled. Floyd, Wisner, Lewis and Alsop tho'
good men, never quit their chairs. You must know the
Importance of these Questions too well not to wish to [be]
present whilst they are debating and therefore I shall say
no more upon the Subject. I have been much engaged
lately upon a plan of a Confederation which Dickenson has
drawn ; it has the Vice of all his Productions to a considerable Degree ; I mean the Vice of Refining too much.
Unless it's greatly curtailed it never can pass, as it is to be
submitted to Men in the respective Provinces who will not
be led or rather driven into Measures which may lay the
Foundation of their Ruin. If the Plan now proposed
should be adopted nothing less than Ruin to some Colonies
will be the Consequence of it— The Idea of destroying all
Provincial Distinctions and making every thing of the most
minute kind bend to what they call the good of the whole,
is in other Terms to say that these Colonies must be subject to the Government of the Eastern Provinces. The
Force of their Arms I hold exceeding Cheap, but I confess
I dread their over-ruling Influence in Council. I dread their
low Cunning, and those . . . Principles which Men
without Character and without Fortune in general possess,
which are so captivating to the lower class of Mankind, and
which will occasion such a fluctuation of Property as to
introduce the greatest disorder. I am resolved to vest the
Congress with no more Power than that is absolutely neces-

sary, and to use a familiar Expression, to keep the Staff in our own Hands; for I am confident if surrendered into the Hands of others a most pernicious use will be made of it. If you can't come let me hear from you by the Return of the Post. Compliments to Livingston & G. Morris. God bless you.

With Esteem & affection
Yrs.
E. RUTLEDGE.

JAY TO EDWARD RUTLEDGE.

6th July, 1776.

DEAR RUTLEDGE :

Your friendly letter found me so engaged by plots, conspiracies, and chimeras dire, that, though I thanked you for it in my head I had no time to tell you so either in person or by letter. Your ideas of men and things (to speak mathematically) run, for the most part, parallel with my own; and I wish Governor Tryon and the devil had not prevented my joining you on the occasion you mentioned. How long I may be detained here is uncertain, but I see little prospect of returning to you for a month or two yet to come. We have a government, you know, to form; and God only knows what it will resemble. Our politicians, like some guests at a feast, are perplexed and undetermined which dish to prefer. Our affairs in Canada have lately become the subject of animadversion; and the miscarriages in that country are, with little reserve, imputed to the inattention of the Congress. Indeed, there is reason to believe that certain military gentlemen who reaped no laurels there are among the patrons of that doctrine. It is to me amazing that a strict inquiry has not been made into the behaviour of those under whose direction we have met with nothing but repeated losses in that country. Nor is the public silent with respect to the inactivity of the fleet ; and reports have gone abroad, that the admiral has refused to comply with the orders of Congress relative to the cannon taken at Providence. I 'll tell you a pretty story of Gen. Wooster. While he was smoking his pipe in the suburbs of Quebec, he took it into his head that he might do wonders with a fire-ship ; and, with an imagination warmed by the blaze of the enemy's vessels, sent for a New-York captain, who, it seems, understood the business of fire-ship building. Under the strongest injunctions of secrecy, he communicated to him the important plan, and ordered him to get the ship in readiness with all the despatch and privacy in his power ; wisely observing, that if the enemy should get any intelligence of his design, they would carry their vessels out of the way of his fire-ship. The captain accordingly set about preparing the materials, &c. necessary for the exploit which was to heroise his general. Some short time after, Wooster was informed that the time for which the York troops were enlisted would expire in a day or two ; he issued orders for them to parade at a certain time and place, and informed them that he would then and there make a speech to them—and a Ciceronian speech it was.

" My lads," says he, " I find your time is almost out, and maybe some of you may think on going ; but surely you won't leave me now ; you must try and stay a little longer. Don't think that I am laying here doing nothing. No, no ; you shall see a fine sight soon. I am busy building a fire-ship ; and as soon as she is ready, we 'll burn all their vessels up." *Cetera desunt.*

The York troops, allured by the promise of a *feu de joie*, staid and were disappointed. Some renegade Frenchmen remembered the speech, and told it as a secret to Governor Carleton. The vessels were put out of harm's way, and the Connecticut Alexander lost his passage in a fire-ship to the temple of fame.

My compliments to Messrs. Braxton, Lynch, and such others as I esteem,—of which number rank yourself, my dear Ned, among the first.

Believe me to be sincerely yours,

JOHN JAY.

JAY TO THE PRESIDENT OF CONGRESS.

NEW YORK, July 6, 1776.

SIR :

The enclosed memorial was yesterday given me by Mr. Bill, with a request that I would transmit it to Congress. He appears much hurt in being omitted in the arrangement of officers intended for the regiment lately ordered to be raised in this Colony ; and I sincerely wish he had less reason to think himself neglected. He is a fine, spirited young gentleman, of one or two and twenty, of an ancient and once opulent family in this Colony. His connexions are extensive in the County, and he seems to possess that generous kind of ambition so essential to the character of a good officer. What renders his case the more unfortunate is, that he is almost the only one of his family who has discovered any degree of ardour in the American cause. His promotion would have contributed as much to increase their zeal as his being laid aside may tend to diminish it. Nor is this the only instance in which that arrangement has given disgust : among others, Mr. Cortlandt, whose family is not only very numerous, but also respectable and wealthy, entered the service last year as Lieutenant-Colonel ; he has done the like this year. Mr. Dubois entered the service last year as a Captain, and this year Captain Dubois is made to command Lieutenant-Colonel Cortlandt. Appointments like these pay ill compliment to those who are thus (as they think unjustly) superseded, and therefore have an unhappy tendency to drive them into a sullen indifference about Congressional measures.[1]

I am, Sir, with great respect, the Congress's and your most obedient servant,

JOHN JAY.

To the Honourable John Hancock, Esq.

---

[1] This question of military appointments occasioned anxiety among officers and others in all the States. Congress had lately nominated officers for a New York battalion, which the Convention of that State believed to be an assumption of power. Jay wrote the Convention's reply, printed in its proceedings, in which he said : " The third reason given for depriving us in this instance of the right of nomination, is the good of the service and the danger of delay. *The necessity of the case*, has in all ages and nations of the world been a fruitful, though dangerous, source of power. It has often sown tares in the fair fields of liberty, and like a malignant blast, destroyed the fruits of patriotism and public spirit. The whole history of mankind bears testimony against the propriety of considering this principle as the parent of civil rights ; and a people jealous of their liberties will ever reprobate it. We believe Congress

RESOLUTIONS OF NEW YORK CONVENTION APPROVING
DECLARATION OF INDEPENDENCE.[1]

> In Convention of the Representatives of
> the State of New York, WHITE PLAINS,
> July 9, 1776.

Resolved, unanimously, That the reasons assigned by the Continental Congress for declaring the *United Colonies* free and independent States, are cogent and conclusive ; and that while we lament the cruel necessity which has rendered that measure unavoidable, we approve the same, and will, at the risk of our lives and fortunes, join with the other Colonies in supporting it.

Resolved, That a copy of the said Declaration, and the aforegoing Resolution, be sent to the Chairman of the Committee of the County of Westchester, with orders to publish the same with beat of drum at this place, on Thursday next, and to give directions that it

---

went into this measure with pure intentions, and with no other wish than that of serving their country ; and we entertain too high an opinion of their virtue and integrity to apologize for a plainness of speech becoming freemen, and which we know can give offence only to that counterfeit and adulterated dignity which swells the pride of those who, instead of lending, borrow consequence from their offices. And, sir, we beg leave to assure Congress, that though we shall always complain of and oppose their resolutions when they injure our rights, we shall ever be ready to risk our lives and fortunes in supporting the American cause."

[1] On July 9, 1776, the day the newly elected Convention of New York, mentioned on p. 59, assembled at White Plains, it received through the delegates at Congress a copy of the Declaration of Independence for approval. This was read and then referred to a Committee, of which Mr. Jay was chairman. At the afternoon session of the same day the Committee reported the above resolutions which were unanimously adopted. Referring to this action Jay's biographer says, vol. i., p. 45 : " Thus, although Mr. Jay was, by his recall from Congress, deprived of the honour of affixing his signature to the Declaration of Independence, he had the satisfaction of drafting the pledge given by his native State to support it ; and this pledge, in his own handwriting, is preserved among the records of New York."

be published with all convenient speed in the several Districts within the said County, and that copies thereof be forthwith transmitted to the other County Committees within the State of *New York*, with orders to cause the same to be published in the several Districts of their respective Counties.

Resolved, That five hundred copies of the Declaration of Independence, with the two last-mentioned Resolutions of this Congress for approving and proclaiming the same, be published in handbills, and sent to all the County Committees in this State.

Resolved, That the Delegates of this State in Continental Congress, be, and they are hereby, authorized to consent to and adopt all such measures as they may deem conducive to the happiness and welfare of the *United States of America*.

JOHN JAY,
ABRAHAM YATES,
JOHN SLOSS HOBART, } Committee on draft of Resolutions.
ABRAHAM BRASHER,
WILLIAM SMITH.

JAY TO MRS. JAY.

SALISBURY, 29th July, 1776.

MY DEAR SALLY:

I am now returning to Poughkeepsie, where I am to meet some members of the Convention on the 7th of August. How long I may stay there is entirely uncertain. Unless some unforeseen business should intervene, I propose returning to the White Plains by the way of Elizabethtown. The journey will be long and fatiguing, but as all the inconveniences of it will be amply compensated by the pleasure of spending a day or two with you, I consider it with satisfaction, and shall pursue it with cheerfulness. Don't, however, depend on it, lest you be disappointed. In these days of uncertainty we can be certain only for the present; the future must be the object rather of hope than expectation. My dear Sally, are you yet provided with a secure retreat in case Elizabethtown should cease to be a place of safety. I shall not be at ease till this be done. You know my happiness depends on your welfare; and therefore I flatter myself your affection for me has, before this will reach you, induced you to attend to that necessary object. I daily please myself with an expectation of finding our boy in health and much grown, and my good wife perfectly recovered and in good spirits. I always endeavour to anticipate good instead of ill fortune, and find it turns to good account; were this practice more general, I fancy mankind would experience more happiness than they usually do. The only danger attending it is, that, by being too sanguine in our expectations, disappointment often punishes our confidence, and renders the sensations occasioned by mortification and chagrin more painful than those arising from anticipated and imaginary enjoyments were pleasing. These, however, are inconveniences which a little prudence will obviate. A person must possess no great share of sagacity who, in this whirl of human affairs, would account that certain which, in the nature of things, cannot be so. But this looks more like writing an essay than a letter. I was thinking loud, my dear wife, which you know is a species of enjoyment which never falls to my lot but when in your company. May I long and often enjoy it! My compliments to all the family.

I am, my dear Sally, and always will be,

Your very affectionate husband,

JOHN JAY.

JAY'S REPORT ON THE PURCHASE OF CANNON.[1]

In pursuance of your Instructions given me at this place on the 22^d July last I immediately repaired to Salisbury Furnace and applied to Messrs. Fitch & Norton, two of the superintendants of the Furnace, Col. Porter the other superintendent being absent, for the cannon and other articles mentioned in the said Instructions. They informed me that there were several cannon and a considerable quantity of shot ready but they were not authorized to dispose of or part with any of the said articles without a licence from Govr Trumbull, that they had no trux [trucks] made and could not order any to be made without his direction. They furnished me with a state of the

[1] Report made to the Secret Committee of the New York Convention about August 7, 1776. This was one of the more important of several committees on which Jay served during that critical period. It was appointed, July 16th, specially to obstruct the channel of the Hudson and annoy the enemy's shipping, and was also authorized " to impress carriages, teams, sloops and horses, and to call out detachments of the militia." Jay was commissioned to secure cannon at Salisbury, Connecticut, for Fort Montgomery in the Highlands.

ordnance and stores they had prepared, and I forthwith proceeded to Govr. Trumbull's at Lebanon.

I gave the Gov. a copy of my instructions and requested the favor of him to furnish the Convention of New York with as many cannon for the defence of Hudson's River as the State of Connecticut could conveniently spare, not exceeding the number mentioned in my Instructions together with a proportionable quantity of shot. I also desired him to give directions for the casting trux for said cannon, and intimated to him that Messrs. Fitch & Norton had informed me it might be done without delaying the making of cannon.

Govr. Trumbull expressed his readiness to contribute all in his power toward the good of the American cause and the safety of this State, but thought it most prudent to summon his Council and submit my request to their consideration.

When the Council convened they concurred with the Govr. in an order for ten twelve pounders and six pounders then at the Furnace at Salisbury to the State of New York, also a suitable proportion of shot for said cannon—said cannon to be replaced and said shot to be returned or accounted for by said State when requested ; and the overseers of said Furnace were required to cast a sufficient number or as many as could be of iron trux or carriage wheels for said cannon to be loaned to said State and returned or accounted for with the cannon aforesaid—all to be delivered to me or my order by said overseers taking proper Receipts for the same. Of this order they gave me the certified copy which is annexed to this Report.

On my return to Salisbury I found Col. Porter there, and the overseers of the Furnace agreed to prepare the cannon mentioned in the above order with the greatest expedition—several of them not being yet bored or drilled. As to the trux, Col. Porter was averse to their entering on that branch of business, objecting that it would impede the casting of cannon, and gave me very satisfactory reasons for his being of that opinion ; and on the same account expressing a desire that Salisbury Furnace might be confined to the making of cannon and Col. Livingston's employed for casting shot and other ordnance stores, adding that he would furnish the Col. with some sand moulders and give him every other assistance in his power. For these reasons I did not think it either reasonable or prudent to insist on a compliance with the Gov$^{r's}$ order respecting the trux.

I then hired teams to carry four twelve pounders which were soon made ready, together with 50 rounds of shot for each of them, to Col. Hoffman's Landing [on Hudson River] at 35 *s* lawful money of Connecticut per ton, and requested Hez$^{h :}$ Fitch, Esq. to forward the remainder as they became ready, with 50 rounds of shot for each cannon to the same place, and engaged to make him a reasonable compensation. He consented to undertake the business and I left with him 28–4–0 lawful money of Connecticut to defray the expenses attending it and to pay the teamsmen then employed in transporting the twelve pounders and shot aforesaid, for which money I took his receipt and have annexed it to this Report.

Being of opinion that application should immediately be made to Col. Livingston for trux and shot, and it being uncertain whether he was at Ancram or the Manor, I went immediately to Ancram, and not finding him there proceeded to the Manor. At my request he has undertaken to furnish the Convention of yᵉ State of New York with proper trux for ten twelve and five (?) six pounders together with cannon shot of various sizes. On my way to this place I overtook the cannon and shot aforesaid going to Col. Hoffman's Landing, and being informed that a sloop was there ready to sail to Fort Montgomery, I ordered the said cannon & shot to be put on board & carried to the said Fort.

[August 7 (?), 1776.]

JOHN MORIN SCOTT[1] TO JAY.

NEW YORK, Sepʳ. 6ᵗʰ, 1776.

DEAR SIR:

I received your Letter about half an hour ago by the Messenger of the honorable Convention, in which you inform me that they are anxious to be informed of any Transactions at this Place that may be of use to the State, or otherwise of Importance. My duty would have directed me to exe-

---

[1] John Morin Scott, a leading lawyer in New York before the war, a warm advocate of the American cause, and at this date Brigadier General of State troops ; subsequently Secretary of State of New York. During the battle of Long Island, fought August 27, 1776, his brigade was ordered over from New York, but took no part in the action.

single inch of ground. *But was soon convinced by the un-answerable Reasons for it.* They were these :—Invested by an Enemy of about double our number from water to water, scant in almost every necessaiy of life & without covering & liable every moment to have the Communication between us and the City cut off by the Entrance of the Frigates into the East River between (late) Governor's Island and Long Island ; which General McDougall assured us from his own nautic Experience was very feasible. In such a situation we should have been reduced to the alternative of desperately attempting to cut our way [through] a vastly superior Enemy with the certain loss of a valuable Stock of Artillery & Artillery Stores which the Government had been collecting with great Pains ; or by Famine & Fatigue been made an easy prey to the Enemy. In either Case the Campaign would have ended in the total Ruin of our army. The Resolution therefore to retreat was unanimous and tho formed late in the Day was executed the following night with unexpected success. We however lost some of our heavy Cannon on the forts at a Distance from the water, the softness of the ground occasioned by the Rains having rendered it impossible to remove them in so short a time. Almost every thing else valuable was saved ; and not a Dozen Men lost in the Retreat. The Consequence of our Retreat was the loss of (late) Gov[rs.] Island which is perfectly commanded by the Fort on Red Hook.—The Enemy however from Fear or other Reasons, indulged [us] with the opportunity of two nights to carry off all except some heavy cannon. The Garrison was drawn off in the afternoon after our Retreat under the fire of the Shipping who are now drawn up just behind (late) Gov[rs.]-Island, & the Fire of some Cannon from Long Island Shore ; but with no other loss than that of one man's arm. What our loss on Long Island was I am not able to estimate. I think the Hills might have been well maintained with 5,000 men. *I fear their natural strength was our Bane by lulling us into a State of Security & enabling the Enemy to steal a march upon us.* I think from the last accounts we must have killed many of the enemy. We are sure that late Col⁰· & afterwards General Grant who was so bitter against us in Parliament, is among the slain. General Parsons late Col⁰· and promoted to the Rank of a General officer escaped from the action & Pursuit as by a miracle. I believe him to be a brave man. He is a Connecticut Lawyer. He told me that in the action he commanded a Party of about 250 men, with orders from Lord Stirling to cover his Flank; and that when the Enemy gave way, he threw into a Heap about thirty of the Enemies dead, and that in advancing a little farther he found a Heap made by the Enemy at least as large as that which he had collected. Lord Stirling had ordered him to maintain his ground till Receipt of the order to retreat. However, finding that no such order came; and finding the Enemy by rallying to increase on his hands, he flew to the Place were Lord Stirling was posted, leaving his Party on the ground with strict orders to maintain it till his Return; but he found his Lordship & his whole Body of Troops gone. There can be no doubt but Lord Stirling behaved bravely; but I wish that he had retreated sooner. He would have saved himself, and a great number of Troops from Captivity; but he refused to retreat for want of orders. We miss him much; he was a very active officer. General Sullivan who was also made a Prisoner in the action on the Heights went some days ago on Parole to Congress to endeavour to procure his Exchange for Prescott. I have not heard of his return. Two or three Days ago the Rose Frigate went up between the Islands and took Shelter, after a severe Cannonade from us, behind Blackwell's Island. She retreated yesterday as far as opposite Corlears Hook, where she was briskly cannonaded till night. I have not heard of her this morning—By the loss on Long Island

and the running away of our Militia, *especially those of Connecticut,* to their respective Homes our Army is much diminished, and I am sure is vastly inferior to that of the Enemy. *The Troops are vastly dispirited—publickly say, but I believe without Reason, that they are sold. In short they have great Diffidence of Head Quarters and the officers of all Ranks suspect two certain Persons near the General, whom I believe to be a good man, to have more influence than their abilities entitle them to. I seldom go to Head Quarters; because I think my visits there not over acceptable.* I content myself with doing my Duty which is very severe, as for some time past I *have been Brigadier of the Day every other Day*—the more severe, as the Hardships to which I was reduced on Long Island, *without Bedding,* almost without Food, and exposed to the rain have much impaired my Health.

The Army is continually praying most ardently *for the arrival of General Lee as their Guardian Angel.* He is daily expected ; his arrival will probably *nerve their Spirits.* The Number of the Army I do not know, probably not so many by one half as Congress intended. Its present Disposition is this. It is divided into three Divisions, one in the City where I am with my Brigade under the Command of Major General Putnam ; the other two under the respective Commands of Majors General Spencer & Heath, one between Haerlem & us, the other at & about Kings Bridge. What the Enemy intend we cannot yet discover. I am inclined to think to choose to avoid a Cannonade & Bombardment of the City & an attempt on West Chester County. Should they make it and succeed the Consequences are obvious, we shall be totally confined to this Island & cut off from all Communication with the Continent. With a View to this danger *I wrote a few days ago to the General,* giving it as *my opinion* that we should abandon the City, make a strong post in the Heights of Kings Bridge and dispose of the bulk of the Army in West Chester County and support the Communication between both, by placing the armed Vessels in the mouth of Spuyten Devil on the East River. *I have rec^d. no answer.* The *Vessels lie in parade before Head Quarters* but some of the artillery & Stores are removing. God knows what will be the Event of this Campaign ; but I beg leave to assure the Honorable Convention that *I will never bring Disgrace on their appointment.*

Poor General Woodhull with a Lieutenant & four men were made Prisoners on Long Island. I had a letter from him dated the 1st Inst, but not dated from any Place, nor does he tell me how he was taken. He has lost all his Baggage and requested of me two Shirts and two Pairs of Stockings, which I should have sent him had not the Flag of Truce been gone before I rec^d the Letter. I shall comply with his Request by the first opportunity. Commend me with all possible Devotion to the Honorable Convention.

I am Sir
Your most obedient Servt.
JNO. MORIN SCOTT.

P. S. *The army badly paid* & *wretchedly fed ;* 1,100 men arrived from the Southward. A Deserter tells me but 3,000 *foreign Troops* on *Staten Island. I know not what the flying Camp is doing.* He says the Enemy on Long Island are 26,000. *I believe this much exagerated ;* & 1,000 in the Shipping.

LEWIS MORRIS TO JAY.

PHIL^A·, Sep^r· 8, 1776.

MY DEAR FRIEND :

I am very anxious about our situation at N. York. I should have gone off this day but Mr. Lewis has taken flight towards that Place in quest of his family, that were on Long Island, and there remain only three of us. I wish you would let me know how matters stand and at what Place our Convention are. Genl. Sullivan brought a mesage from Lord Howe to Congress in consequence of which they have sent Doctor Franklin, John Adams and Ned Rutledge. I doubt in my own mind any good effect that it can have, as he was desirous to meet them in their favorite character. I will enclose you the resolve of Congress. Sullivan says that L. Howe said he was ever against taxing of us, and that they had no right to interfere with our internal Police, and that he was very sure America could not be conquered, and that it was a great pitty so brave a nation should be cutting one another to pieces. Mr. Linch yesterday asked me if you would part with your chestnut horse. I told him I did not know ; I thought I had heard you say once in this Place that if you did sell him you would have seventy pounds. He beged of me to write to you and get your answer. Poor Mr. Lawrence remains very unwell ; he joins me in our best regards to you and all friends.

Yours Most sincerely

Lewis Morris.

ROBERT MORRIS TO JAY.

Philad^{a.}, Septr. 23rd, 1776.

Dear Sir:

Altho' your express delivered me your favour last Wednesday or Thursday, yet I did not receive the letter from Mr. Deane untill this day and shall now send after the Express that he may convey this safe to your hands ; should he be gone I must find some other safe conveyance. You will find enclosed both M^{r.} D—nes letters as you desired and I shall thank you for the Copy of the Invisible part. He had communicated so much of this Sceret to me, before his departure as to let me know he had fixed with you a mode of writing that would he invisible to the rest of the World ; he also promised to ask you to make a full communication to me, but in this use your pleasure.   The secret so far as I do or shall know it will remain so to all other persons.   It appears clear to me that we may very soon involve all Europe in a War by managing properly the apparent forwardness of the Court of France; it 's a horrid consideration that our own Safty should call on us to involve other nations in the Calamities of War.   Can this be morally right or have Morality & Policy nothing to do with each other?   Perhaps it may not be good Policy to investigate the Question at this time.   I will therefore only ask you whether General Howe will give us time to cause a diversion favorable to us in Europe.   I confess as things now appear to me the prospect is gloomy indeed.   Therefore if you can administer Comfort do it ;   Why are we so long deprived of your abilitys in Congress?   Perhaps they are more usefully exerted where you are.   That may be the case, but such men as you, in times like these, should be every where.   I am with true sentiments of respect & esteem

   Dr. Sir

    Your Obedt. hble. Servt.

      Robt. Morris.

John Jay, Esqr.

JAY TO ROBERT MORRIS.

FISHKILLS, Octr. 6, 1776.

DEAR SIR :

The enclosed is a part of the late invisible parts of Mr. Deane's letters.   You will perceive some blanks in it.   Mr. D. it seems did not write with his usual care and accuracy.   There are many blots in one of the letters and in one or two instances the lines cross and run into one another.   Little material is however illegible. I am happy to find our affairs wear so pleasing an aspect in France.

This most certainly will not be the last campaign, and in my opinion Lord Howe's operations cannot be so successful and decisive as greatly to lessen the ideas which foreign nations have conceived of our importance. I am rather inclined to think that our declaring Independence in the face of so powerful a fleet and army will impress them with an opinion of our strength and spirit ; and when they are informed how little our country is in the enemy's possession, they will unite in declaring us invincible by the arms of Britain.

If the works carrying on by the General for obstructing the navigation of Hudson's River at Mount Washington prove effectual, Lord Howe must rest content with the City of New York for this campaign. For altho it is not impossible for him to land a large body of troops on the shores of the Sound and thereby divide our forces, yet no great matters can by that means be achieved. Our communication with the army by the Sound is already cut off by the ships of war ; and any strong Post they might take on the shore would not much injure our communication by land. But should they on the contrary be able suddenly to penetrate the North River with a few ships of war and a number of transports, they would effectually destroy all communication between the upper country and the army by land and water. For before the shores would be put in such a state of defence as to prevent their landing with success, they the river even below the mountains, I think I foresee that a retreat would become necessary, and I can't forbear wishing that a desire of saving a few acres may not lead us into difficulty. Such is the situation of this State at present and so various and I may say successful have been the arts of Govr. Tryon and his adherents to spread the seeds of disaffection among us that I cannot at present obtain permission to return to Congress. Our Convention continues unanimous in all its measures and to do them justice are diligent as well as zealous in the cause.

As long as your whimsical constituents shall permit the gentleman to whom I am writing to remain among the number of those honest and able patriots in Congress, in whose hands I think the Interest of America' very safe, the Congress will possess too great a stock of abilities to perceive the absence of my little mite. It gives me pleasure however to reflect that your remarks on this subject, however ill founded, would have been dictated only by that friendly partiality which you have shown me, and which in this instance has been permitted to impose on your judgment. I wish the Secret Committee would communicate no other intelligence to the Congress at large, than what may be necessary to promote the common weal, not gratify the curiosity of individuals. I hint this, because a copy of a letter from A. L. to that Committee has lately been sent by a member of Congress to a gentleman of his acquaintance who is not a member of Congress. I came by this intelligence in such a way as to speak with certainty, for I have seen the copy, but at the same time in such a way as not to be able with propriety to mention names. You will be pleased therefore to make no other use of this information than to induce the greater caution in the Committee. For as to binding certain members in the house to secresy by oaths or otherwise would be just as absurd as to swear Lee (no matter which of them) to look or feel like Ned Rutledge.

Had M^r. Deane mentioned to me his having conversed with you relative to the mode of writing I communicated to him, I should most certainly have spoken to you on the subject, and will when we meet give you the same information respecting it that I did to him. I am D^r. Sir, with respect and esteem your most ob^t. serv^t.

JOHN JAY.

FREDERICK JAY TO JAY.[1]

HARRISONS PURCHASE, 19th Oct^r., 1776.

DEAR JOHN:

Papa has directed me to have all the Stock removed from Rye to the Fish Kills—at foot you have a list of those now sent. He intends to sett off this Day or to-morrow with Mama & Nancey & some of the servants—the rest will sett off in a day or two. He thinks it best for me to stay & remove everything. I could wish you were here to go with them. Jos. Purdy Senr. has partly engaged to go; if he does not I shall attend them. They mean to take the

[1] Upon the advance of the British into Westchester County in October, 1776, Jay's father withrew with his family from the homestead at Rye and settled at Fishkill.

Crompond Road; if you could meet them it would be a satisfaction.—Endeavor to provide provender for the Cattle &c, this winter; if you could any ways send the Waggon down it would assist me greatly. No Carts to be had at this present time they being all engaged in the Service. I wish papa had taken my advice & moved by water when you first hired the place—it would have saved both trouble and expense—When ye things are all moved Peter will go up— I shall take care of myself—I imagine you 'l be full.

I am in great haste,
Yours &c

FR. JAY.

JAY TO THE GENERAL COURT OF NEW HAMPSHIRE.

FISHKILL, October 31, 1776.

GENTLEMEN :

The Committee appointed by the Convention of this State for the purpose of inquiring into, detecting, and defeating all conspiracies which may be formed therein against the liberties of America, find it indispensably necessary to remove a number of dangerous and disaffected persons, some of whom have been taken in arms against America, to one of the neighbouring States.[1]

On conferring with Lieutenant-Colonel Welch relative to sending them to New Hampshire, he was

---

[1] More important than the Secret Committee, referred to in note on p. 75, was the committee "for inquiring into, detecting, and defeating all conspiracies which may be formed in this State against the liberties of America." This was appointed by the New York Convention, after much debate, on September 21, 1776, the report in its favor being offered by Mr. Duer. The Committee, consisting of one member from each county, elected by the Convention, stood as follows : William Duer, Chairman ; Zephaniah Platt, Pierre Van Cortlandt,

of opinion that the zeal which your honourable body have uniformly manifested for the American cause, would induce you cheerfully to receive and dispose of them, in such manner as to prevent the further execution of their wicked and malicious designs.

The Committee desire that all such of the prisoners as are not directed to be confined, and not in circumstances to maintain themselves, be put to labour and compelled to earn their subsistence. And they have directed the bearer, Egbert Benson, Esquire, chairman of the Committee of this County, to pay you two hundred dollars on account of the expenses you may be put to by complying with their request.

The Committee beg leave to recommend this gentleman to your notice and confidence. He will communicate to you the instructions given him by the Committee, and readily give you any information that may be necessary to enable you to form a judgment of the characters of the several prisoners and the degrees of restrictions proper to enjoin.

By order of the Committee, I am, gentlemen, your most obedient, humble servant,

JOHN JAY, Chairman.

To the honourable the General Court
of the State of New Hampshire.

Nathaniel Sackett, John Jay, Charles De Witt, and Leonard Gansevoort. On November 9th Jay was made Chairman, *vice* Duer, and apparently continued as such until the dissolution of the Committee, February 27, 1777, when a new body known as the " Commissioners for detecting conspiracies," &c., was appointed. Mr. Jay did not serve on the latter. A portion of the minutes of the first Committee, in Jay's handwriting, is preserved in the New York Historical Society Library. See " Life of Jay," vol. i., pp. 48, 49.

JAY TO EDWARD RUTLEDGE.

Fishkill, 11th Oct., 1776.

Dear Rutledge :

Be so kind as to forward the enclosed by the first opportunity to your brother. It is in answer to one from him to Mess.ʳˢ Duane, Wm. Livingston, and myself, mentioning the losses sustained by General Lee in consequence of entering into the American service, and recommending a compliance with the resolution of Congress for indemnifying him. As he has doubtless written to you on the subject, I forbear enlarging on the propriety, policy, or justice of the measure. I am for my own part clear for it, and wish with all my heart that it may take place : I shall write to my colleagues on the subject.

Let no considerations induce you to excuse General Mifflin from the office of quartermaster-general. Moyland acted wisely and honestly in resigning. Try no new experiments : you have paid for the last. Let me repeat it—keep Mifflin.

Although extremely anxious to be with you, the circumstances of this State will not admit of my leaving it. Governor Tryon has been very mischievous : and we find our hands full in counteracting and suppressing the conspiracies formed by him and his adherents.

What is your fleet amd noble admiral doing ? What meekness of wisdom and what tender-hearted charity ! I can't think of it with patience. Nothing but more than lady-like delicacy could have prevailed on your august body to secrete the sentence they passed upon that pretty genius. I reprobate such mincing, little, zigzag ways of doing business : either openly acquit, or openly condemn.

If General Lee should be at Philadelphia, pray hasten his departure—he is much wanted in New York. I wish our army well stationed in the highlands, and all the lower country desolated; we might then bid defiance to all the further efforts of the enemy on that quarter.

I am, my dear Rutledge,
Your friend,
JOHN JAY.

EDWARD RUTLEDGE TO JAY.

PHILADELPHIA, Nov. 24th, 1776.

MY DEAR JAY :

I expected long ere this to have been seated quietly at home; but the progress which the enemy had made, and seemed likely to make, into your country, induced me to suspend my resolution which I came to several months ago, and assist with the whole of my power (little enough, God knows) a State which appeared to be marked for destruction. The storm, however, has passed away; and though I have reason to dread its bursting upon the heads of my countrymen, I cannot but most sincerely congratulate you upon the event. I wish you may improve the time; and if you can concur with me in sentiment, it will be improved in the following manner. Let Schuyler, whose reputation has been deeply wounded by the malevolence of party spirit, immediately repair to Congress, and after establishing himself in the good opinion of his countrymen, by a fair and open inquiry into his conduct, concert with the House such a plan as he shall think will effectually secure all the upper country against the attacks of the enemy; which plan being agreed to by the House, give him full power to effect it, and send him off with all possible despatch to carry it into execution. Let steps be taken to place *real* obstructions in the North River, at least in that part of it which can be commanded by Fort Montgomery, and the other fort in the highlands. If these things be done, and that soon, your country, I think, will be safe; provided you establish a good government, with a strong executive. A pure democracy may possibly do, when patriotism is the ruling passion; but when the State abounds with rascals, as is the case with too many at this day, you must suppress a little of that popular spirit. Vest the executive powers of government in an individual, that they may have vigour, and let them be as ample as is consistent with the great outlines of freedom. As several of the reasons which operated against you or Livingston's leaving the State are now removed, I think you would be of vast service in Congress. You know that body possesses its share of human weakness; and that it is not impossible for the members of that House to have their attention engrossed by subjects which might as well be postponed for the present, whilst such as require despatch have been, I had almost said neglected. This may be the case with the measures which should be taken for the defence of your State. It is therefore your interest and your duty, (if you are not prevented by some superior public concern) to attend the House, and that soon; you have a right to demand their attention, and I trust they will give you early assistance. Every intelligence from New York for the last ten days convincing me that the enemy are preparing to attack the State with a large body of troops, I shall take the wings of the morning, and hasten to my native home; where I shall endeavour to render my country more service in the field than I have been able to render her in the cabinet. I have therefore very little time to write, and none to lengthen this letter. I could not however think of quitting this part of the continent without writing you what appeared to me of consequence, especially when I consider that it is probable, or at least possible, that this may be the last time I may have it in my power to give you any evidence of my affection. I shall add no more than that you have my best wishes for your happiness, and that if I fall in the defence of my country it will alleviate my misfortune to think that it is in support of the best of causes, and that I am esteemed by one of the best of men. God bless you, Adieu my friend.

Yours Truly,

E. RUTLEDGE.

COLONEL McDOUGALL TO JAY.

PEEKS KILL, Decr. 2^{d.}, 1776.

MY DEAR SIR :

I have much to say to you, which the moveable state of the army prevented and still prevents. General Lee in consequence of positive orders from General Washington, is to cross the North river to Jersey to-morrow with about three small Brigades of the Continental army, illy cloathed, many of the men without Blankets, Shirts or Shoes. Mine is the most wanting in those articles. Those troops have been so fatigued in marching from the Plains by rains & deep roads that they are almost beat out, and to continue a forced march of near 100 miles will ruin them. With the present low and dissolved State of the army it's Idle to attempt an attack on the Enemy. All that should be aimed at with any tolerable prospect of Success ought to be to take strong Posts to stop the Progress of the Enemy, and bend our utmost attention to recruiting our army. Instead of this, we are carrying the most of the officers who are to effect it out of the Country where alone it can be done ; and harrassing the Troops the last moment of the Campaign, to deter them by severe toil & service from enlisting. Sir, I tremble for the consequences. The levies will be greatly retarded by this movment. God grant this may be the worst consequence of this moment. General officers with a few militia is the only force now below Crotten river ; except about 400 men General Woster has about Mamarinek, and these a Squadron of light Horse and three Companies of light Troops would frighten out of the County, which will soon below that be all under the command of the Enemy. The Highlands should be better guarded than I fear they will be in the winter. The Northern expedition cost me my eldest son ; and the other, Ronald McDougall, was made a Prisoner in Canada. He is now on his parole to Govr. Carlton ; and is extremely uneasey lest he should be called upon to deliver himself up. As he was at the taking of the Prisoners, taken at St. Johns, whenever they are released, he is entitled to the Benefit of them in preference to those, who were not there ; and who have been prisoners for a much less time than he has. I have therefore to beg you to write to Congress on his behalf, lest he should in the exchange of those prisoners be forgot : the sooner you do it, the more you will oblige me. He was a second Lieut. in my old Regiment. If I should do otherwise than well I pray remember this boy. Mr. John Laurence, my son in Law, is now Paymaster to my old Regiment, but as it will soon be dissolved I spoke to Col. Livingston of the 4th. to get him appointed for his. He assured me he would write to Convention on the Subject. If he has, I should be glad you would speak to the members, if it should be judged necessary. May God bless you, and save my bleeding distressed Country.

I am your affectionate

ALEXR. McDOUGALL.

SILAS DEANE TO JAY.[1]

PARIS, 3rd December, 1776.

DEAR JAY:

If my letters arrive safe they will give you some idea of my situation—without intelligence, without orders, and without remittances, yet boldly plunging into contracts, engagements and negotiations, hourly hoping that something will arrive from *America*. By General *Coudray* I send thirty thousand fusils, two hundred pieces of brass cannon, thirty mortars, four thousand tents, and clothing for thirty thousand men, with two hundred tons of gunpowder, lead, balls, &c., &c., by which you may judge we have some friends here. A war in *Europe* is inevitable. The eyes of all are on you, and the fear of your giving up or accommodating is the greatest obstacle I have to contend with. Mons. *Beaumarchais* has been my Minister in effect, as this Court is extremely cautious, and I now advise you to attend carefully to the articles sent you. I could not examine them here. I was promised they should be good, and at the lowest prices, and that from persons in such station that had I hesitated it might have ruined my affairs. But as in so large a contract there is room for impositions, my advice is that you send back to me samples of the articles sent you. Cannon, powder, mortars, &c., are articles known ; but clothes, the fusils, &c., by which any imposition may be detected. Large remittances are necessary for your credit, and the enormous price of tobacco, of rice, of flour, and many other articles, gives you an opportunity of making your

---

[1] On November 29, 1775, the Continental Congress appointed a committee consisting of Messrs. Harrison, Franklin, Johnson, Dickinson, and Jay to conduct a correspondence with friends of America in Great Britain, Ireland, and other parts of the world. It was known as the Secret Committee, and the results following from its correspondence were highly important. Deane was their principal agent abroad during 1776, several of whose letters appear in Force's "Archives" for that year. The original of the above, addressed to Jay in person, is among his papers.

remittances to very great advantage. Twenty thousand hogsheads of tobacco are wanted immediately for this kingdom, and more for other parts of *Europe*.

I have written you on several subjects, some of which I will attempt briefly to recapitulate. The destruction of the *Newfoundland* fishery may be effected, by two or three of your frigates, sent there early in *February*, and by that means a fatal blow given to *Great Britain*—I mean by destroying the stages, boats, &c., and by bringing away the people left there as prisoners. *Glasgow*, in *Scotland*, may be plundered and burnt with ease, as may *Liverpool*, by two or three frigates, which may find a shelter and protection in the ports of *France* and *Spain* afterwards. Blank commissions are wanted here to cruise under your flag against the *British* commerce. This is a capital stroke and must bring on a war. Hasten them out I pray you. *France* and *Spain* are friendly, and you will greatly oblige the latter by seizing the *Portuguese* commerce wherever it is found. I have had overtures from the King of *Prussia* in the commercial way, and have sent a person of great confidence to his Court in person with letters of introduction from his agent here, with whom I am on the best of terms. A loan may be obtained, if you make punctual remittances for the sums now advanced, for any sums at five per cent. interest, perhaps less. The western lands ought to be held up to view as an encouragement for our soldiers, especially foreigners, and are a good fund to raise money on. You may, if you judge proper, have any number of *German* and *Swiss* troops; they have been offered me, but you know I have no proposals to treat. A number of frigates may be purchased at *Leghorn*, the Grand Duke of *Tuscany* being zealously in favor of *America*, and doing all in his power to encourage its commerce. Troubles are rising in *Ireland*, and with a little assistance much work may be cut out for *Great Britain*, by sending hence a few priests, a little money, and plenty of arms. *Omnia tentanda* is my motto, therefore I hint the playing of their own game on them, by spiriting up the *Caribs* in *St. Vincents*, and the negroes in *Jamaica*, to revolt.

On all these subjects I have written to you. Also on various particulars of commerce. Our vessels have more liberty in the ports of *France* and *Spain* and *Tuscany*, than the vessels of any other nation, and that openly. I presented the Declaration of Independence to this Court, after indeed it had become an old story in every part of *Europe ;* it was well received, but as you say you have articles of alliance under consideration, any resolution must be deferred until we know what they are. The want of intelligence has more than once well nigh ruined my affairs ; pray be more attentive to this important subject, or drop at once all thoughts of a foreign connection.

I must mention a few trifles. The Queen is fond of parade, and I believe wishes a war, and is our friend. She loves riding on horseback. Could you send me a fine *Narrotoheganset* horse or two, the present might be money exceedingly well laid out. *Rittenhouse's* orrery, or *Arnold's* collection of insects ; a phæton of *American* make, and a pair of bay horses. A few barrels of apples, of walnuts, of butternuts, &c., would be great curiosities here, where everything *American* is gazed at, and where the *American* contest engages the attention of all ages, ranks, and sexes.

Had I ten ships here I could fill them all with passengers for *America*. I hope the officers sent will be agreeable ; they were recommended by the Ministry here, and are at this instant really in their army ; but this must be a secret. Do you want heavy iron cannon, sea officers of distinction, or ships? Your special orders will enable me to procure them. For the situation of affairs in *England* I refer you to Mr. *Rogers*, Aid-de-Camp to Mons. *Du Coudray*. I have presented a number of memoirs, which have been very favourably received, and the last by his Majesty, but my being wholly destitute of other than accidental and gratuitous assistance will not permit my sending you copies. Indeed I was obliged to make them so as to explain the rise, the nature, and the progress of the dispute. I have been assured by the Ministers, that I have thrown much light on the subject, and have obviated many difficulties ; but his Majesty is not of the disposition of his great grandfather *Louis* XIV. If he were, *England* would soon be ruined. Do not forget or omit sending me blank commissions for privateers ; under these, infinite damage may be done to the *British* commerce, and as the prizes must be sent to you for condemnation the eventual profits will remain with you. Tell Mrs. *Trist* that her husband and Captain *Fowler* were well on the 16th instant. I had a letter from the latter. Pray be careful who you trust in *Europe*. One *Williamson*, a native of *Pennsylvania*, is here as a spy ; yet I believe he corresponds with very good people on your side of the water. The villain returns to *London* about once in six weeks to discharge his budget.

Doctor *Bancroft* has been of very great service to me ; no man has better intelligence in *England* in my opinion, but it costs something. The following articles have been shown to me ; they have been seen by both the Courts of *France* and *Spain*, and I send them to you for speculation :

1st. The Thirteen *United Colonies*, now known by the name of the *Thirteen United States of North-America*, shall be acknowledged by *France* and *Spain*, and treated with as independent States, and as such shall be guaräntied in the possession of all that part of the Continent of *North-America*, which by the last treaty of peace was ceded and confirmed to the Crown of *Great Britain*.

2dly. The *United States* shall guaranty and confirm to the Crowns of *France* and *Spain*, all and singular their possessions and claims in every other part of *America* whether north or south of the equator, and of the islands possessed by them in the American seas.

3dly.   Should *France* or *Spain*, either or both of them, possess themselves of the islands in the *West-Indies* now in the possession of the Crown of *Great Britain*, (as an indemnity for the injuries sustained in the last war, in consequence of its being commenced on the part of *Great Britain* in violation of the laws of nations,) the *United Colonies* shall assist the said Powers in obtaining such satisfaction, and shall guaranty and confirm to them the possession of such acquisition.

4thly.   The fisheries on the banks of *Newfoundland*, of *Cape-Breton*, and parts adjacent, commonly known and called by the name of the cod fishery, shall be equally free to the subjects of *France*, *Spain*, and the *United States*, respectively, and they shall mutually engage to protect and defend each other in such commerce.

5thly.   The more effectually to preserve this alliance, and to obtain the great object, it shall be agreed that every and any *British* ship or vessel found or met with on the coasts of *North-America*, of *South-America*, or of the islands adjacent, and belonging thereto, and within a certain degree or distance to be agreed on, shall be forever hereafter considered as lawful prize to any of the subjects of *France*, *Spain*, or the *United Colonies*, and treated as such, as well in peace as in war, nor shall *France*, *Spain*, or the *United Colonies*, ever hereafter admit *British* ships into any of their ports in *America*, North and South, or the islands adjacent. This article never to be altered or dispensed with, but only by and with the consent of each of the three contracting States.

6thly.   During the present war between the *United States* and *Great Britain*, *France* and *Spain* shall send into *North-America*, and support there, a fleet to defend and protect the coasts and the commerce of the *United States*, in consequence of which if the possessions of *France* or *Spain* should be attacked in *America* by *Great Britain*, or her allies, the *United States* will afford them all the aid and assistance in their power.

7thly. No peace or accommodation shall be made with *Great Britain* to the infringement or violation of any one of these articles.

I am, with the utmost impatience to hear from you, dear sir, yours, &c.,

SILAS DEANE.

ADDRESS OF THE CONVENTION OF THE REPRESENTATIVES OF THE STATE OF NEW YORK TO THEIR CONSTITUENTS.[1]

At this most important period, when the freedom and happiness, or the slavery and misery, of the present and future generations of Americans, is to be determined on a solemn appeal to the Supreme Ruler of all events, to whom every individual must one day answer for the part he now acts, it becomes the duty of the Representatives of a free people to call their attention to this most serious subject, and the more so at a time when their enemies are industriously endeavoring to delude, intimidate, and seduce them by false suggestions, artful misrepresentations, and insidious promises of protection.

---

[1] The misfortunes and defeats experienced by the American troops in the campaign of 1776 produced so much despondency that the Continental Congress and some of the State bodies issued spirited and encouraging addresses to the people, which, with the victories at Trenton and Princeton, wonderfully revived faith and confidence. Among the addresses was the above from the New York Convention, Jay being the author of it. The Continental Congress so far adopted it as its own as to recommend its " serious perusal " by all the people of America, and ordered it to be translated into the German language.

You and all men were created free, and authorized to establish civil government, for the preservation of your rights against oppression, and the security of that freedom which God hath given you, against the rapacious hand of tyranny and lawless power. It is, therefore, not only necessary to the well-being of Society, but the duty of every man, to oppose and repel all those, by whatever name or title distinguished, who prostitute the powers of Government to destroy the happiness and freedom of the people over whom they may be appointed to rule.

Under the auspices and direction of Divine Providence, your forefathers removed to the wilds and wilderness of America. By their industry they made it a fruitful, and by their virtue a happy country. And we should still have enjoyed the blessings of peace and plenty, if we had not forgotten the source from which these blessings flowed ; and permitted our country to be contaminated by the many shameful vices which have prevailed among us.

It is a well known truth, that no virtuous people were ever oppressed ; and it is also true, that a scourge was never wanting to those of an opposite character. Even the Jews, those favourites of Heaven, met with the frowns, whenever they forgot the smiles of their benevolent Creator. By tyrants of Egypt, of Babylon, of Syria, and of Rome, they were severely chastised ; and those tyrants themselves, when they had executed the vengeance of Almighty God, their own crimes bursting on their own heads, received the rewards justly due to their violation of the sacred rights of mankind.

You were born equally free with the Jews, and have as good a right to be exempted from the arbitrary domination of Britain, as they had from the invasions of Egypt, Babylon, Syria, or Rome. But they, for their wickedness, were permitted to be scourged by the latter; and we, for our wickedness, are scourged by tyrants as cruel and implacable as those. Our case, however, is peculiarly distinguished from theirs. Their enemies were strangers, unenlightened, and bound to them by no ties of gratitude or consanguinity. Our enemies, on the contrary, call themselves Christians. They are of a nation and people bound to us by the strongest ties—a people, by whose side we have fought and bled; whose power we have contributed to raise; who owe much of their wealth to our industry, and whose grandeur has been augmented by our exertions.

It is unnecessary to remind you that during the space of between one and two hundred years, every man sat under his own vine and his own fig-tree, and there was none to make us afraid—that the people of Britain never claimed a right to dispose of us, and everything belonging to us, according to their will and pleasure, until the reign of the present King of that Island—and that to enforce this abominable claim they have invaded our country by sea and land. From this extravagant and iniquitous claim, and from the unreasonable as well as cruel manner in which they would gain our submission, it seems as though Providence were determined to use them as instruments to punish the guilt of this country, and bring us back to a sense of duty to our Creator.

You may remember that to obtain redress of the many grievances to which the King and Parliament of Great Britain had subjected you, the most dutiful petitions were presented, not only by the several Assemblies, but by the Representatives of all America in General Congress. And you cannot have forgot with what contempt they were neglected; nay, the humblest of all petitions, praying only to be heard, was answered by the sound of the trumpet and the clashing of arms. This, however, is not the only occasion on which the hearts of kings have been hardened; and in all probability it will add to the number of those instances in which their oppression, injustice and hardness of heart have worked their destruction.

Being bound by the strongest obligations to defend the inheritance which God hath given us, to Him we referred our Cause, and opposed the assaults of our taskmasters, being determined rather to die free than live slaves and entail bondage on our children.

By our vigorous efforts and by the goodness of Divine Providence, those cruel invaders were driven from our country in the last Campaign. We then flattered ourselves that the signal success of our arms, and the unanimity and spirit of our people, would have induced our foes to desist from the prosecution of their wicked designs, and disposed their hearts to peace. But peace we had not yet deserved. Exultation took place of thanksgiving, and we ascribed that to our own prowess which was only to be attributed to the great Guardian of the innocent.

The enemy with greater strength again invade us

—invade us not less by their arts than their arms. They tell you that if you submit you shall have protection; that their king breathes nothing but peace; that he will revise (not repeal) all his cruel acts and instructions, and will receive you into favour. But what are the terms on which you are promised peace? Have you heard of any except absolute, unconditional obedience and servile submission? If his professions are honest—if he means not to cajole and deceive you, why are you not explicitly informed of the terms, and whether parliament means to tax you hereafter at their will and pleasure? Upon this and the like points, these military commissioners of peace are silent; and, indeed, are not authorized to say a word, unless a power to grant pardon implies a power to adjust claims and secure privileges; or unless the bare possession of life is the only privilege which Americans are to enjoy. For a power to grant pardon is the only one which their parliament or prince have thought proper to give them. And yet they speak of peace, but hold daggers in their hands. They invite you to accept of blessings, and stain your habitations with blood. Their voice resembles the voice of Jacob, but their hands are like the hands of Esau.

If their Sovereign intends to repeal any of the acts we complain of, why are they not especially named? If he designs you shall be free, why does he not promise that the claim of his parliament, to bind you in all cases whatsoever, shall be given up and relinquished? If a reasonable peace was intended, why did he not empower his Commissioners to treat with the Congress, or with Deputies from all the Assemblies ; or why was not some other mode devised, in which America might be heard ? Is it not highly ridiculous for them to pretend that they are authorized to treat of a peace between Britain and America with every man they meet ? Was such a treaty ever heard of before ? Is such an instance to be met with in the history of mankind ? No! The truth is, peace is not meant ; and their specious pretentions and proclamations are calculated only to disunite and deceive.

If the British king really desires peace, why did he order all your vessels to be seized, and confiscated ? Why did he most cruelly command, that the men found on board such vessels should be added to the crews of his ships of war, and compelled to fight against their own countrymen—to spill the blood of their neighbours and friends ; nay, of their fathers, their brothers and their children ; and all this before these pretended ambassadors of peace had arrived on our shores ! Does any history, sacred or profane, record any thing more horrid, more impious, more execrably wicked, tyrannical or devilish ? If there be one single idea of peace in his mind, why does he order your cities to be burned, your country to be desolated, your brethren to starve, and languish, and die in prison ? If any thing were intended besides destruction, devastation, and bloodshed, why are the mercenaries of Germany transported near four thousand miles to plunder your houses ; ravish your wives and daughters ; strip your infant children ; expose whole families naked, miserable, and forlorn, to want, to hunger, to inclement skies, and wretched deaths? If peace were not totally reprobated by him, why are those pusillanimous, deluded, servile wretches among you, who, for present ease or impious bribes, would sell their liberty, their children, and their souls ; who, like savages, worship every devil that promises not to hurt them ; or obey any mandates, however cruel, for which they are paid ? how is it, that these sordid, degenerate creatures, who bow the knee to this king, and daily offer incense at his shrine, should be denied the peace so repeatedly promised them ? Why are they indiscriminately abused, robbed, and plundered, with their more deserving neighbours ? But in this world, as in the other, it is right and just that the wicked should be punished by their seducers.

In a word, if peace was the desire of your enemies, and humanity their object, why do they thus trample under foot every right and every duty, human and divine ? Why, like the demons of old, is their wrath to be expiated only by human sacrifices ? Why do they excite the savages of the wilderness to murder our inhabitants and exercise cruelties unheard of among civilized nations ? No regard for religion or virtue remains among them. Your very churches bear witness of their impiety ; your churches are used without hesitation as jails, as stables, and as houses of sport and theatrical exhibitions. What faith, what trust, what confidence, can you repose in these men, who are deaf to the call of humanity, dead to every sentiment of religion, and void of all regard for the temples of the Lord of Hosts?

And why all this desolation, bloodshed, and un-paralleled cruelty? They tell you to reduce your obedience. Obedience to what? To their will and pleasure! And then what? Why, then you shall be pardoned, because you consent to be slaves. And why should you be slaves now, having been freemen ever since this country was settled? Because, for-sooth, the king and parliament of an island three thousand miles off, choose that you should be hewers of wood and drawers of water for them. And is this the people whose proud domination you are taught to solicit? Is this the peace which some of you so ardently desire? For shame! for shame!

But you are told that their armies are numerous, their fleet strong, their soldiers valiant, their resources great; that you will be conquered; that victory ever attends their standard; and therefore that your oppo-sition is vain, your resistance fruitless. What then? You can but be slaves at last, if you should think life worth holding on so base a tenure. But who is it that gives victory? By whom is a nation exalted? Since what period hath the race been always to the swift and the battle to the strong? Can you be persuaded that the merciful King of kings hath sur-rendered His crown and sceptre to the merciless tyrant of Britain and committed the affairs of this lower world to his guidance, control and direction? We learned otherwise from our fathers; and God himself hath told us that strength and numbers avail not against Him. Seek then to be at peace with Him; solicit His alliance, and fear not the boasted strength and power of your foes.

You may be told that your forts have been taken, your country ravaged, and that your armies have retreated, and therefore that God is not with you. It is true that some forts have been taken, that our country hath been ravaged, and that our Maker is displeased with us. But it is also true that the King of Heaven is not like the King of Britain, implacable. If His assistance be sincerely implored, it will surely be obtained. If we turn from our sins, He will turn from His anger. Then will our arms be crowned with success, and the pride and power of our enemies, like the arrogance and pride of Nebuchadnezzar, will vanish away. Let us do our duty and victory will be our reward. Let a general reformation of manners take place; let no more widows and orphans, compelled to fly from their peaceful abodes, complain that you make a market of their distress, and take cruel advantage of their necessities; when your country is invaded and cries aloud for your aid, fly not to some secure corner of a neighbouring State and remain idle spectators of her distress, but share in her fate and manfully support her cause; let universal charity, publick spirit and private virtue be inculcated, encouraged and practised; unite in preparing for a vigorous defence of your country, as if all depended on your own exertions; and when you have done these things, then rely upon the good Providence of Almighty God for success, in full confidence, that without His blessing all our efforts will evidently fail.

A people moving on these solid principles never have been, and never will be, subjected by any tyrant whatever. Cease, then, to desire the flesh-pots of Egypt, and remember their taskmasters and oppressions. No longer hesitate about rejecting all dependence on a king who will rule you only with a rod of iron. Tell those who blame you for declaring yourselves independent that you have done no more than what your late king had done for you; that he declared you to be out of his protection; that he absolved you from all allegiance; that he made war upon you, and instead of your king he became your enemy and destroyer. By his consent, by his own act, you became independent of his crown. If you are wise you will always continue so. Freedom is now in your power. Value the heavenly gift. Remember, if you dare to neglect or despise it, you offer an insult to the Divine Bestower. Nor despair of keeping it. Despair and despondency mark a little mind and indicate a grovelling spirit. After the armies of Rome had been repeatedly defeated by Hannibal, that Imperial City was besieged by this brave and experienced general at the head of a numerous and victorious army. But so far were her glorious citizens from being dismayed by the loss of so many battles and of all their country, so confident in their own virtues and the protection of Heaven, that the very land on which the Carthaginians were encamped was sold at public auction for more than the usual price. Those heroic citizens disdained to receive his protection or to regard his proclamations. They remembered that their ancestors had left them free—ancestors who had bled in rescuing their country from the tyranny of kings. They invoked the protection of the Supreme Being. They bravely defended their city with undaunted resolution ; they repelled the enemy and recovered their country. Blush, then, ye degenerate spirits, who give all over for lost, because your enemies have marched over three or four counties in this and a neighbouring State—ye who basely fly to have the yoke of slavery fixed upon your necks and to swear that you and your children after you shall be slaves forever ! Such men deserve to be slaves, and are fit only for beasts of burden to the rest of mankind. Happy would it be for America if they were removed away, instead of continuing in this Country to people it with a race of animals who, from their form, must be classed among human species, but possess none of those qualities which render man more respectable than the brutes.

There never yet was a war in which victory and success did not sometimes change sides. In the present, nothing has happened either singular or decisive. Inquire dispassionately, and be not deceived by those artful tales which emissaries so industriously circulate.

A powerful and well-disciplined army, supported by a respectable fleet, invade this country. They are opposed by an army which, though numerous and brave, is quite undisciplined. Notwithstanding this manifest disparity, they have never thought it prudent to give us battle, though they have often had the fairest opportunities. True it is, that taking advantage of that critical moment when our forces are almost disbanded, they have penetrated into *Jersey*, and marched a considerable distance without being attacked. If any are alarmed at this circumstance, let them consider that we do not fight for a few acres of land, but for freedom—for the freedom and happiness of millions yet unborn.

Would it not be highly imprudent to risk such important events upon the issue of a general battle, when it is certain *Great Britain* cannot long continue the war, and by protracting it we cannot fail of success ? The *British* Ministry, sensible of this truth, and convinced that the people of *England* are aware of it, have promised that the present campaign shall be the last. They are greatly and justly alarmed at their situation. A country drained of men and money, the difficulties of supplying fleets and armies at so great a distance, the danger of domestic insurrections, the probability that *France* will take advantage of their defenceless condition, the ruin of their commerce by our privateers—these are circumstances at which the boldest are dismayed. They are convinced that the people will not remain long content in such a dangerous situation : hence it is that they press so hard to make this campaign decisive ; and hence it is that we should endeavor to avoid it. Even suppose that *Philadelphia*, which many believed to be of such great importance, suppose it was taken or abandoned, the conquest of *America* will still be at a great distance. Millions, determined to be free, still remain to be subdued—millions who disdain to part with their liberties, their consciences, and the happiness of their posterity in future ages, for infamous protections and dishonourable pardons.

But amidst all the terror and dismay which have taken hold of some weak minds, let us consider the advantage under which we prosecute the present war. Our country supplies us with every commodity which is necessary for life and defence. Arms and ammunition are now abundantly manufactured in almost all the *American* States, and our armies will be abundantly supplied with all military stores. We have more fighting men in *America* than *Britain* can possibly send. Our trade is free, and every port of *France* and *Spain* affords protection to our ships. Other nations, invited by the advantages of the commerce, will doubtless soon follow their example ; and experience must convince the most incredulous that the *British* Navy cannot exclude us from the sea. If their armies have invaded, ravaged and plundered our dominions and our people, have we not successfully attacked them on their boasted empire of the ocean ? Have not our privateers brought into our ports of America *British* property to the amount of more than fifteen hundred thousand pounds? And do we not daily receive the most valuable cargoes from foreign countries in spite of those fleets whose colours have waved in triumph over the globe? The article of salt, about which some of you have been uneasy, will soon be fully supplied. The shores of *America* are washed by the ocean for more than two thousand miles. Works for manufacturing salt have been erected and proved successful, and many cargoes of it are expected, and have arrived, in the neighbouring States. Provisions of every kind abound among us. From our plenteous stores *Great Britain* hath heretofore supplied her necessities, though she now most wantonly and ungratefully abuses the kind hand which hath ministered to her wants and alleviated her distress. As to clothing, the rapid increase of our manufacturers, and the supplies we obtain from abroad, quiet all fears upon that subject. By the most authentic intelligence from Europe, we are informed that the people of *France* are ripe for a war with *Britain*, and will not omit the present opportunity of extending their commerce, and humbling their rival. Every State in *Europe* beheld with a jealous eye the growing power of the *British* empire, and the additional strength she daily received from this amazing continent; for they could not but perceive that their own security was diminished in proportion as her power to injure them increased. Whence is it, then, that some persons pretend to assure you that *France*, *Spain*, and the other *European* States, are not disposed to favour you? The wise and virtuous of all nations have pronounced our cause to be just, and approved the manner in which our resistance hath been conducted.

Whoever, therefore, considers the natural strength and advantage of this country, the distance it is removed from *Britain*, the obvious policy of many *European* Powers, the great supplies of arms and amunition cheerfully afforded us by the *French* and *Spaniards*, and the feeble and destitute condition of *Britain*—that she is drained of men and of money, obliged to hire foreign mercenaries for the execution of her wicked purposes; in arrears to her troops for a twelvemonth's pay, which she cannot or will not discharge: her credit sunk; her trade ruined; her inhabitants divided; her King unpopular, and her Ministers execrated; that she is overwhelmed with a monstrous debt; cut off from the vast revenue heretofore obtained by taxes on *American* produce; her *West India* Islands in a starving condition; her ships taken; her merchants involved in bankruptcy; her design against us wicked, unjust, cruel, contrary to the laws of God and man, pursued with implacable, unrelenting vengeance, and in a manner barbarous and opposed to the usage of civilized nations;—whoever considers that we have humbly sought peace and been refused; that we have been denied even a hearing; all our petitions rejected; all our remonstrances disregarded; that we fight not for conquest but only for security; that our cause is the cause of God, of human nature and posterity: whoever we say seriously considers these things, must entertain very improper ideas of the Divine justice to which we have appealed, and be very little acquainted with the course of human affairs, to harbour the smallest doubt of our being successful.

Remember the long and glorious struggle of the

United Netherlands against the power of *Spain*, to which they had once been subjected. Their extent was small, their country poor, their people far from numerous, and unaccustomed to arms, and in the neighbourhood of their enemies. *Spain*, at that time the most powerful kingdom in *Europe*, her fleet formidable, her armies great, inured to war, and led by the best generals of the age, and her Treasury overflowing with the wealth of *Mexico* and *Peru*— endeavoured to enslave them. They dutifully remonstrated against the design. Their petitions were treated with contempt, and fire and sword was carried into their country to compel submission. They nobly resolved to be free. They declared themselves to be independent States, and after an obstinate struggle, frustrated the wicked intentions of *Spain.*

Switzerland presents us with another instance of magnanimity. That country was oppressed by cruel tyrants, but the people refused to continue in bondage. With arms in their hands they expelled those tyrants, and left to their descendants the portion of freedom.

Even *England*, whose Genius now blushes for the degeneracy of her sons, hath afforded examples of opposition to tyranny which are worthy to be imitated by all nations. His sacred Majesty *Charles* the First, lost his head and his crown by attempting to enslave his subjects; and his sacred Majesty *James* the Second, was for the same reason expelled the kingdom, with his whole family, and the Prince of *Orange* chosen king in his stead. The *English* were too wise to believe that the person of any tyrant could be sacred, and never suffered any man to wear the crown who attempted to exercise the powers of royalty to the destruction of the people from whom those powers were derived.

This practice is not only consistent with human reason, but perfectly consonant to the will and practice of God himself. You know that the Jews were under his peculiar direction, and you need not be informed of the many instances in which he took the crown from such of their kings as refused to govern according to the laws of the Jews.

If then, God hath given us freedom, are we responsible to him for that, as well as other talents? If it be our birthright, let us not sell it for a mess of pottage, nor suffer it to be torn from us by the hand of violence! If the means of defence are in our power and we do not make use of them, what excuse shall we make to our children and our Creator? These are questions of the deepest concern to us all. These are questions which materially affect our happiness, not only in this world but in the world to come. And surely, "if ever a test for the trial of spirits can be necessary, it is now. If ever those of liberty and faction ought to be distinguished from each other, it is now. If ever it is incumbent on the people to know truth and to follow it, it is now."

Rouse, therefore, brave Citizens! Do your duty like men! and be persuaded that Divine Providence will not permit this Western World to be involved in the horrours of slavery. Consider that, from the earliest ages of the world, Religion, Liberty and

Empire, have been bounding their course toward the setting sun. The Holy Gospels are yet to be preached to those western regions, and we have the highest reason to believe that the Almighty will not suffer Slavery and the Gospel to go hand in hand! It cannot, it will not be.

But if there be any among us, dead to all sense of honour, and love of their country; if deaf to all the calls of liberty, virtue, and religion; if forgetful of the magnanimity of their ancestors, and the happiness of their children; if neither the examples nor the success of other nations, the dictates of reason and of nature, or the great duties they owe to their God, themselves, and their posterity, have any effect upon them; if neither the injuries they have received, the prize they are contending for, the future blessings or curses of their children, the applause or the reproach of all mankind, the approbation or displeasure of the Great Judge, or the happiness or misery consequent upon their conduct, in this and a future state, can move them;—then let them be assured, that they deserve to be slaves, and are entitled to nothing but anguish and tribulation. Let them banish from their remembrance the reputation, the freedom, and the happiness they have inherited from their forefathers. Let them forget every duty, human and divine; remember not that they have children: and beware how they call to mind the justice of the Supreme Being: let them go into captivity, like the idolatrous and disobedient Jews, and be a reproach and a by-word among the nations.

But we think better things of you. We believe,

and are persuaded, that you will do your duty like men, and cheerfully refer your cause to the great and righteous Judge. If success crown your efforts, all the blessings of Freedom will be your reward. If you fail in the contest, you will be happy with God and Liberty in Heaven.

By the unanimous order of the Convention:

AB'M TEN BROECK, *President.*

FISHKILL, December 23$^{d.}$ 1776.

ROBERT MORRIS TO JAY.

PHILADELPHIA, Feb. 4, 1777.

DEAR SIR:

Your favour of the 7th ult. came safe to hand. Timothy Jones is certainly a very entertaining, agreeable man; one would not judge so from any thing contained in his cold insipid letter of the 17th Sept., unless you take pains to find the concealed beauties therein: the cursory observations of a sea captain would never *discover* them, but transferred from his hand to the penetrating eye of a *Jay*, the diamonds stand confessed at once. It puts me in mind of a search after the philosopher's stone, but I believe not one of the followers of that phantom have come so near the mark as you, my good friend.[1] I handed a copy of your discoveries to the committee, which now consists of Harrison, R. H. Lee, Hooper, Dr. Witherspoon, Johnson, you, and myself;

---

[1] Reference is made here to the secret correspondence between Silas Deane and the committee of Congress mentioned in note, p. 97. Deane wrote his letters with invisible ink, which the committee were to decipher through some chemical preparation. To mislead the enemy in case of the interception of the letters, Deane would write a brief and unimportant note over an assumed name on the upper portion of the sheet of paper on which the hidden communication was entered. Timothy Jones, in Morris' letter above, was one of Deane's fictitious signatures. See "Life of Jay," vol. i., p. 64.

and honestly told them who it was from, because measures
are necessary in consequence of it ; but I have not received
any directions yet.

I should never doubt the success of measures conducted
by such able heads as those that take the lead in your Convention. I hate to pay compliments, and would avoid the
appearance of doing it, but I cannot refrain from saying I
love Duane, admire Mr. Livingston, and have an epithet for
you if I had been writing to another. I wish you had done
with your Convention ; you are really wanted exceedingly
in Congress : they are very thin. Adieu, my dear sir ; God
bless you, and grant success to America in the present contest, with wisdom and virtue to secure peace and happiness
to her sons in all future ages.

I am, with true regard
Your most obedient servant,
ROBERT MORRIS.

GENERAL WASHINGTON TO JAY.

[Private.]

MIDDLEBROOK, March 1st, 1777.

DEAR SIR :

I have been a little surprised, that the several important
pieces of intelligence lately received from Europe (such
parts of it, I mean, as are circulated without reserve in conversation), have not been given to the public in a manner
calculated to attract the attention and impress the minds of
the people. As they are now propagated, they run through
the country in a variety of forms, are confounded in the
common mass of general rumours, and lose a real part of
their effect. It would certainly be attended with many
valuable consequences if they could be given to the people
in some more authentic and pointed manner. It would
assist the measures taken to restore our currency, promote

the recruiting of the army and our other military arrangements, and give a certain spring to our affairs in general.

Congress may have particular reasons for not communicating the intelligence officially (which would certainly be the best mode if it could be done), but if it cannot, it were to be wished that as much as is intended to be commonly known could be published in as striking a way, and with as great an appearance of authority as may be consistent with propriety.

I have taken the liberty to trouble you with this hint, as sometimes things the most obvious escape attention. If you agree with me in sentiment, you will easily fall upon the most proper mode for answering the purpose.

With great esteem and regard, I am, dear sir,
Your most obedient servant,
GEO. WASHINGTON.

JAY TO WILLIAM LIVINGSTON.

KINGSTON, 22d March, 1777.

DEAR SIR :

Your obliging letters of the 18th ult. and 3d inst., after passing through various hands and places, were at length delivered to me two days ago. Your elegant panegyric on the amiable character and benevolent designs of his Britannic majesty meets with general approbation ; and some do not hesitate to predict that it will stimulate your gracious prince to embrace the first opportunity of exalting you. On reading the proclamation against picking and stealing I could not forbear wishing there had been one pasted on the foreheads of some of our late protectors. Nothing but the chance of their being predestined to go to heaven, can save them from a campaign in the opposite regions. The least they can expect with any degree of modesty is to be decimated. They seem to have acted as if they thought themselves tenants in common in all the good things they met with, and that posterior instead of prior occupancy enabled them to hold in severalty. The affectionate manner in which you speak of our little boy is very obliging. I hope he may live to thank you for your kind attention and deserve it. Sally's rheumatism continues now and then to pay her short visits; her health however is much mended and I flatter myself the approaching season will remove all her fears on that head.

At a time when the most strenuous efforts are necessary to our political salvation it is to be regretted that any of our measures should bear the marks of feeble or dispirited councils. Your militia bill should have been so framed as to give birth to strong and decisive executive powers. I should have thought the spirit of the speech added to the remembrance of the barbarous ravages of the enemy would have diffused thro' the Legislature a degree of resentment, determination and enthusiasm which would have been productive of regulations better adapted to the times.

Our convention has now under consideration the report of the committee for preparing a form of government for their State, and unless my expectations are very ill founded, our constituents will have great reason to be satisfied.

The "Impartial Intelligence" does honor to the wit as well as the invention of its author.

Our printer for £200 a year bond or subscriptions etc., can afford only to publish a two-penny half sheet, filled for the most part with accounts of desertions for which he is paid, instead of interesting publications by which the public might be gratified ; these and other considerations have induced the convention to take Holt into their service ; and when he begins to print I may probably often have the pleasure of sending you a paper worth reading.

   I am my dear sir,

     With the greatest respect and esteem,

       Your most obedient Servant,

         JOHN JAY.

      FROM JAY TO MRS. JAY.

         KINGSTON, 25th March, 1777.

MY DEAR SALLY :

Accept my thanks for your affectionate letters of the 17th and 21st instants. I am happy to hear of the health of yourself and son and am pleased with your candour and sincerity on that subject. . . .

We have lately received an uncertain though unpleasant account of the enemy's landing at Peekskill—How did your nerves bear the shock ? My father and mother I apprehend were very uneasy. I should be happy were it in my power to bear all their as well as all your misfortunes. The infirmities of age added to the terrours and calamities of war conspire in depriving them of ease and enjoyment. I most sensibly feel for and pity them. God grant them the only remedy against the evils inseparable from humanity—fortitude founded on resignation. The moment I may suspect you to be exposed to danger I shall set out for Fishkill. As yet I think you very safe, for if the reports we have heard be true, the enemy's force is not sufficient to penetrate the country.

I congratulate Peter on his recovery and return; remind him of sending to Captain Platt's for the barley. Let not the fear of the enemy deter him from pursuing the business of the farm. The same Providence which enables us to sow may enable us to reap. Present my compliments to our good friends the Doctor and Mrs. Wyche.

My love to Cate.

I am, my dear wife,

Your very affectionate

JOHN JAY.

ROBERT MORRIS TO JAY.

PHILAD^A, April 1st, 1777.

D^{R.} SIR:

The enclosed letters came by a French Ship to New Hampshire and were sent under cover to me by Mr. Langdon with many others; I believe they are from England and wish they may convey agreeable tidings. Last week a Brig^{t.} arrived here with 6,800 muskets & 2100 Gun Locks; another in Mary^{ld.} with 633 bbls Powder & this ship into Portsmouth brought with her about 12,000 muskets, 1000 bbls Powder a number of Blankets & cloathing; all these are for Continental account and many others may be daily looked for. An offer was made to our Com^{rs.} at Paris of two Millions of Livres without interest to be repaid when these United States have established their Independancy in Peace & quietness; no Security or Condition required. You may be sure they accepted this noble Bounty & 500,000 Livres was paid down the 20th Jany·; 500,000 more was to be paid every three months until compleated or sooner if our affairs require it. The Commissioners were well received & promised protection of the Court and that their propositions should all be duly attended to.

Great armaments & preparations for war &c. I fancy however, we must try our strength alone for a while longer, altho I firmly believe a general war will & must eventually take place in Europe this summer. I wish our army was in the field; we want nothing else to make the day our own.

With great regard & esteem I am
Dr. Sir
Your affectionate & ob. Ser.
Robt. Morris.

P. S. My best Compts· to Mr· Duane & Mr· Livingston.

R. R. LIVINGSTON AND G. MORRIS TO JAY.[1]

Dear Sir :

We were much surprised at your letter to Mr. Hobart, as we could not perceive the danger which would result from

---

[1] The first Constitution of the State of New York, with which Jay's name is closely associated, was adopted April 20, 1777. Unfortunately no record of the deliberations of the committee that framed it is known to exist, and the debate upon its adoption in the Convention was but meagrely reported, while the only material bearing upon any of its features found among Jay's papers consists of the above letter from Livingston and Morris, Jay's reply following, and the letter from Duane of May 28, 1777. The main facts in the history of the Constitution are well known. A committee to draft the instrument, in accordance with a general recommendation from the Continental Congress (see note, p. 58), was appointed as early as August 1, 1776, but events delayed the submission of its report until March 11, 1777. This committee, a majority of

permitting the several courts to appoint their own clerks, while on the other hand great inconveniences must arise from suffering them to be independent of such Courts, and of consequence frequently ignorant, always inattentive. Neither had we the most distant idea that a clause of this sort could meet with your disapprobation since you was so fully of the opinion to appoint by judges of the Supreme Court not only clerks but all other civil officers in the government.

As to what you mention about the licensing of Attornies there might perhaps be a propriety in permitting one court to do this drudgery for the rest if we could agree upon the proper court, but as the Gentlemen who preside in each may think themselves qualified to determine as well upon the abilities of the several advocates as upon the merits of the causes advocated, it will not be quite easy to persuade them that they have not an equal right with others to say who shall and who shall not be entitled to practice.

The division of the State into Districts was in your own opinion as you will well remember improper as a part of the Constitution and only to be taken up by the Legislature. If this opinion was well founded there can be no great evil in the omission. Neither had you any ground to suppose that we would go into the Connecticut Plan of holding up which we have declared to be in our opinion inconvenient

whom were prominent lawyers, was composed of Messrs. Jay, Hobart, Smith, Duer, Morris, Livingston, Broome, Scott, Abraham and Robert Yates, Wisner, DeWitt, and Townhsend. According to Jay's biographer, Chancellor Kent, and others, the first draft of the Constitution was presented in Jay's handwriting, and reflected the committee's mature deliberations. That he devoted much attention to it himself and stamped it largely with his own views is evident from the debate in the Convention and his letter of April 29, 1777. During the debate changes were made and amendments adopted. Jay, for example, moved the substitution of the ballot for the previous *viva-voce* method of electing representatives ; he also proposed the Council of Appointment for the nomination of civil officers. Morris, Livingston, Scott, and others figure in the proceedings.

and by reason of the rotatory mode of electing entirely useless.

But if we had been so fortunate as to agree in all or any of your ideas yet as the Government was not only agreed to but solemnly published, it would have been highly improper to attempt any reconsideration.   Besides this the difficulties we were obliged to wade thro' in order to get any Government at all merely by reason of reconsiderations were so great and by us so highly reprobated that no persons could have stood in a more aukward situation to propose them. . . .

We wish you would get here soon, as many matters of considerable importance are on the carpet.

We are yours &c,
Robt. R. Livingston.
Gouv. Morris.

Kingston, 26 April, 1777.

JAY TO LIVINGSTON AND MORRIS.[1]

Fishkill, 29 April, 1777.

Gentlemen :

Your letter of the 26th instant was this evening delivered to me.   When I was called east from Convention, a clause in the report of the form of Government had been by a very great majority agreed to instituting a council for the appointment of military and many civil officers, *including clerks of courts ;* and though I publicly advocated and voted for that clause, you express much surprize at my disapproving a material alteration of it.

Had you retained the most distant idea of the part I took relative to the various modes proposed for the

---

[1] See note to preceding letter.

appointment of officers, I am confident you would not have asserted " *that I was fully of opinion to appoint by judges of the Supreme Court, not only clerks, but all other civil officers in the Government.*" Had such a representation of my opinion relative to the best mode of appointing those officers, fallen from some persons whom I could name, I should have called it very disingenuous and uncandid.

The fact was thus—The clause directing the Governor to *nominate* officers to the Legislature for their approbation being read and debated, was generally disapproved. Many other methods were devised by different members, and mentioned to the House merely for consideration. I mentioned several myself, and told the Convention at the time, that however I might then incline to adopt them, I was not certain but that after considering them, I should vote for their rejection. While the minds of the members were thus fluctuating between various opinions, Capt. Platt moved for the only amendment which was proposed to the House for introducing the judges. I told the House I preferred the amendment to the original clause in the report, but that I thought a better mode might be devised. I finally opposed the adoption of Capt. Platt's amendment, and well remember that I spent the evening of that day with Mr. Morris at your lodgings, in the course of which I proposed the plan for the institution of the Council as it now stands, and after conversing on the subject, we agreed to bring it into the House the next day. It was moved and debated and carried with the only amendment that the Speaker of the General Assembly for the time being was then (to avoid the Governor's having frequent opportunities of a casting vote) added to the Council.

As to the alteration in question, vizt., transferring the appointment of clerks, etc., of courts from the Council to the respective judges, I dislike it for many reasons which the limits of a letter will not admit of being fully enumerated and discussed.

You say that "*great inconveniencies must arise from suffering clerks to be independent of such courts, and of consequence frequently ignorant, always inattentive.*" If ignorance and inattention would by some necessary consequence unknown to me, characterize all such clerks as the Council (of which the Governor is President, and consisting of the Speaker of the General Assembly and four senators elected in that House) should appoint, I grant that the appointment ought to be in other hands. But I am at a loss and unable to conjecture by what subtle refinement or new improvement in the science of politics it should be discovered that a council acknowledged to be competent to the choice and appointment of the first judges of the land, was insufficient to the nomination of clerks of courts; or from whence it is to be inferred that they, by whose will and pleasure the duration of many other offices is limited by the Constitution, would either appoint or continue in office ignorant or inattentive clerks, more than ignorant or inattentive judges, sheriffs or justices of the peace. Nor can I perceive why the clerks in chancery appointed by the Council, should be more ignorant and inattentive than the examiners, who you are content should still be appointed by that body ; unless ignorance and inattention be supposed less dangerous and important in the one than the other.

That clerks should be *dependent* is agreed on all hands. On whom ? is the only question. I think not on the judges.[1]

Because,

The chancellor, and the judges of the Supreme Court holding permanent commissions, will be *tempted* not only to give those appointments to their children, brothers, relations, and favourites, but to continue them in office against the public good. You, I dare say, know men of too little probity, abilities, and industry to fill an office well, and yet of sufficient art and attention to avoid such gross misbehaviour as might justify loud clamours against them.

Besides, men who appoint others to offices, generally have a partiality for them, and are often disposed, on principles of pride as well as interest, to support them.

By the clerks of court being dependent on the judges collusion becomes more easy to be practised, and more difficult to be detected, and instead of

---

[1] A letter in the "Calendar of New York Historical MSS.," vol. i., pp. 678, 679, March 24, 1777, contains this reference :

"Mr. Jay is exceedingly unhappy about the 27th paragraph of the form of Government which puts the appointm.t of the clerks of courts in the power of the respective Judges. . . . He alleges that 't is putting in their power to provide for Sons, Brothers, creatures, Dependants, &c—That it will prevent obtaining Evidence against the most wicked Judge should such be appointed. Corrupt bargains may be made for appointments to those offices," etc.

publishing and punishing each other's transgressions, will combine in concealing, palliating, or excusing these mutual defects or misdemeanours.

From the clerks, etc., being appointed by the Council, these advantages would result—

The Council might avail themselves of the advice of the judges without being bound by their prejudices, or interested in their designs.

Should the Council promote their favourites at the expense of the public, that body, having a new set of members every year, a bad officer thus appointed would lose his office on his patrons' being removed from the Council.

It would avoid that odium to which that part of the Constitution will now be exposed, viz., that it was framed by lawyers, and done with design to favour the profession.

The new claims respecting the licensing of attorneys, to speak plain, is in my opinion the most whimsical, crude and indigested thing I have met with.

There will be now between thirty and forty courts in this State, and, as that clause now stands, an attorney (however well qualified and licensed by the Supreme Court) must, before he can issue a writ in a little borough or mayor's court, obtain their license also. The reasons assigned for this seem to be: that it would be improper for one court to do this drudgery for the rest; that it would be difficult to distinguish which court it would be most proper to impose it upon; that the judges of the inferior courts might be offended at being relieved from this drudgery, thinking themselves as capable of judging of the merits of an attorney as of a cause, and that they had equal right with others to say who shall and who shall not be entitled to practise.

To say that it would be improper for one to do this drudgery for the rest, is begging the question. Other courts than the Supreme Court *never* had this drudgery to do ; and I believe never will have in any part of the world, except in the State and by the Constitution of New York. Why the examination and licensing of attorneys should with more propriety be styled *a drudgery* than striking a jury, or any other business incident to the office of judge, I know not. If it be, I should think it ought not to be multiplied by thirty or forty, and then imposed on all in the State, compelling them to solicit and pay fees for admission to thirty or forty courts when one would have sufficed.

How it should be difficult to distinguish the proper court for the purpose, is to me mysterious.

The Supreme Court controls all the courts in the State which proceed according to the course of the common law, and its jurisdiction is bounded only by the limits of the State. An attorney is an officer of a common-law court. That court, therefore, which, by the Constitution, is made superior to the others, must be supposed most competent, not only to the determination of causes, but of the qualification of the attorneys who manage them.

The lesser courts cannot be deemed equally qualified for either ; and, being dependent and inferior in every other respect, ought not to have concurrent, independent, or equal authority in this. Justice as well as decency forbids that a mayor and four aldermen should constitutionally have a right to refuse admission to attorneys licensed by the Supreme Court.

Whence is it to be inferred that the judges of the inferior courts, unless gratified with this novel, unprecedented power, would *complain?* It is not to be found among the rights enjoyed by them prior to the Revolution ; and I must doubt whether, unless within this fortnight or three weeks, there was a single man in the State who ever thought of such a thing.

It would be arrogance in them to expect to be indulged in a right to examine, question, and reject the judgment of the Supreme Court respecting the qualifications of attorneys, when that very court is appointed, among other things, to correct their errors in all other cases. Nay, in this case the mere will of these little courts is to be the law ; and an attorney of reputation and eminence in the Supreme Court is without remedy in case an inferior court should unjustly refuse to admit him.

According to the present system an attorney must, if he chooses to have *general* license, obtain admission into the Supreme Court, three mayors' courts, thirteen inferior courts of common pleas for counties, fourteen courts of sessions for the peace, and the Lord knows how often or in how many courts of oyer and terminer and gaol delivery.

Remember that I now predict that this same clause which thus gives inferior courts uncontrolled and unlimited authority to admit as many attorneys as they please, will fill every county in the State with a swarm of designing, cheating, litigious pettifoggers, who, like leeches and spiders, will fatten on the spoils of the poor, the ignorant, the feeble, and the unwary.

The division of the State into districts for the purposes of facilitating elections, I well remember, was agreed to be referred to the Legislature; and I well remember, too, several members as well as myself were of the opinion that a short clause should be inserted in the Constitution which would give the people a claim on the Legislature for it.

The Connecticut plan of nominating or holding up senators I ever warmly espoused. I thought it bore strong marks of wisdom and sound policy; nor have I forgot that others opposed it, or that I undertook, with the leave of the House, to reduce it to writing and offer it to their consideration. The opinion that the rotatory mode of electing renders it entirely useless, I have neither heard nor can I perceive any reason for.

The difficulty of getting any governor at all, you know, has long been an apprehension of little influence on my mind, and always appeared to be founded less in fact than in a design of quickening the pace of the House.

What the secretary may have written to Mr. Benson I know not. I expressed the same sentiments to him that were inserted in my letter to Mr. Hobart, and no others.

The other parts of the Constitution I approve, and only regret that, like a harvest cut before it was all ripe, some of the grains have shrunk.

Exclusive of the clauses which I have mentioned, and which I wish had been added, another material one has been omitted, viz., a direction that all persons holding offices under the government should swear allegiance to it, and renounce all allegiance and subjection to foreign kings, princes, and states in all matters, ecclesiastical as well as civil.

I should also have been for a clause against the continuation of domestic slavery,[1] and the support and encouragement of literature, as well as some other matters, though perhaps of less consequence.

Though the birth of the Constitution is, in my opinion, premature, I shall nevertheless do all in my power to nurse and keep it alive, being far from approving the Spartan law which encouraged parents to destroy such of their children as perhaps by some cross accident might come into the world misshapen.

I am, etc.,

JOHN JAY.

To Robt. R. Livingston and Gouverneur Morris, Esqrs.

JAY TO ABRAHAM YATES.[2]

16th May, 1777.

DEAR SIR:

From the information you were pleased to give me, before you left this place, that it would be proposed

---

[1] Such a recommendation was introduced by Gouverneur Morris and passed, but subsequently omitted. It was in the form of a call upon " the future Legislatures of the State to take the most effectual measures, consistent with the public safety and private property of individuals, for abolishing domestic slavery within the same, so that in future ages every human being who breathes the air of this State shall enjoy the privileges of a freeman." Jay, who, on account of his mother's illness, was absent from the Legislature during the last days of the debate, does not appear to have been aware of the clause offered by Morris. It was during Jay's term as governor, however, that slavery was finally abolished in New York.

[2] Abraham Yates, of Albany, member of the New York Convention.

to hold me up as a candidate for the office of govern-
or, I think it necessary to be very explicit on that
subject. That the office of first magistrate of this
State will be more respectable, as well as more lucrative, and consequently more desirable than the place
I now fill, is very apparent. But, sir, my object in
the course of the present great contest neither has
been, nor will be, either rank or money. I am persuaded that I can be more useful to the State in the
office I now hold than in the one alluded to, and
therefore think it my duty to continue in it. You are
acquainted with the reasons which induce me to be
of this opinion, and although I entertain a high sense
of the honour which my friends are disposed to confer
upon me, I must request the favour of them not to encourage my being named as a candidate for that
office, but to endeavour to unite the votes of the
electors in the county of Albany in favour of some
other gentleman.

I am, dear sir,

Your most obedient and humble servant,

JOHN JAY.

WILLIAM DUER[1] TO JAY.

[PHILA.] May 28th, 1777.

MY DEAR SIR:

You have been undoubtedly surprised at my long silence,
but when I assure you what is fact, that my principal
reasons for not writing have been want of time, and of
satisfactory matter, I flatter myself I shall stand acquitted,

---

[1] William Duer, of Charlotte County, lately member of the New York Convention, and now delegate in Congress.

(if not with honor) at least as a wilful offender against the laws of friendship.

As General Schuyler expects to deliver this letter in person I shall refer you to him for the particular [intelligence] respecting his own affairs, and for the political complexion of affairs in Congress. From a very low ebb at which our affairs were when we arrived here we have recover'd surprisingly; and I may venture to say that the eyes of all those who are not willfully blind are open, and that we may expect [something] to take place with respect to our State.

I congratulate you on the completion of the task of forming and organizing our new Government. I think it upon the maturest reflection the best system which has as yet been adopted, and possibly as good as the temper of the times would admit of. If it is well administered, and some wise and vigorous laws pass'd at the opening of the [session] for watching, and defeating the machinations of the enemy and their abettors, and for supporting by taxes, and other means the credit of the circulating money, it will be a formidable engine of opposition to the designs of our tyrannical enemies; but I assure you I am not without my fears concerning the choice which will be made of those who are to set the machine in motion.

Our all depends on it. It is very observable that in almost every other State where Government has been formed, and establish'd either from the convention of parties, or from a want of proper power being vested in the executive branches, disaffection has encreased prodigiously, and an unhappy langour has prevailed in the whole political system. I sincerely wish that this may not be the case with us, but that the new Government may continue to act with that spirit, integrity, and wisdom which animated the councils of the old!

In this State [Penn.] toryism, or rather treason, stalks

triumphant; the credit of our money is sapp'd by the arts and advances of the malignants, and monopolists (?), and such is the desperate situation of affairs that nothing but desperate remedies can restore these people to reason, and virtue.

The assembly is now conven'd, but I am afraid will not dare to lay a tax to call in part of the large sums of money circulating in this State, or to pass vigorous laws to crush the disaffected.—All my hope is that the spirit of Whiggism will at length break forth in some of the populace, which (if well directed) may affect by quackery or cure what the regular State physicians, are either not adequate to, or unwilling to attempt.

A spirit of this kind under the name of Joyce has made his appearance in Boston; I should not be surprised if he was to travel Westward. It would be attended with good effects.

What think you of an Episcopalian Clergyman in this City praying last Sunday for the Lords Spiritual and Temporal—or rather what think you of the Congregation which heard him with patience?— If in the midst of your political business you can now and then drop me a line I will esteem it as a favor, and (if not regularly) I will by starts, when there is any thing worth communicating, write to you.

A word in the ear of a friend: When I was sent here I had some idea that I was entring into the temple of public virtue. I am disappointed and chagrined. Genl. Schuyler will communicate my sentiments and his own at large.

Col. Lee will I am credibly inform'd be left out of the next delegation for Virginia which is now in agitation. The mere contemplation of this event gives me pleasure; my mind is full, and I wish to unburthen it, but prudence forbids me.

I condole with you on the loss of your aged mother; or rather should I not congratulate you that she is arrived in a secure and pleasant Haven, from a storm, which she was little calculated to bear? This reflection I believe has alleviated your distress.—May we be as virtuous as your parents should we live to be as old.—From the rapid increase of villainy both moral and political, it is to be fear'd that we shall not increase in virtue, as we may in years—Remember me to all my friends, particularly to my fellow-labourers in the Council of *Conspiracy*. Adieu and believe me

Yours with much esteem and affection

W^{M.} DUER.

I have delivered Genl. Schuyler a letter from your friend Mr. Dean in France; I have had it some time by me, but waited a safe mode of conveyance.

JAY TO LEONARD GANSEVOORT.[1]

KINGSTON, 5th June, 1777.

DEAR SIR:

Mr. Cuyler informs me that some of my friends in your county have done me the honour of naming me, among other candidates, for the office of governor.

In my opinion I can be more useful in the place I now hold; and therefore, though the other is far more respectable as well as lucrative, yet, sir, the regard due to the public good induces me to decline this promotion.

I thought it necessary that you and others should be informed of my sentiments on this subject; and it would give me pleasure to hear that the electors in Albany had united in a design of voting for some one

---

[1] Leonard Gansevoort, of Albany County, member of the New York Convention.

gentleman whose spirit, abilities, and reputation might recommend him to that important office.

Our Constitution is universally approved, even in New England, where few New York productions have credit. But, unless the government be committed to proper hands, it will be weak and unstable at home, and contemptible abroad. For my own part, I know of no person at present whom I would prefer to General Schuyler.

I am, dear sir,

Your most obedient and humble servant,

JOHN JAY.

FROM JAY TO MRS. JAY.

KINGSTON, 6th June, 1777.

MY DEAR SALLY:

I was extremely happy to be informed by Mr. Morris' letter that you arrived safe at Troy. The length of the journey and the improbability of your having good accommodations on the road gave me no little anxiety. Elmendolph tells me the little boy behaved very well. I fear the bones of our sister Kate were sore vexed, and that the memory of this jaunt will influence her to decline paying a second visit to Fishkill. Employ all your eloquence to induce her to return; if it has as much influence on her as on me you will be successful.

Let me remind you of consulting your health in all things—ride, bathe, etc.; should a horse be wanting, buy one at any price. Let your returning with Mr. Morris be determined entirely by your own inclination. A court is directed to be held in Dutchess, and

I expect the like order will be given for other counties, so that should you not hear from me so frequently, ascribe it to my absence from here. The family at Fishkill continue as usual, my father weak and his spirits much depressed.

The Tories desert in great numbers to take the benefit of our act of grace. Mr., or rather the Rev., Parson Beardsley and others of some note have come in. Adieu, my dear Sally. Remember me to all the family.

I am, with the most sincere affection, Yours,

JOHN JAY.

JAY TO GENERAL SCHUYLER.

ESOPUS, 20th June, 1777.

DEAR SIR :

It would have given me pleasure to have acknowledged the receipt of your letters of the 10th and 14th inst. I returned on Tuesday last from Fishkill, and postponed writing till I could collect a little information.

The elections in the middle district have taken such a turn as that, if a tolerable degree of unanimity should prevail in the upper counties, there will be little doubt of having, erelong, the honour of addressing a letter to your Excellency.[1]

Clinton by being pushed for both offices may have neither; he has many votes for the first and not a

---

[1] Although Jay had declined to stand as a candidate in this first gubernatorial election in New York, he received a considerable number of votes, as appears from the following note on p. 164 " Civil List, State of New York, 1886 " : " A fragment of the canvass of 1777 shows the returns from Albany, Cumberland,

few for the second. Scott, however, has carried a number from him, and you are by no means without a share. The conclusions to be drawn from such divisions are obvious.

A report that Albany designed General Ten Broeck for Lieutenant-Governor excited jealousy. What influence it may have had is difficult to conjecture. I believe not very great, as it had not time to spread wide or take root deep.

I have casually hinted at holding the first session of the Legislature at Albany, and find a general disinclination to it. Some object to the expense of living there as most intolerable, and others say that should Albany succeed in having both the great officers, the next step would be to make it the capital of the State. In my opinion the election should be determined before it will be proper to say much on this subject, and then should the governor only come from Albany, and could assurances be given that the members might live as cheap there as here, a removal may be practicable and prudent; but should such a measure be occasioned by a coalition of the upper counties, and carried by a slender majority, it would be productive of more evil than its advantages would probably compensate.

You may rely on receiving by express the earliest notice of the event alluded to.

Dutchess, Tryon, Ulster, Westchester as follows : George Clinton, 865 ; John Morin Scott, 386 ; Philip Schuyler, 1,012 ; John Jay, 367 ; Philip Livingston, 5 ; Robert R. Livingston, 7. The votes from Orange and other Southern counties gave the election to Clinton. The returns were made to the Council of Safety, July 9, and the Governor was sworn in on the 30th at Kingston."

GENERAL SCHUYLER TO JAY.

ALBANY, June 30, 1777.

DEAR SIR:

Your favor of the 20th Instant I received on the 26th and I have not been able to snatch a moment to give you a line in answer.

General Clinton I am informed has a majority of votes for the Chair. If so he has played his cards better than was expected.

The enemy have opened the ball in every quarter. It is pretty certain that they will pay us a visit from the westward as well as from the North. I am in much pain about Ticonderoga; little or nothing has been done there this spring. However if the garrison escapes, or if it does not and we get a reinforcement from below and are spiritedly seconded by the Militia we shall prevent them from [advancing] on the side of the Lakes. It would greatly inspire the people with confidence to see the whole Council of Safety here; as I shall be to the Northward somebody ought to be here to give advice and assistance to our people in the western quarter. I therefore earnestly wish to see you and your brethren.[1]

My compliments to all friends,

I am Dr. Sir

Very Sincerely Your

Most obedient humble Servant,

PH. SCHUYLER.

---

[1] Before it dissolved in May, 1777, the New York Convention appointed a Council of Safety to provide for the military necessities of the State until the meeting of the first Legislature in September. Jay was a member of this Council. Its published proceedings show that the suppression of toryism, the mustering of the militia, and the general defence of the State were the principal matters absorbing its attention.

ALEXANDER HAMILTON TO JAY.

HEAD QUARTERS, POMPTON PLAINS [N. J.],
July 13th, 1777.

D[R]. SIR :

I received your favour and one from M[r]. Morris last night by Express. The stroke at Ticonderoga is heavy, unexpected and unaccountable.[1]—If the place was untenable why not discovered to be so before the Continent had been put to such an annoying expence, in furnishing it with the means of defence ? If it was tenable, what, in the name of common sense could have induced the evacuation ? I would wish to suspend my judgement on the matter; but certainly present appearances speak either the most [despicable] cowardice, or treachery. What can have become of St. Clair and the army? did they venture to return without knowing where the enemy were, or what rout to take ?—Or did they wilfully run into their mouths ?—All is mystery and dark beyond conjecture.—But we must not be discouraged at a misfortune—we must rather exert ourselves the more vigorously to remedy the ill consequence of it. If the army gets off safe, we shall soon be able to recover the face of affairs—I am in hope that Burgoigne's success will precipitate him into measures that will produce his ruin. The enterprizing spirit he has credit for, I suspect, may easily be fanned by his vanity into rashness.

The day before yesterday, our whole army marched to this place, computed to be about eighteen miles from Morris Town ; as soon as the weather will permit we shall continue our march to Peeks-Kill. Howe's army we are told are all embarked. We suppose they will shortly make an excursion up the North River.—If we can get there before them all will be well.

The most we have to fear is that a panic will seize the people, and disqualify them for giving their aid. It

---

[1] Evacuation of Ticonderoga by Gen. St. Clair on the approach of Burgoyne, July 4, 1777.

behoves their leaders to put on a cheerful countenance, and combat their fears by a spirited and manly example.

I am, Dr. Sir,

Your most obed. servant,

A. HAMILTON.

GENERAL SCHUYLER TO JAY.

FORT EDWARD, July 14th, 1777.

DEAR SIR:

I am much obliged by your two favors of the —— and 11th Instant. I am happy that the Council of Safety have written the letter to Gen. Putnam, a copy whereof you were so good as to send me.—I feel myself so superior to my malicious enemies from the happy reflection that I have zealously done my duty to my country, that I shall as you very [wisely] recommend not discompose myself in the occupation. This calumny will bring shame and confusion on themselves.

I am in such a situation that it is necessary for me to conciliate the affections of all about me, I dare not speak my sentiments on the evacuation of Tyconderoga. You will perceive I have not done it to Gen. Washington. In the Council of Safety, to your secrecy, I can confide them. They are that it was an ill judged measure not warrented by necessity, and carried into execution with a precipitation that could not fail of creating the greatest panic in our troops and inspiriting the enemy. I am confident that with a moderate degree of foresight and exertion the far greater part of the valuable stores might have been saved, even if it had been really necessary to have abandoned the posts. From my letters to Gen St. Clair he had the greatest reason to believe that I would have joined him in a few days with a very considerable body of troops, and I believe I should have been with him at the head of four or five thousand men by this time if not before ; but all this is *Entre nous*. I hope Gen. Clinton's having the chair of Government will not cause any divisions amongst the friends of America. Altho' his family and connections do not entitle him to so distinguished a predominance; yet he is virtuous and loves his country, has abilities and is brave, and hope he will experience from every patriot what I am resolved he shall have from me, support, countenance and comfort. I think I am neither enthusiastical or superstitious but I cannot help informing you that I am impressed with a presentiment that all will go well, that amidst the multiplicity of business which engages my attention this friendly guest intrudes at every hour, with the 'be of good cheer,' and so amazingly raises my spirits that I feel like a conqueror. You will laugh at me ; do if you please and let our friends laugh with you, but remember if all I feel should be caused by some dreadful and flattering divinity, such as removed the pilot Athamos from Ithaca which he thought he beheld and approached, I am still happy whilst the illusion lasts.

Adieu—my best wishes attend you and my other friends.

I am

Your most Obt. Servt.

PH. SCHUYLER.

FREDERICK JAY TO JAY.

FISH KILL, 18th July, 1777.

DEAR JOHN :

Both your letters are come to hand—I have been to Kent & provided Accommodations for the Family in case of a retreat.

I have done every thing in my power to get your Books removed, but in vain; not a waggon or Cart to be hired at any rate, the People here being busy in their Harvests.

I shall speak to Coll. Hughes to day for two Continental teams; if he has them, I make no doubt he 'll be ready to assist us.—The peas are not yet come to hand. The Family as usual, except Peggy who has been ill with a fever ever since you left us, which is the reason of my not writing to you sooner.

Genl. Sullivan with 2000 Continental Troops are now encamped in the Town of Fishkill; this affair makes the old Gentleman imagine that the Enemy will certainly attempt the River. I could wish he was as easy about the matter as myself—M^r. Platt of Kent informs me that there is a Farm of about 160 Acres with a Comfortable House to be sold near him for about £700, Lawful [money]. Would it not be better to purchase it than have the family in different houses; had I the money of my own, the farm should be mine. The old Gentleman I believe would soon come into the measure if you was to give him only a hint about it.

I am Your Aff^t. Brother
FRED JAY.

JAY TO GENERAL SCHUYLER.

KINGSTON, 21st July, 1777.

DEAR SIR :

Your favour of the 14th inst. came safe to hand. I am happy to see so much cheerfulness diffused through it. I hope your sweet smiling genius won't play the coquette. The confidential part of your letter shall remain secret. Putnam's answer was cautious; he believed there was a fault somewhere, but neither excused nor accused anybody; nor did he take any notice of that part of our letter which respected you.

This kind of reserve is not friendly.   The evacuation of Ticonderoga continues to be the subject, not only of general speculation, but also of general censure and reproach.   The public, not being furnished with the reasons for that measure, are left to form their own conjectures, and seem very universally to impute it to treachery and practice with the enemy; nor are the four generals alone the objects of suspicion; it reaches you.

It is unnecessary to observe that, like many other worthy characters, you have your enemies; and it is also true that countenance is indirectly given to the popular suspicions by persons from whom I should have expected more candour, or I may say more honesty.

It is said, but I know not with what truth, that St. Clair, on being asked by some of his officers why the fort was evacuated, replied generally, that he knew what he did; that on his own account he was very easy about the matter, and that he had it in his power to justify himself.   From hence some inferred that he must have alluded to orders from you.

Another report prevails, that some short time before the fort was left, a number of heavy cannon were by your order dismounted and laid aside, and small ones placed in their room.   This is urged as circumstantial proof against you.

The ship-carpenters have come down, much dissatisfied and clamorous.   In short, sir, that jealousy which ever prevails in civil wars, added to the disappointment and indignation which the people feel on

this occasion, together with the malice of your enemies, require that the integrity and propriety of your
conduct be rendered so evident, as that there may not
be a hook or loop whereon to hang a doubt.

I forgot to mention that stress is also laid on your
distance from the fort at the time of the enemy's
approach, and from this circumstance unfavourable
conclusions are drawn.

Your friends in the mean time are not idle; they
argue that you would have been highly reprehensible,
if you had, by being in a fort besieged, deprived the
other parts of the department of your services and
superintendence.   That they are assured of your having neither ordered nor been privy to the evacuation
of the fort, etc., etc., etc.   A clear, short, and authentic
statement of facts can alone do the work; while the
people remain uninformed they will suspect the
worst. I think the generals (who are *mortal* if honest)
ought to give you a certificate that Ticonderoga was
left without your direction, advice, or knowledge; and
I submit to you whether it would not be expedient to
write such a letter to the Council of Safety on this
subject, as they could with propriety publish.   I think
it should not look like a defence, though it should
amount to it.   It should take no notice of accusations, and yet remove all grounds for them.   Charges
may be answered without seeming to know of any; a
defence more pointed and particular would give a
certain degree of consequence even to calumny, and
resemble an implied admission that there was apparent
room for suspicion.

In one of your late letters to the council was this sentiment. "You wished the evacuation might not be too much depreciated"; and your reasons for this caution may have weight; but, sir, a certain gentleman at that board, whom I need not name, and from whom I do *not* desire this information should be concealed, is in my opinion your secret enemy. He professes much respect, etc., for you; he can't see through the business; he wishes you had been nearer to the fort, though he does not doubt your spirit; he thinks we ought to suspend our judgment, and not censure you rashly; he hopes you will be able to justify yourself, etc., etc. Observe so much caution, therefore, in your letters, as to let them contain nothing which your enemies may wrest to their own purposes.

I must also inform you that the flying seals of your letters to General Washington often arrive there broken. That from the different colour of the wax, if not from the clumsy manner in which they are often put up by the secretaries, it can be no difficult matter for those who receive them to perceive that they have been inspected. I wish some other mode was devised.

Thus, sir, I have performed the unpleasing task of writing to you with much freedom on a very disagreeable subject, and of acquainting you with facts that will give you pain, and put your equanimity to a trial.

I won't apologize for the liberty I have taken, being persuaded that you will consider it as a proof of the regard with which I am, dear sir,

Your friend and humble servant,

JOHN JAY.

TO THE GENERAL COMMITTEE OF TRYON COUNTY.[1]

(*In Council of Safety.*)

GENTLEMEN :   KINGSTON, 22d July, 1777.

We have received your letter, and several others from different parts of your county, and are no less affected by the dangers than the fears of the people of Tryon. It is with the utmost concern that we hear of the universal panic, despair, and despondency which prevail throughout your county. We flattered ourselves that the approach of the enemy would have animated, and not depressed their spirits. What reason is there to expect that Heaven will help those who refuse to help themselves ; or that Providence will grant liberty to those who want courage to defend it. Are the great duties they owe to themselves, their country, and posterity, so soon forgotten ? Let not the history of the present glorious contest declare to future generations that the people of your county, after making the highest professions of zeal for the American cause, fled at the first appearance of danger, and behaved like women. This unmanly conduct gives us great concern. We feel too much for your honour and reputation not to be uneasy. Instead of supplicating the protection of your enemies, meet them with arms in your hands—make good your professions, and let not your attachment to freedom be manifested only in your words.

We could scarcely have believed that a man among

---

[1] The above letter is credited by his biographer to Mr. Jay, vol. i., p. 71. Jay seems to have conducted a large part of the correspondence for the Council of Safety ; its proceedings contain or refer to drafts of letters by him to Washington, Clinton, Schuyler, Trumbull, and others.

you would have thought of *protections* (as they are falsely called) from the enemy. Of what advantage have they been to the deluded wretches who accepted them in Jersey, New York, Westchester, and Long Island ? After being seduced from their duty to their country, they were plundered, robbed, cast into prison, treated as slaves, and abused in a manner almost too savage and cruel to be related. We ought to profit by the woful experience of others, and not with our eyes open run to destruction. Nor imagine you will remain unsupported in the hour of trial. We consider you as part of the State, and as equally entitled with other counties to the aid of the whole. . . .

Let all differences among you cease. Let the only contest be, who shall be foremost in defending his country. Banish unmanly fear, acquit yourselves like men, and with firm confidence trust the event with that Almighty and benevolent Being who hath commanded you to hold fast the liberty with which he has made you free ; and who is able as well as willing to support you in performing his orders. If you can prevail on your people to exert their own strength, all will be well. Let us again beseech and entreat you, for the honour and reputation, as well as the safety of the State, to behave like men.

JAY TO GENERAL SCHUYLER.

DEAR SIR : KINGSTON, 26th July, 1777.

Your favour of the 24th instant, covering a letter from General St. Clair, was delivered to me this evening. I have sent the letter to the press ; it will be printed entire. Extracts might be followed by suspicions. The malicious might remark, that parts were concealed which, if made known, would probably give a different colour to the whole. A number of Holt's papers shall be sent to you, and care taken to transmit others to Congress, to headquarters, to Peekskill, etc. I shall also request Loudon to reprint it.

This attack on your reputation will, I hope, do you only a temporary injury. The honest though credulous multitude, when undeceived, will regret their giving way to suspicions which have led them to do you injustice.

I have reason to suspect that the Council of Safety believed that Ticonderoga was left by your direction or advice, or with your knowledge. They appear fully satisfied of the contrary, and, in my opinion, St. Clair's letter will remove all doubts on that head.

The propriety of appointing a committee to inquire into your conduct appears to me very questionable. Supposing it unexceptionable in point of delicacy with respect to you (which I by no means think it), yet as this Council and the late Convention have, on certain occasions, made your cause their own, your enemies would not fail to insinuate that the proposed inquiry was a mere contrivance to give a favourable complexion to your conduct. Your readiness to submit to such an inquiry is no doubt a strong argument of innocence and conscious rectitude ; but whether it would not be assuming in the Council to propose it, and inconsistent with the dignity of your station to accede to it, are questions of importance. Besides, a proposition so apparently officious and out of their line might perhaps be maliciously ascribed to their apprehensions of mismanagement, and consequently cast weight in the scale against you.

A temperate statement of facts, formed from the materials you mention, would doubtless set your conduct in its true point of view. Although a strict scrutiny may be eligible, yet how far it would be proper to *press* Congress to adopt that measure is worth consideration. The affairs of the northern department have lately engaged much of their time and attention. The evacuation of Ticonderoga will naturally bring about an inquiry. The country will not be satisfied without it. You will then have a fair opportunity of vindicating your conduct. The manner in which you account for the removal of the cannon mentioned in my letter is very satisfactory. Mr. Morris returned this afternoon. The Council were displeased with the last letter from him and Mr. Yates. They have passed a resolution declaring it disrespectful and unsatisfactory, and dissolved that committee. They have, nevertheless, joined Mr. Morris with me, and directed us to repair to headquarters, to confer with his Excellency on the state of your army, the means of reinforcing it, etc. We set out to-morrow. With the best wishes for your health and prosperity,

   I am, dear sir,

    Your friend and obt. servant,

      John Jay.

JAY TO GENERAL ST. CLAIR.

KINGSTON, 28th July, 1777.

SIR :

Your letter of the 25th July inst., which does no less honour to your candour than justice to the reputation of General Schuyler, was very acceptable. Agreeable to what I apprehend to have been your intention, I have sent it to the press, and flatter myself the purposes for which it was written will be fully answered.

The evacuation of Ticonderoga was an event very unexpected as well as important, and has given occasion to much speculation and discontent. How far it was necessary or prudent, can only be determined by gentlemen acquainted with the forts, grounds about them, strength of both parties, and many other circumstances essential to a proper discussion of that subject.

I hope the expediency of the measure may, contrary to the general expectation, derive proof from the event, and that the determination of the general officers on that head may on inquiry be found undeserving the censure it at present meets with.

I am, sir, your most obedient and humble servant,

JOHN JAY.

Brigadier-General St. Clair.

TO JAY FROM HIS FATHER.

FISH KILL, 29 July, 1777.

DEAR JOHNNY,

I have received your letter of the 21 Inst :—The evacuation of Ticonderoga is very alarming ; I wish it may soon be made to appear in a less gloomy light.

Hitherto Fady has not been able to succeed in providing waggons to remove your Books to Kent.—My thoughts have been much imployed of late about removing from hence in case of need, but the more I consider of it the more I am perplex^{d.}, for my present state of health admits of my undergoing no fatigue. Besides I conceive my going to Kent will be attended with an immense expence, for there I can hire no Farm to raise necessarys for my numerous Family, but must lodge them in different Houses and buy daily food &c for them, I suppose at the same exorbitant rate that is extorted from the distressed in other parts of the Country; so that unless I can get a Farm in order to raise so much as will in some measure answer the expence of the Necessarys of life, I am very apprehensive it will have too great a tendency to our ruin, for we may long continue in our present distressed situation before a Peace takes place. I am indeed at a loss what steps to take and therefore I could wish you were nearer at hand to consult with you and Fady what to do. Hitherto my present abode appears to me as safe as elsewhere, and it may be most prudent to continue here till we know what rout the Regulars take & their success if any they have; but in the mean time it may be best to remove some of my most valuable things by way of precaution, which we'll consider of when you come here. If we can purchase another Waggon it shall be done.

Johnny Strang was here about a fortnight or three weeks ago when we was expect^{g.} the Regulars were about coming up the River; he then proposed to send a box or two he has of yours at his Father's to Salem, and promised to remove them from there in case of need & said he would be very careful of them. Nancy is now unwell & Peggy is very sick with an intermitting fever ever since her return from Albany.

I am y^{r.} affect^{e.} Father

PETER JAY.

JAY'S CHARGE TO THE GRAND JURY OF ULSTER COUNTY.[1]

GENTLEMEN :

It affords me very sensible pleasure to congratulate you on the dawn of that free, mild, and equal government which now begins to rise and break from amid those clouds of anarchy, confusion, and licentiousness which the arbitrary and violent domination of Great Britain had spread in greater or less degree throughout this and the other American States. And it gives me particular satisfaction to remark that the first fruits of our excellent Constitution appear in a part of this State, whose inhabitants have distinguished themselves by having unanimously endeavoured to deserve them. This is one of those signal instances in which Divine Providence has made the tyranny of princes instrumental in breaking the chains of their subjects, and rendered the most inhuman designs productive of the best consequences to those against whom they were intended.

The infatuated sovereign of Britain, forgetful that kings were the servants, not the proprietors, and

---

[1] Upon the adoption of the State Constitution, April 20, '77 (see note p. 126), the New York Convention appointed a committee, distinct from the Council of Safety, to establish the authority of the new government in all its branches. As the situation required the organization of the judiciary without delay, the convention itself proceeded, on May 3d, to name the officers, and elected, among others, John Jay, as Chief-Justice of the Supreme Court. He received nineteen votes, against fifteen cast for John Morin Scott. The Supreme Court was not formally opened until September 9th following, at Kingston, when Jay delivered the above charge to the grand jury, a body described at the time as " composed of the most respectable characters in the County, no less than twenty-two of whom attended and were sworn." The charge was published at the jury's request.

ought to be the fathers, not the incendiaries of their people, hath, by destroying our former constitutions, enabled us to erect more eligible systems of government on their ruins ; and, by unwarrantable attempts to bind us in all cases whatever, has reduced us to the happy necessity of being free from his control in any.

Whoever compares our present with our former Constitution will find abundant reason to rejoice in the exchange, and readily admit that all the calamities incident to this war will be amply compensated by the many blessings flowing from this glorious revolution—a revolution which, in the whole course of its rise and progress, is distinguished by so many marks of the Divine favour and interposition, that no doubt can remain of its being finally accomplished.

It was begun and has been supported in a manner so singular, and I may say miraculous, that when future ages shall read its history they will be tempted to consider a great part of it as fabulous. What, among other things, can appear more unworthy of credit than that, in an enlightened age, in a civilized and Christian country, in a nation so celebrated for humanity as well as love of liberty and justice as the English once justly were, a prince should arise who, by the influence of corruption alone, should be able to reduce them into a combination to reduce three millions of his most loyal and affectionate subjects to absolute slavery, under a pretence of a right, appertaining to God alone, of binding them in all cases whatever, not even excepting cases of conscience and religion ?

What can appear more improbable, although true, than that this prince and his people should obstinately steel their hearts and shut their ears against the most humble petitions and affectionate remonstrances, and unjustly determine by violence and force to execute designs which were reprobated by every principle of humanity, equity, gratitude, and policy—designs which would have been execrable if intended against savages and enemies, and yet formed against men descended from the same common ancestors as themselves—men who had liberally contributed to their support and cheerfully fought their battles even in remote and baleful climates. Will it not appear extraordinary that thirteen colonies, the object of their wicked designs, divided by variety of governments and manners, should immediately become one people, and though without funds, without magazines, without disciplined troops, in the face of their enemies, unanimously determine to be free, and, undaunted by the power of Britain, refer their cause to the justice of the Almighty, and resolve to repel force by force, thereby presenting to the world an illustrious example of magnanimity and virtue scarcely to be paralleled? Will it not be matter of doubt and wonder, that notwithstanding these difficulties, they should raise armies, establish funds, carry on commerce, grow rich by the spoils of their enemies, and bid defiance to the armies of Britain, the mercenaries of Germany, and the savages of the wilderness? But, however incredible these things may in the future appear, we know them to be true; and we should

always remember that the many remarkable and unexpected means and events by which our wants have
been supplied and our enemies repelled or restrained,
are such strong and striking proofs of the interposition of Heaven, that our having been hitherto
delivered from the threatened bondage of Britain
ought, like the emancipation of the Jews from Egyp-
tian servitude, to be forever ascribed to its true cause ;
and instead of swelling our breasts with arrogant ideas
of our powers and importance, kindle in them a flame
of gratitude and piety which may consume all remains
of vice and irreligion.

Blessed be God ! the time will now never arrive
when the prince of a country in another quarter of
the globe will command your obedience, and hold
you in vassalage. His consent has ceased to be
necessary to enable you to enact laws essential to
your welfare ; nor will you in future be subject to
the imperious sway of rulers instructed to sacrifice
your happiness whenever it might be inconsistent
with the ambitious views of their royal master. The
Americans are the first people whom Heaven has
favoured with an opportunity of deliberating upon,
and choosing the forms of government under which
they should live. All other constitutions have derived their existence from violence or accidental circumstances, and are therefore probably more distant
from their perfection, which, though beyond our
reach, may nevertheless be approached under the
guidance of reason and experience.

How far the people of this State have improved

this opportunity, we are at a loss to determine. Their constitution has given general satisfaction at home, and been not only approved but applauded abroad. It would be a pleasing task to take a minute view of it, to investigate its principles and remark the connection and use of its several parts; but that would be a work of too great length to be proper on this occasion. I must therefore confine myself to general observations, and among those which naturally arise from a consideration of this subject, none are more obvious than that the highest respect has been paid to those great and equal rights of human nature, which should forever remain inviolate in every society, and that such care has been taken in the disposition of the legislative, executive, and judicial powers of government, as to promise permanence to the constitution, and give energy and impartiality to the distribution of justice. So that while you possess wisdom to discern and virtue to appoint men of worth and abilities to fill the offices of the State, you will be happy at home and respectable abroad. Your lives, your liberties, your property, will be at the disposal only of your Creator and yourselves. You will know no power but such as you will create; no authority unless derived from your grant; no laws but such as acquire all their obligation from your consent.

Adequate security is also given to the rights of conscience and private judgment. They are by nature subject to no control but that of the Deity, and in that free situation they are now left. Every man is permitted to consider, to adore, and to worship his Creator in the manner most agreeable to his conscience. No opinions are dictated, no rules of faith prescribed, no preference given to one sect to the prejudice of others. The constitution, however, has wisely declared, that the "liberty of conscience thereby granted shall not be so construed as to excuse acts of licentiousness, or justify practices inconsistent with the peace or safety of the State." In a word, the convention by whom that constitution was formed were of opinion that the gospel of Christ, like the ark of God, would not fall, though unsupported by the arm of flesh; and happy would it be for mankind if that opinion prevailed more generally.

But let it be remembered that whatever marks of wisdom, experience, and patriotism there may be in your constitution, yet like the beautiful symmetry, the just proportion, and elegant forms of our first parents before their Maker breathed into them the breath of life, it is yet to be animated, and till then may indeed excite admiration, but will be of no use : from the people it must receive its spirit and by them be quickened. Let virtue, honour, the love of liberty and of science be and remain the soul of this constitution, and it will become the source of great and extensive happiness to this and future generations. Vice, ignorance, and want of vigilance will be the only enemies able to destroy it. Against these be forever jealous. Every member of the State ought diligently to read and to study the constitution of his country, and teach the rising generation to be free. By knowing their rights, they will sooner perceive when they are violated, and be the better prepared to defend and assert them.

This, gentlemen, is the first court held under the authority of our constitution, and I hope its proceedings will be such as to merit the approbation of the friends, and avoid giving cause of censure to the enemies of the present establishment.

It is proper to observe that no person in this State, however exalted or low his rank, however dignified or humble his station, but has a right to the protection of, and is amenable to, the laws of the land ; and if those laws be wisely made and duly executed, innocence will be defended, oppression punished, and vice restrained. Hence it becomes the common duty, and indeed the common interest of those concerned in the distribution of justice, to unite in repressing the licentious, in supporting the laws, and thereby diffusing the blessings of peace, security, order and good government, through all degrees and ranks of men among us.

I presume it will be unnecessary to remind you that neither fear, favour, resentment, or other personal and partial considerations should influence your conduct. Calm, deliberate, reason, candour, moderation, a dispassionate and yet a determined resolution to do your duty, will, I am persuaded, be the principles by which you will be directed.

You will be pleased to observe that all offences committed in this country against the people of this State, from treason to trespass, are proper objects of your attention and inquiry.

You will pay particular attention to the practice of counterfeiting bills of credit, emitted by the General Congress, or either of the American States, and of knowingly passing such counterfeits—practices no less criminal in themselves than injurious to the interests of that great cause, on the success of which the happiness of America so essentially depends.

ROBERT TROUP [1] TO JAY.

CAMP 3 MILES ABOVE STILL-WATER,
Sept. 14, 1777. 11 o'clock at night.

MY DEAR SIR :

On the 9th Instant about 8 o'clock A.M. the army marched from Van Shaack's Islands, & London's Ferry ; at 3 in the afternoon it incamped at Forts Mills, and early next morning reached Still-water.

We took Post on the Heights, began to open Communications and throw up a few small redoubts principally with a view of amusing the Enemy. On the 11th we recd. Intelligence that Gen. Burgoyne had called in his Out-posts, collected his Carriages, and was making every Preparation to advance. The General conceiving the Ground we occupied was not calculated for Defence went to reconnoitre & 3 Miles in Front discovered a Spot which fully answered his wishes.—On the 12, he marched the Army upon it and made the necessary dispositions for Action. But in this he was disappointed.

Gen. Burgoyne, like his Colleague, seems to be exceedingly embarrassed. For some time past, he has had his Army in Point, without making a single Motion, till to-day. By the Information of our Scouts he has brought the main

---

[1] Colonel Robert Troup, *aide-de-camp* to General Gates. Subsequently Judge United States District Court of New York.

Body of his Army to Saratoga. They declare they distinctly counted 800 Tents on the West Side of the River near General Schuyler's House. From this Circumstance, with a variety of others we conclude he means to attack us. Should he be so rash as to adopt this Plan, I think we shall end the War in the Northern Department. I speak with Confidence because our Army is truly respectable, & every thing wears the most flattering aspect. We have now on the Ground 9000 Men, well armed, in good Health, high Spirits, & eager for Action. The horrid Barbarities committed by the Enemy, & the Sacredness of our Cause seem to have stamped in every Countenance the glorious words —conquer or die. Permit me to add to these considerations the Strength of our post. There are two Roads only which lead to our Encampment. The one to our Flank by Saratoga Lake, thro a thick marshy swamp; and the other to our Front along Hudsons River. I am inclined to think they will advance on both in order to divide our attention. In the former their Artillery will be of little service; we have obstructed the Pass already by felling Trees, and shall secure it properly to-morrow by fortifying a commanding Eminence. The latter is also favorable to our Designs. Within Musket Shot of it, on the left, is a Ridge which extends very far; this the Riflemen, Infantry, & a large Detachment of the Army will take Possession of, about 4 or 5 Miles in Front, to gall the Enemy *sorely* before they engage the Main Body. In one word—if the action becomes general, they will be obliged to contend with Hills, Rocks, Gullies & Trees on *all sides*. I have impartially considered the different accounts relative to the number of the Enemy. I make a large allowance when I estimate them at 7000. These compose a motley Crew of Englishmen, Germans, & Tories quarrelling with each other & discontented with the Service. From Men void of Principle, and destitute of Harmony can Victory be expected?

Reason & Justice say no. Gen. Lincoln is near Skeens-borough with a numerous Body of Militia. The object of his Expedition is to push *in the Enemy's Rear.*—This he will completely effect, if the delicate, polite, & humane Colonel of the Queen's Dragoons Attempts to get more *elbow Room.*

This much for Military Matters.

When I saw Mrs. Jay last I promised to write to her. I am extremely sorry the great Hurry of Business will not permit me to enjoy *that Pleasure.* I beg you will present my best respects to her, at the same Time apologise for me. How is your little Boy? Does he grow cleverly? Can he talk so as to be understood? Pray, let me hear from your Family, when you have nothing of more Importance to do. —I am in perfect Health, & hope I shall not, in the critical hour, disgrace you, or any of my good Friends.

I am, my dear Sir,

With Respect, yours

R. TROUP.

GENERAL SCHUYLER TO JAY.

SARATOGA, November 6th, 1777.

MY DEAR SIR:

When I did myself the pleasure to write you on the 17th ult., I was not apprized of the enemy's progress up Hudson's River, nor of the barbarous devastation they have been guilty of committing at Kingston, and other places in the vicinity. It is no consolation to me that I have so many fellow-sufferers; I feel, however, a very sensible one, in the fate which has attended General Burgoyne.

Is it not probable that the enemy, in a future campaign, will make another attempt to sail up Hudson River? If they do, and at the same time attack the Eastern States, will there not be a want of bread in those States? As in that case little or none can be conveyed to that quarter, would it not be prudent to form very considerable magazines of flour on the east side of the Green Mountains? and does it not appear necessary to throw such obstructions in Hudson River, as to render it impracticable for shipping to penetrate beyond the highlands? Perfectly to obstruct the navigation of Hudson River is certainly a very arduous task, but not attended with so many difficulties as may at first view be imagined. And I am persuaded, that a spirited director, at the head of four hundred men, would completely prepare every thing in the course of the winter, so as to sink the works in the course of six weeks after the ice shall have quitted the river. The British engineers and officers confess, that if the works on the Lake, at Ticonderoga had been completed, it would have been impossible to have opened a passage in less than ten days, if they had been possessed of every requisite for such a business, and if not the least molestation had been given them. Very early in the war I urged the necessity of securing Hudson River; I have repeated my wish more than once, and I shall be extremely happy to see a business completely executed, on which I am persuaded much of the safety of the United States in general, and this in particular, depends. If I had any interest with the Senate and Assembly, I should venture to address them on the subject; but as I have not, I must leave it to you, if you are in sentiment with me on the necessity of the work, to mention it to your friends in both Houses.

As I shall shortly be altogether out of public life, I am earnestly engaged in building me a house at this place, that I may be as far out of the noise and bustle of the great world as possible. I am confident (provided we repel the enemy), that I shall enjoy more true felicity in my retreat, than ever was experienced by any man engaged in public life. My hobby-horse has long been a country life; I dismounted with reluctance, and now saddle him again with a very considerable share of satisfaction (for the injurious world has not been able to deprive me of the best source of happiness, the approbation of my own heart), and hope to canter him gently on to the end of the journey of life.

When Congress will send for me to inquire into my conduct, I cannot even make a guess at. I have entreated that it may be soon, and respectfully observed, that from my past services I ought not to remain longer than needs must be in the disagreeable situation in which I now stand.

Where are you lodged—and where is your father's family? Can I be of any service? Some tory tenants of mine have lost fine farms, either for grain or stock, between this and Albany; two or three of them in good fence, with small tenements on them. If these or any of them can be of any use, I am sure they are much at your service. What further buildings are necessary may be cheaply and speedily erected, as the frame of a whole house can be sawed, boards and every other material procured at the cheapest rates. I will not let any of these farms, except such as I am confident would not do for you, until I have the pleasure of hearing from you; or rather, until I have had the happiness of giving you a bed in the new house, which I began upon on the 1st instant, and which will be under cover, and have two rooms finished by the 15th instant, unless the weather should prove remarkably wet: but observe that it is only a frame house, sixty feet long, twenty-one broad, and two stories high, filled in with brick.

I hope pains will be taken to recruit our army; we ought not to grow negligent, and trust too much to our good fortune: there is danger in too much confidence, and I apprehend that Britain, like a desperate gamester whose affairs are on the brink of ruin, will make a bold push to retrieve the loss, if yet it is possible.

Pray make my compliments to the governor, the chancellor, speaker, R. Yates, and such other of my friends as are in your quarter. I do not mention Morris, because I hear he has gone to relieve Mr. Duane. It is rather hard upon the latter to be obliged to such a constant attendance. Adieu : my best wishes attend you through life.

I am, dear sir, with great esteem and affection,

Your obedient humble servant,

PHILIP SCHUYLER.

JAY TO GENERAL SCHUYLER.

FISHKILL, 11th December, 1777.

DEAR GENERAL :

Your very friendly letter of the 6th ult. was this moment delivered. I am happy to find your firmness unimpaired, and your attachment to your country unabated by its ingratitude. Justice will yet take place, and I do not despair of seeing the time when it will be confessed that the foundation of our success in the northern department was laid by the present commander's predecessor. I am nevertheless anxious that such authentic evidence of the propriety of your conduct should be transmitted to posterity as may contradict the many lies which will be told them by writers under impressions and under an influence unfriendly to your reputation. This subject merits attention. Facts, and not a single resolution of Congress, will in my opinion be effectual to do the business. I have thought much of this matter, but more of this when we meet.

Your offer of a farm, etc., is very obliging : be pleased to accept my thanks for it. I am at present at a loss how to determine. Let not my delay, how-

ever, be injurious to you. This place, at which all the
family now reside, is by no means agreeable or convenient, if secure, which is also doubtful.   I purpose
doing myself the pleasure of seeing you this winter,
and shall then avail myself of your advice.

The rapidity with which the desolation of your seat
at Saratoga is repairing does not surprise me.   I remember the despatch with which the preparations for
our first expedition into Canada were completed.   I
wish the repair of our forts, etc., in the river was in the
same train.

As to your loss of influence among a certain body,
it is less so than you may imagine.   The virtuous and
sensible still retain their former sentiments.   The
residue ever will be directed by accident and circumstances.   Few possess honesty or spirit enough openly
to defend unpopular merit, and by their silence permit
calumny to gain strength.   These, however, are temporary evils, and you do well to despise them.

I am, my dear sir, very sincerely
Your friend and obedient servant,

JOHN JAY.

JAY TO JAMES DE LANCEY.[1]

SIR,

Nothwithstanding the opposition of our sentiments
and conduct relative to the present contest, the friendship which subsisted between us is not forgotten ; nor

---

[1] A Westchester County loyalist and an officer in Oliver De Lancey's corps
recruited in New York and Long Island. Surprised and captured by a party of
Americans in the fall of 1777, he was taken to and confined at Hartford. See
his answer following.

will the good offices formerly done by yourself and family cease to excite my gratitude.

How far your situation may be comfortable and easy, I know not : it is my wish, and shall be my endeavour, that it be as much so as may be consistent with the interest of that great cause to which I have devoted every thing I hold dear in this world. I have taken the liberty of requesting Mr. Samuel Broome immediately to advance you one hundred dollars on my account.

Your not having heard from me sooner was unavoidable. A line by the first opportunity will oblige me. Be explicit, and avail yourself without hesitation of the friendship which was entertained as well as professed for you by

Your obedient and humble servant,
JOHN JAY.

POUGHKEEPSIE, 2d January, 1778.

JAMES DE LANCEY TO JAY.

HARTFORD, Jany. 14th, 1778.

DR. SIR :

I rec^{d.} your kind Letter of the 2^d Inst. with 100 Dollars from Mr. Saml. Broome which with the many other obligations I am under to you will never be forgot; as I have had a plentifull supply of money from home returned it Mr. Broome.

The gentlemen of the Army particularly Genl. Parsons & some of the inhabitants of this place have been very civil to me; the Genl. has made application to the Governor & Councill to have me permitted to go on Parole to New York to settle my affairs there & to try if I could effect an exchange between Col. Ely & myself, but could not succeed

and commissary departments are in a most lamentable situation. Opportunities have been neglected last campaign which were truly golden ones, but omnipotent fatality had, it seems, determined that the American capital should fall. Our sentiments on this occasion are so perfectly coincident that I will not enlarge. The mighty Senate of America is not what you have known it. The Continental currency and Congress have both depreciated, but in the hands of the Almighty Architect of empires, the stone which the builders have rejected may easily become head of the corner. The free, open, and undisturbed communication with the city of Philadelphia debauches the minds of those in its vicinage with astonishing rapidity. O, this State is sick even unto the death, and in Sir William [Howe] they have certainly got a most damnable physician. Just before the reduction of the forts, the enemy balanced exactly upon the point of quitting the city, and a straw would have turned in either scale. Our troops; *Heu Miseros!* The skeleton of an army presents itself to our eyes in a naked, starving condition, out of health, out of spirits. But I have seen Fort George in the summer of 1777. Next campaign I believe we shall banish these troublesome fellows. For Heaven's sake, my dear friend, exert yourself strenuously in the great leading business of taxation. To that great wheel " a thousand petty spokes and small annexments are morticed and adjoined." I earnestly entreat you and my other friends, *fortia opponere pectora* to that fatal system of limitation, which, if carried into execution, would be downright ruin, and in the ineffectual attempt will carry us to the brink of it. Yorktown and its neighbourhood, although nearly ninety miles from Philadelphia, already considers our money almost as waste paper. At taverns, take as specimen the following rates : breakfast and supper each, seven shillings and sixpence ; dinner, ten shillings ; one night's hay for one horse, seven shillings and sixpence ; oats, per quart, one shilling ; toddy, per bowl, ten shillings ;

rum, per gill, seven shillings and sixpence ; wine, per bottle, from thirty to forty shillings, and the like ; you will observe this is proclamation. Hay, they tell me, hath been sold in some places at £20 proc. per ton. My love to Livingston. I shall write to him by this opportunity, if I can find time to send a long letter, which, indeed, I owe him. Remember me to Mrs. Jay, and believe me, yours,

GOUVERNEUR MORRIS.

JAY TO GENERAL SCHUYLER.

POUGHKEEPSIE, 12th February, 1778.

DEAR GENERAL :

I hope you will seriously determine to serve your country, at least in a legislative capacity. Class yourself with those great men of antiquity, who, unmoved by the ingratitude of their country, omitted no opportunities of promoting the public weal. In this field malice cannot prevent your reaping laurels, and remember that the present state of our affairs offers you a plentiful harvest. Set about it then, my dear sir, in earnest. I know not who will be the bearer of this letter, and therefore forbear enlarging.

I am, dear sir,

Your most obedient servant,

JOHN JAY.

JAY TO GENERAL SCHUYLER.

26th February, 1778.

DEAR SIR :

As an opportunity of going to Albany will not probably be given me during the session of the Legislature, and as I have too long kept you in suspense relative to the farm you was so kind as to offer me, I ought now to acquaint you that I am under a necessity of denying myself the pleasure of being your neighbour. My father's infirmities have so increased as to render a removal to Saratoga so inconvenient and painful, if practicable, that he cannot prevail upon himself to undertake it. So that, my dear sir, filial obligations will constrain me to continue in his neighbourhood.

He is greatly obliged by your friendly offer, and believe me, it will ever excite the gratitude of your obliged and

Affectionate friend and servant,
John Jay.

JAY TO GOUVERNEUR MORRIS.

11th March, 1778.

Dear Morris:

Your favour of the 1st of February came to hand last week. It gives me pleasure to hear you were then at headquarters, especially on business so important and perplexed. It is time that inquiries, as well as punishments, should become more frequent. I wish better, or rather more, use was made of courts-martial. Why is the inquiry directed to be made into the causes to which we are to ascribe the loss of Fort Montgomery, etc., so long delayed? Had it been immediately after that event took place, the river would now have been well fortified, and a general at the head of the troops in the southern part of the State.

Pennsylvania, I believe, is sick unto death.   It will nevertheless recover, though perhaps not soon.   Weak and bad constitutions incline to chronical disorders.

Were I sure that this letter would reach you uninspected, I should commit many things to paper worth your knowledge, but which would give you little pleasure or surprise ; but as it is uncertain who will be the bearer, they must be reserved for the present. God bless you, and give you diligence and patience. Where you are, both are necessary.

I am your friend,

JOHN JAY.

GOUVERNEUR MORRIS TO JAY.

YORKTOWN [YORK, PA.], 28th April, 1778.

DEAR JAY :

I won't dispute who has written most.   I have written more than twice what you acknowledge to have received, but this is of no consequence.

I am sorry for your session, but I wish you had marked out what taxes have been laid, what salaries given, and a few more striking outlines of legislation.   These, with what I know of your men, would have enabled me to imagine proper lights and shades.

I choose that my friends should write freely, and those who know me must know that such freedoms need no apology.   I never thought the person you allude to so steady as could be wished.   We have all of us our weak sides ; would to God that were the worst.

What you mention relative to our plan of rights shall be attended to.   I am a busy man, though, as heretofore, a pleasurable one.

Let your governor cleanse the Augean stable in his State,

which no public body would do though it stink under their noses. I am labouring at arrangements of various kinds. God prosper me, and give me patience and industry. It was a good wish from one who knew my wants.

We have ordered troops from the highlands, but we will send thither a general, who shall be empowered to call forth the swarms of the eastern hive. Men were necessary at the Valley Forge. I have a good knack at guessing. I guess the enemy won't attempt Hudson River.

I do think of Vermont : and unless I mistake, matters shall be managed to effect, without bellowing in the forum, which I believe hath been a little too much the case. But why should I blame impetuous vivacity,—hath it never led me into an error ?

Putnam will soon be tried. The affair of Schuyler and St. Clair laboured under awkward circumstances. Their friends and their enemies appear to me to have been equally blind. I enclose extracts from the minutes made the other night to possess myself of the real state of facts. There are some other entries from time to time. It was erroneous to order a committee simply to collect facts ; they should have been directed to state charges. This morning, my colleague being absent, I got a committee appointed for the latter purpose : Sherman, Dana (Massachusetts), and Drayton (South Carolina). This was unanimous, and yet I would have undertaken to argue for it in a style which would absolutely have ruined the measure. You know it would have been easy to say, *justice to those injured gentlemen*, instead of *justice to an injured country* requires, &c.

Great Britain seriously means to treat. Our affairs are most critical, though not dangerously so. If the minister from France were present as well as him from England, I am a blind politician if the thirteen States (with their extended territory), would not be in peaceable possession of their independence three months from this day. As it is, expect a long war. I believe it will not require such aston-

ishing efforts after this campaign to keep the enemy at bay.
Probably a treaty is signed with the house of Bourbon ere
this ; if so, a spark hath fallen upon the train which is to
fire the world. Ye gods! what havoc doth ambition make
among your works.

My dear friend, adieu. My love to your wife. Remember me to all my friends of every rank and sex.

I am yours,

GOUVERNEUR MORRIS.

P.S. I meant to have said, the present is within the
spirit of our constitution, a *special occasion.*

JAY TO GOUVERNEUR MORRIS.

ALBANY, April 29, 1778.

DEAR MORRIS :

My last to you was written about a week ago. I
am now engaged in the most disagreeable part of my
duty, trying criminals. They multiply exceedingly.
Robberies become frequent : the woods afford them
shelter, and the tories food. Punishments must of
course become certain, and mercy dormant—a harsh
system, repugnant to my feelings, but nevertheless
necessary. In such circumstances lenity would be
cruelty, and severity is found on the side of humanity.

The influence of Lord North's conciliatory plan is
happily counterbalanced by the intelligence from
France. There was danger of its creating divisions.
A desire of peace is natural to a harassed people ;
and the mass of mankind prefer present ease to the
arduous exertions often necessary to ensure permanent tranquillity.

What the French treaty may be, I know not. If Britain would acknowledge our independence, and enter into a liberal alliance with us, I should prefer a connexion with her to a league with any power on earth. Whether those objects be attainable, experience only can determine. I suspect the commissioners will have instructions to exceed their powers, if necessary. Peace, at all avents, is, in my opinion, the wish of the minister. I hope the present favorable aspect of our affairs will neither make us arrogant nor careless. Moderation in prosperity marks great minds, and denotes a generous people. Your game is now in a delicate situation, and the least bad play may ruin it. I view a return to the domination of Britain with horror, and would risk all for independence ; but that point ceded, I would give them advantageous commercial terms. The destruction of Old England would hurt me ; I wish it well : it afforded my ancestors an asylum from persecution.

Parties here are still in a ferment. I hope it will be the means of purging off much scum and dross. I can't be particular. This letter may never reach you.

I expect in a few days to see General Schuyler ; and my importunities shall not be wanting to urge him to join you without delay. The people grow more reconciled to him.

The military departments here, I believe, are well managed. The commissary deserves credit. Handsome things are said of the quarter-master ; and there is one at the head of the artillery, who appears to me to have much merit. The park elaboratory and stores are in high order. There is the appearance of regularity, care, and attention in all the public works. As to the hospital I can say little, not being as yet well informed. Conway is pleased with Schuyler, and manages the Vermont troops properly ; but of this say nothing. I fancy he does not well understand the views of his patron. Neither of them ought to know this.

The clothier-general, once the Duke of Bolton's butler, is an anti-Washington. An ignorant butcher is issuing commissary. Let me again hint to you the propriety of restraining the staff from trade : besides general reasons, there are particular ones. Many good cannon remain yet at Ticonderoga—strange neglect. Remember Vermont. Why do the marine committee keep Tudor in pay ? I can't hear that he does any thing for it.

I am, and will be your friend,

John Jay.

JAY TO PETER VAN SCHAACK.[1]

Poughkeepsie, 26th June, 1778.

Dear Sir :

It is but three days since your favour of the 3d instant was delivered to me. A fair wind, good company, the prospect of a short passage, and thereby avoiding the fatigue and inconvenience of a journey by land, induced me to return from Albany by water.

---

[1] A well-known loyalist, one of Jay's friends before the war, now a prisoner on parole. See " Life of Van Schaack," by his son.

The letter you mention to have written on the subject of a pass, etc., has never come to hand. On conversing with the governor yesterday on that subject, he told me he lately had the pleasure of seeing you, and had settled that matter to your satisfaction.

I am of the number of those who think exercise and change of air and company essential to your health. I might add a third requisite—a mind at ease. The two first conduce to the other. Misfortunes, and severe ones, have been your lot. The reflection that they happened in the course of a providence that errs not, has consolation in it. I fear, too, that your sensibility is wounded by other circumstances—but these are wounds not to be probed in a letter. Could we now and then smoke a few pipes together, you would perhaps be in a better humour with many things in the world than I think you now are. I suspect your imagination colours high and shades too deep. But more of this another time.

You mistake me much if you suppose the frequency of your letters or applications troublesome to me. I assure you it would give me pleasure were opportunities of being useful to you more frequent than either. When you were last here, fourteen miles more would have carried you to Fishkill. That little ride would have been a gratification to me, and not unpleasant to you. What detained you? Was you not sure I would be glad to see you? God bless you and give you health. I am, dear Peter, affectionately yours, etc.,

JOHN JAY.

EDWARD RUTLEDGE TO JAY.

CHARLESTON, Dec. 25th, 1778.

MY DEAR JAY:

It is a long time since we have had any correspondence, but I see no reason why it should be longer, when we have any thing to say, and leisure to say it in. Such is just my situation ; for it is Christmas-day, and all the world (*i. e.* my clients) being either at their devotions or their amusements, I have time to tell you, and I fear with some reason (as it comes north about), that a damned infamous cabal is forming against our commander-in-chief, and that whenever they shall find themselves strong enough they will strike an important blow. I give you this hint, that you may be on your guard ; and I know you will excuse me for doing so, when you recollect that there are some men of our acquaintance who are in possession of all the qualities of the devil, his cunning not excepted. Recollect the indirect attempts that were repeatedly made against the command and reputation of poor Schuyler, and the fatal stab that was at last aimed at both ; and let us be taught how necessary it is to oppose a cabal in its infancy. Were it in my power, I would stifle it in its birth. Conway, the ****, and ******* are said to be at the bottom of this, besides an abundance of snakes that are concealed in the grass. If these are not encouraged to come forward, they will continue where they are ; but if the former are permitted to bask in the sunshine of Congressional favour, the latter will soon spread themselves abroad, and an extended field will be immediately occupied by the factious and the ambitious. The fate of America will then be like the fate of most of the republics of antiquity, where the designing have supplanted the virtuous, and the worthy have been sacrificed to the views of the wicked. Indeed, my friend, if the Congress do not embrace every opportunity to extinguish that spirit of cabal and unworthy ambition, it will finally be more essentially injurious to the well-being of this continent than the sword of Sir Harry and his whole army. I view the body of which we were for a long time members, as possessing, in a very eminent degree, the powers of good and evil. It depends on those who manage the machine to determine its object. I hear you have returned to Congress, and I hope you will have your full share in the management. I do not know what gentleman we shall send from this State. We have some fine plants, nay, saplings, that will do wondrous well in a few years, but are too tender at present to bear up the weight of this continent. Were it now to be imposed upon them, it might check their growth, or, as they are the production of a southern clime, it is possible they might be blighted by a northern wind. When you write me, let me know how Robert R. Livingston is. Remember me to him, for I esteem him highly. God bless you, my dear Jay, and believe me to be, with great sincerity,

Your affectionate friend,
EDWARD RUTLEDGE.

TO JAY FROM MRS. JAY.

PERSIPINEY, Decb^{r.} 28th, 1778.

MY DEAR MR. JAY:

.   .   .   .

I had the pleasure of finding by the newspaper that you are honor'd with the first office on the Continent, and am still more pleased to hear this appointment affords general satisfaction.[1] Will you be so kind as to inform me whether

---

[1] This "appointment" was Jay's election to the presidency of the Continental Congress, December 10, 1778. Under the New York Constitution the Chief Justice was debarred from holding any other office except that of delegate to Congress on "a special occasion." The irritating Vermont controversy presented such an occasion, and on November 4th the New York Legislature elected Jay a delegate without vacating his judicial office. Three days after taking his seat in Congress he was elected president of that body, succeeding Henry Laurens, of South Carolina, who had resigned.

our State has prolonged your stay beyond the first of March or not? As by your present appointment your personal attendance upon Congress I imagine can't be dispensed with, I am very solicitous to know how long I am still to remain in a state of widowhood. Upon my word I sincerely wish these three months may conclude it; however, I mean not to influence your conduct, for I am convinced that had you consulted me as some men have their wives about public measures, I should not have been *Roman matron* enough to have given you so entirely to the public, and of consequence your reputation and claim to the gratitude of your country would have been as much diminished as theirs who have acted so imprudent tho' tender a part.

It will give you pleasure to be informed that your son and myself are still favored with health, and if you can spare time to give me the same grateful tidings of yourself, you can hardly imagine what happiness you 'll confer upon your   Affec^{te.} wife,

SARAH JAY.

JAY TO GENERAL LAFAYETTE.

PHILADELPHIA, 3d January, 1779.

SIR :

The Congress have directed me to observe to you, that the plan for emancipating Canada [1] was conceived at a time when, from various movements of the enemy, there was the highest reason to expect a speedy and total evacuation of all the ports they held in these States. These indications, however, proved false, and the probability of their quitting this country

---

[1] Respecting the proposed Canada expedition see Washington to Jay, April 14, 1779.

in the course of the winter is become very slender ; nor is it by any means certain that they will do it in the spring. Prudence therefore dictates that the arms of America should be employed in expelling the enemy from her own shores before the liberation of a neighbouring province is undertaken, as the proportion of force necessary for our defence must be determined by the future operations and designs of the enemy, which cannot now be known ; and as, in case of another campaign, it may happen to be very inconvenient if not impossible for us to furnish our proposed quota of troops for the emancipation of Canada. Congress think they ought not, under such circumstances, to draw their good ally into a measure the issue of which, depending on a variety of contingencies, is very uncertain, and might be very ruinous.

JOHN JAY.

Major-General the Marquis de Lafayette.

JAY TO ROBERT R. LIVINGSTON.

PHILADELPHIA, 13th January, 1779.

DEAR ROBERT :

Not a single line have you received from me since my arrival. This, as you say, does not look very friendly. I confess it, and, what is more in my favour, feel it.

Business, I know, cannot excuse a total silence, though it may palliate a partial one. I won't plead it, for I never admitted it ; nor do I now write merely to keep fair with my own principles. Inclination more than consistency prompts me on this occasion.

I presume your Legislature is by this time convened. Now is the season for exertion. Attend regularly. Confirm those who esteem you and their country. Convert or confound those who would sacrifice either to private views.

Will any consideration induce you to visit another quarter of the globe? I don't know that you will be called upon, but I am not sure that you may not. My conduct will be greatly influenced by your inclination.

I had almost persuaded myself to write a letter to your brother Ned, urging him to come to this college, and offering my service to prepare the way for his reception. But as, on reflection, I apprehend it might stimulate him to a measure in which, perhaps, his mamma or brother might not concur, I decline it for the present. I cannot forbear, however, observing to you that, in my opinion, his genius and his years call for a further degree of cultivation than can be obtained at Hurley. I wish to be useful to every lad of talents and cleverness; and I assure you that desire will always be increased when these recommendations are possessed by one so nearly connected with a gentleman and a family who have particular claims to my esteem and respect.

I am, your friend,

John Jay.

P.S.—Don't be too lazy or too busy to let me know how you do.

PHILADELPHIA, 15th February, 1779.

SIR :

When characters rendered amiable by virtues and important by talents, are exposed to suspicions, and become subjects of investigation, the sensibility of individuals as well as the interest of the public are concerned in the event of the inquiry.[1]

It gives me, therefore, great pleasure to transmit to you an unanimous act of Congress of the 11th instant, not only acquitting your conduct in the transaction it relates to of blame, but giving it that express approbation, which patriotism in the public, and integrity in every walk of life always merit and seldom fail ultimately to receive.

I am, sir, with great respect and esteem, your most obedient servant,

JOHN JAY,
President of Congress.

JAY TO ROBERT R. LIVINGSTON.

PHILADELPHIA, 16th February, 1779.

DEAR ROBERT :

Your favour of the third instant came to hand this morning. The satisfaction my letter afforded you flatters as well as pleases me. It argues a remembrance of former times ; for which, and other reasons,

---

[1] In a letter to Congress of January 28, 1779, Robert Morris called attention to "insinuations" thrown out against his integrity as a member of the Secret Committee of Congress, and demanded an investigation of his conduct and accounts. He was completely vindicated.

I shall give you no more opportunities of joining the assembly of angels in rejoicing over penitent mortals. Not that I mean, on the one hand, to enter the state of reprobation and become a hardened sinner, or, on the other, enlist with those saints who slip not with their foot.

This letter, written on the very day I received yours, will become evidence of my having gone through the whole process of amendment. Divines, you know, describe it as consisting of conviction, contrition, and conversion. Whether I shall persevere or not is a subject on which time will utter the surest prophecies.

The complexions of resignation, of soft complaint, and joyless sensibility, are so blended in your letter, that, if anonymous, one would suppose it written by a wayworn traveller through this vale of tears, who, journeying towards his distant haven through sultry and dreary paths, at length lays his languid limbs under some friendly shade, and permits the effusions of his soul to escape in words. My friend, a mind unbraced and nerves relaxed are not fit company for each other. It was not a *man* whom the poet tells us *pined in thought, and sat like patience on a monument smiling at grief.* In such rugged times as these other sensations are to be cherished. Rural scenes, domestic bliss, and the charming group of pleasures found in the train of peace, fly at the approach of war, and are seldom to be found in fields stained with blood, or habitations polluted by outrage and desolation. I admire your sensibility, nor would I wish to see less milk in your veins ; you would be less amiable. In my opinion, however, your reasoning is not quite just. I think a man's happiness requires that he should condescend to keep himself free from fleas and wasps, as well as from thieves and robbers.

When the present session of your Legislature is ended, take a ride and see us. You will find many here happy to see you. I have something, though not very interesting, to say to you on the subject of politics, but as it is now very late, and I have been writing letters constantly since dinner, I am really too much fatigued to proceed. Make my compliments to Mrs. Livingston, who I presume is with you. Adieu.

I am, your friend,

JOHN JAY.

JAY TO KITTY LIVINGSTON.[1]

PHILADELPHIA, 27th February, 1779.

DEAR KITTY :

    .   .   .   .   .   .

A report has just reached here that the enemy have visited Elizabethtown, and burnt your father's house. This, if true, is a misfortune to the family, which I hope they will bear with proper fortitude and dignity. Similar losses have been my lot ; but they

---

[1] Mrs. Jay's sister. The report of the burning of Gov. Livingston's house proved not to be true. His daughter Susan, it appears, bravely stood her ground in the mansion and succeeded in inducing the British officers to spare it. Hearing of this, Jay wrote a few days later in a note to his wife.: " I wish to know the particulars of Susan's convention with Lord Cathcart. It is said she had the advantage of him in the treaty, and displayed much fortitude as well as address on the occasion. Pray how did John Lawrence fare ? We hear he was in the house and was made a prisoner ? Did they release or carry him off ? "

never have, and I hope never will, cost me an hour's sleep. Perseverance in doing what we think right, and resignation to the dispensations of the great Governor of the world, offer a shield against the darts of this sort of affliction to every body that will use it. Adieu.

I am, dear Kitty, your affectionate friend and brother,

JOHN JAY.

ALEXANDER HAMILTON TO JAY.

HEAD-QUARTERS, March 14th, 1779.

DEAR SIR:

Colonel Laurens, who will have the honour of delivering you this letter, is on his way to South Carolina, on a project which I think, in the present situation of affairs there, is a very good one, and deserves every kind of support and encouragement. This is to raise two, three, or four battalions of negroes, with the assistance of the government of that State, by contributions from the owners, in proportion to the number they possess. If you should think proper to enter upon the subject with him, he will give you a detail of his plan. He wishes to have it recommended by Congress to the State; and, as an inducement, that they would engage to take those battalions into continental pay.

It appears to me that an expedient of this kind, in the present state of southern affairs, is the most rational that can be adopted, and promises very important advantages. Indeed, I hardly see how a sufficient force can be collected in that quarter without it; and the enemy's operations there are growing infinitely serious and formidable. I have not the least doubt that the negroes will make very excellent soldiers with proper management; and I will venture to pronounce that they cannot be put into better hands than those of Mr. Laurens. He has all the zeal, intelligence, enterprise, and every other qualification necessary to succeed in such an undertaking. It is a maxim with some great military judges, that with sensible officers, soldiers can hardly be too stupid ; and, on this principle, it is thought that the Russians would make the best troops in the world, if they were under other officers than their own. The King of Prussia is among the number who maintain this doctrine, and has a very emphatical saying on the occasion, which I do not exactly recollect. I mention this, because I hear it frequently objected to the scheme of imbodying negroes, that they are too stupid to make soldiers. This is so far from appearing to me a valid objection, that I think their want of cultivation (for their natural faculties are probably as good as ours) joined to that habit of subordination, which they acquire from a life of servitude, will make them sooner become soldiers than our white inhabitants. Let officers be men of sense and sentiment, and the nearer the soldiers approach to machines, perhaps the better.

I foresee that this project will have to combat much opposition from prejudice and self-interest. The contempt we have been taught to entertain for the blacks, makes us fancy many things that are founded neither in reason nor experience ; and an unwillingness to part with property of so valuable a kind, will furnish a thousand arguments to show the impracticability, or pernicious tendency, of a scheme which requires such a sacrifice. But it should be considered, that if we do not make use of them in this way, the enemy probably will ; and that the best way to counteract the temptations they will hold out, will be to offer them ourselves. An essential part of the plan is to give them their freedom with their muskets. This will secure their fidelity, animate their courage, and, I believe, will have a good influence upon those who remain, by opening a door to their emancipation. This circumstance, I confess, has no small weight in inducing me to wish the success of the project; for the dictates of humanity and true policy equally interest me in favour of this unfortunate class of men.

With the truest respect and esteem,

I am, sir, your most obedient servant,

ALEX. HAMILTON.

JAY TO GENERAL SCHUYLER.

PHILADELPHIA, 21st March, 1779.

DEAR SIR:

So uncertain has been the fate of letters during the course of this war, that I very seldom write one without adverting to the possibility and consequences of its miscarriage and publication. This precaution has on a late occasion given me much consolation. Two of my letters to Mrs. Jay fell into the enemy's hands at Elizabethtown; they contained nothing that would give me uneasiness if published. Prudential considerations of this kind have, since my arrival here, restrained me from writing several confidential letters to you; and I should now be equally cautious had I not full confidence in the bearer of this, and under little apprehension of danger from accidents on the road.

Congress has refused to accept your resignation. Twelve States were represented. New England and Pennsylvania against you. The delegates of the latter are new men, and not free from the influence of the former. From New York south you have fast friends. Mr. *****'s disposition is at least questionable. Delaware was unrepresented.

What is now to be done ? You best can answer this question. Were I in your situation, I should not hesitate a moment to continue in the service. I have the best authority to assure you that the commander-in-chief wishes you to retain your commission. The propriety of your resignation is now out of question. Those laws of honour which might have required it are satisfied : are you certain they do not demand a contrary conduct? You have talents to render you conspicuous in the field ; and address to conciliate the affections of those who may now wish you ill. Both these circumstances are of worth to your family, and, independent of public considerations, argue forcibly for your joining the army. Gather laurels for the sake of your country and your children. You can leave them a sufficient share of property ; leave them also the reputation of being descended from an incontestably great man—a man who, uninfluenced by the ingratitude of his country, was unremitted in his exertions to promote her happiness. You have hitherto been no stranger to these sentiments, and therefore I forbear to enlarge. Would it not do you honour to inform Congress that, while in their opinion your services ought not to be withheld from your country, neither the der ngement of your private affairs, the severities you have experienced, nor regard to your health already impaired in their service, shall restrain you from devoting yourself to the execution of their commands ; but that whenever the situation of our affairs may cease to call you to the field, you hope they will permit you to retire and attend to the duties you owe your family.

Should this be your resolution, would not the main army be your proper object ? there you may be best known, and there best acquire military influence. Consider : this campaign will in all human probability be decisive, and the last. Can you, therefore, employ six or eight months better ?

I will not apologize for the freedom with which I write, being persuaded that although our opinions may vary, you will consider this letter as some evidence of the sincerity with which I am

Your friend and servant,

JOHN JAY.

JAY TO GENERAL LINCOLN.

PHILADELPHIA, 2d April, 1779.

SIR :

Although I have not the honour of a personal acquaintance with you, yet I am so well informed of your character as to believe you will always be happy in leading a young soldier to glory, and to afford him that countenance and protection which a brave and generous youth seldom fails to invite. Permit me, therefore, to recommend to you Major Matthew Clarkson, who is now going to place himself under your command ; and be assured that you will confer an obligation on me by becoming his friend as well as his general.

I am, with great respect and esteem,

Your most obedient and humble servant,

JOHN JAY.

JAY TO GENERAL WASHINGTON.

PHILADELPHIA, 6th April, 1779.

Mr. Jay presents his compliments to General Washington, and encloses an extract from a letter in a certain degree interesting.

Extract of a letter from Major-General Gates, of the 15th March, 1779, to the President of Congress.

" The enclosed copy of my letter to General Washington, of the 4th instant, in answer to his of the 14th ult. from Middlebrook, will give Congress a true idea of my opinion respecting our entering Canada, and the only route which we can take with reasonable hopes of success. Individuals, and not the public, will be benefited by an expedition into Canada by either of the routes from Albany. That of Co-os alone is practicable, but not without the co-operation of the allied fleet.

" General Washington's letter of the 14th of February is enclosed. It being the only letter I have received from his excellency since December, Congress will immediately judge of the extent or limitation which it is proper to observe in their instructions to me."

GENERAL WASHINGTON TO JAY.

[Private.]

HEAD-QUARTERS, MIDDLEBROOK,
April 14th, 1779.

I have received your several favours of the 2d, 3d, and 28th of March, and 6th of April. I thank you for them all, but especially for the last, which I consider as a distinguishing mark of your confidence and friendship.

Conscious that it is the aim of my actions to promote the public good, and that no part of my conduct is influenced by personal enmity to individuals, I cannot be insensible to the artifice employed by some men to prejudice me in the public esteem. The circumstance of which you have obliged me with a communication, is among a number of other instances of the unfriendly views which have governed a certain gentleman from a very early period. Some of these have been too notorious not to have come to your knowledge; others, from the manner in which they have been conveyed to me, will probably never be known, except to a very few. But you have perhaps heard enough yourself to make any further explanation from me unnecessary.

The desire, however, which it is natural I should feel to preserve the good opinion of men of sense and virtue, conspiring with my wish to cultivate your friendship in particular, induces me to trouble you with a statement of some facts which will serve to place the present attack in its proper light. In doing this I shall recapitulate and bring into view a series of transactions, many of which have been known to you; but some of which may possibly have escaped your memory.

An opinion prevailing that the enemy were likely, shortly, to evacuate these States, I was naturally led to turn my thoughts to a plan of operations against Canada, *in case that event should take place.* A winter campaign, before the enemy could have an opportunity of reinforcing and putting themselves in a more perfect state of defence, appeared to promise the most speedy and certain success, and the route by Co-os offered itself as most direct and practicable. In this I fully agreed with General Gates and some other gentlemen whom I consulted on the occasion; and on the 12th of September last I wrote to Congress accordingly, submitting it to them, whether it would not be advisable to be laying up magazines, opening a road, and making other preparations for the undertaking. They approved the project, and authorized me to carry it into execution. I the more readily entered into it from a consideration, that if circumstances should not permit us to carry on the enterprise, preparations towards it could easily be converted into another channel, and made serviceable to our operations elsewhere *without any material addition of expense to the continent*, because provisions, which would compose the principal part of the expense, were at all events to be purchased on Connecticut River, the only doubt being whether they should be used in an expedition against Canada, or transported to Boston—circumstances to determine this: with truth it may be added, that, excepting the articles of provision and forage, which, as before observed, would have been bought if no expedition by the way of Co-os had been in contemplation, the " incredible expense," mentioned by General Gates in his letter of March 4th, amounted to the purchase of a few pair of men's shoes, and some leather for moccasins *only*. If any other expense has been incurred, it is unknown to me—must have been by his order, and he alone answerable for it.

In October following, Congress entered into arrangements with the Marquis de la Fayette for co-operating with the court of France, in an expedition against that country. In this scheme, one body of troops was to proceed from Co-os and penetrate by way of the river St. Francis : others forming a junction at Niagara, were to enter Canada by that route ; and while these were operating in this manner, a French fleet and a body of French troops were to go up the river St. Lawrence, and take possession of Quebec.

You are well acquainted with the opposition I gave to this plan, *and my reasons at large for it*. From what has since happened, they seem to have met the full approbation of Congress. The ideas I held up were principally these : that we ought not to enter into any contract with a foreign power, unless we were sure we should be able to fulfil our engagements—that it was uncertain whether the enemy would quit the States or not; and in case they did not, it would be impracticable to furnish the aids which we had stipulated—that even if they should leave us, it was doubtful whether our own resources would be equal to the supplies required; that therefore it would be impolitic to hazard a contract of the kind, and better to remain at liberty to act as future conjunctures should point out. I recommended, nevertheless, as there were powerful reasons to hope the enemy might go away, that eventual preparations should be made to take advantage of it, to possess ourselves of Niagara and other posts in that quarter, for the security of our frontiers, and to carry our views still further with respect to a conquest of Canada, if we should find ourselves able to prosecute such an enterprise.

This Congress, in a subsequent resolve, approved, and directed to be done. It was not the *least motive* with me for recommending it, that operations of this nature seemed to be a very favourable object with this honourable body. The preparations on Hudson River were undertaken in consequence.

Upon a nearer view of our finances and resources, and when it came to be decided that the enemy would continue for some time longer to hold the posts they were in possession of, in the course of the conferences with which I was honoured by the committee of Congress in Philadelphia, I suggested my doubts of the propriety of continuing our northern preparations upon so extensive a plan as was first determined. The committee were of opinion with me, that the state of our currency and supplies in general would oblige us to act on the defensive next campaign, except so far as related to an expedition into the Indian country for chastising the savages, and preventing their depredations on our back settlements; and that though it would be extremely desirable to be prepared for pushing our operations further, yet our necessities exacting a system of economy forbade our launching into much extra expense for objects which were remote and contingent. This determination having taken place, all the northern preparations were discontinued, except such as were necessary towards the intended Indian expedition.

Things were in this situation when I received a letter from General Bailey (living at Co-os), expressing some fears for the safety of the magazine at Co-os ; in consequence of which I directed the stores to be removed lower down the country. This I did to prevent the possibility of accident, though I did not apprehend they were in much danger. Sometime afterward I received the letter (No. 1) from General Gates, expressing similar fears, to which I returned him the answer of 14th February, transmitted by him to Congress (No. 2). Knowing that preparations had been making at Albany, and unacquainted with their true design, he inferred, from a vague expression in that letter, that the intention of attacking Canada was still adhered to, but that I had changed the plan, and was going by way of Lake Champlain or Ontario : either of these routes he pronounces impracticable, and represents that by Co-os as the *only* practicable one. He goes further, and declares, that " in the present state of our army, and the actual situation of our magazines, to attempt a serious invasion of Canada by whatever route, would prove unsuccessful, unless the fleet of our allies should at the same time co-operate with us, by sailing up the river St. Lawrence." Though I differ with him as to the impracticability of *both* the other routes, I venture to go a step beyond him respecting our ability to invade Canada ; and am convinced, that in our present circumstances, and with the enemy in front, we cannot undertake a serious invasion of that country at all, even *with the aid of an allied fleet.*

You will perceive, sir, that I have uniformly made the departure of the enemy from these States *an essential con-*

dition to the invasion of Canada, and that General Gates
has entirely mistaken my intentions. Hoping that I had
embarked in a scheme which our situation would not justify,
he eagerly seizes the opportunity of exposing my supposed
errors to Congress; and in the excess of his intemperate
zeal to injure me, exhibits himself in a point of view from
which I imagine he will derive little credit. The decency
of the terms in which he undertakes to arraign my conduct,
both to myself and to Congress, and the propriety of the
hasty appeal he has made, will, I believe, appear at least
questionable to every man of sense and delicacy.

The last paragraph of the extract with which you favour
me, is a pretty remarkable one. I shall make no comments
further than as it implies a charge of neglect on my part, in
not writing to him but once since December. From the
beginning of last campaign to the middle of December, about
seven months, I have copies of near fifty letters to him, and
about forty originals from him. I think it will be acknowledged the correspondence was frequent enough during that
period; and if it has not continued in the same proportion
since, the only reason was, that the season of the year, the
troops being in winter-quarters, and General Gates's situation unfruitful of events, and unproductive of any military
arrangements between us, afforded very little matter for
epistolary intercourse; and I flatter myself it will be readily
believed, that I am sufficiently occupied with the necessary
business of my station, and have no need of increasing it
by multiplying letters without an object. If you were to
peruse, my dear sir, the letters that have passed between
General Gates and myself for a long time back, you would
be sensible that I have no great temptation to court his
correspondence, when the transacting of business does not
require it. An air of design—a want of candour in many
instances, and even of politeness, give no very inviting
complexion to the correspondence on his part. As a speci-

men of this, I send you a few letters and extracts, which at your leisure, I shall be glad you will cast your eye upon.

Last fall it was for some time strongly suspected that the enemy would transport the whole, or the greater part, of their force eastward, and combine one great land and sea operation against the French fleet in Boston harbour : on this supposition, as I should go in person to Boston, the command next in importance was the posts on the North River. This properly would devolve on General Gates ; but from motives of peculiar scrupulousness, as there had been a difference between us, I thought it best to know whether it was agreeable to him, before I directed his continuance. By way of compliment, I wrote him a letter containing the extract No. 3, expecting a cordial answer and cheerful acceptance. I received the evasive and unsatisfactory reply, No. 4. A few days after this, upon another occasion, I wrote him the letter No. 5, to which I received the extraordinary answer No. 6, which was passed over in silence.

The plan of operations for the campaign being determined, a commanding officer was to be appointed for the Indian expedition. This command, according to all present appearance, will probably be of the second, if not of the first importance for the campaign. The officer conducting it has a flattering prospect of acquiring more credit than can be expected by any other this year, and he has the best reason to hope for success. General Lee, from his situation, was out of the question. General Schuyler, who, by the way, would have been most agreeable to me, was so uncertain of continuing in the army, that I could not appoint him. General Putnam I need not mention. I therefore made the offer of it (for the appointment could no longer be delayed) to General Gates, who was next in seniority, though perhaps I might have avoided it, if I had been so disposed, from his being in a command by the special appointment of Congress. My letter to him on the occasion you will find in No. 7. I believe you will think it was conceived in very candid and polite terms, and merited a different answer from the one given it in No. 8.

I discovered, very early in the war, symptoms of coldness and constraint in General Gates's behaviour to me. These increased as he rose into greater consequence ; but we did not come to a direct breach till the beginning of last year. This was occasioned by a correspondence, which I thought made rather free with me, between him and General Conway, which accidentally came to my knowledge. The particulars of this affair you will find delineated in the packet herewith, endorsed " Papers respecting General Conway." Besides the evidence contained in them of the genuineness of the offensive correspondence, I have other proofs, still more convincing, which, having been given me in a confidential way, I am not at liberty to impart.

After this affair subsided, I made it a point of treating General Gates with all the attention and cordiality in my power, as well from a sincere desire of harmony, as from an unwillingness to give any cause of triumph to our enemies from an appearance of dissension among ourselves. I can appeal to the world and to the whole army, whether I have not cautiously avoided every word or hint that could tend to disparage General Gates in any way. I am sorry his conduct to me has not been equally generous, and that he is continually giving me fresh proofs of malevolence and opposition. It will not be doing him injustice to say, that besides the little underhand intrigues which he is frequently practising, there has hardly been any great military question in which his advice has been asked, that it has not been given in an equivocal and designing manner, apparently calculated to afford him an opportunity of censuring me, on the failure of whatever measures might be adopted.

When I find that this gentleman does not scruple to take

the most unfair advantages of me, I am under a necessity of explaining his conduct to justify my own. This, and the perfect confidence I have in you, have occasioned me to trouble you with so free a communication of the state of things between us. I shall still be as passive as a regard to my own character will permit. I am, however, uneasy, as General Gates has endeavoured to impress Congress with an unfavourable idea of me, and as I only know this in a private confidential way, that I cannot take any step to remove the impression if it should be made. I am aware, sir, of the delicacy of your situation, and I mean this letter only for your own private information ; you will therefore not allow yourself to be embarrassed by its contents, but with respect to me, pass it over in silence.

With the truest esteem and personal regard,

I am, dear sir,

Your obliged and obedient servant,

GEO. WASHINGTON.

JAY TO GENERAL WASHINGTON.

PHILADELPHIA, 21st April, 1779.

DEAR SIR :

Accept my thanks for the long and friendly letter of the 14th inst. which I have had the pleasure of receiving from you. It was, for many reasons, grateful to me. I value the esteem and regard of the wise and virtuous ; and had wished to know the particulars of transactions respecting which only vague and unsatisfactory reports had come to my knowledge. Delicacy forbade my breaking the subject to you when here. I was sure of your politeness, but not certain of more than a usual degree of confidence. The latter has now become manifest, and permit me to assure you it shall be mutual. The impression attempted to be made has not taken. It passed without a single remark. Your friends thought it merited nothing but silence and neglect. The same reason induced me to take no notice of it in my answer.

I have perused the several papers with which you favoured me. The delicacy, candour, and temper diffused through your letters form a strong contrast to the evasions and design observable in some others. Gratitude ought to have attached a certain gentleman to the friend who raised him; a spurious ambition, however, has, it seems, made him your enemy. This is not uncommon. To the dishonour of human nature, the history of mankind has many pages filled with similar instances; and we have little reason to expect that the annals of the present or future times will present us with fewer characters of this class. On the contrary, there is reason to expect that they will multiply in the course of this revolution. Seasons of general heat, tumult, and fermentation favour the production and growth of some great virtues, and of many great and little vices. Which will predominate, is a question which events not yet produced nor now to be discerned can alone determine. What parties and factions will arise, to what objects be directed, what sacrifices they will require, and who will be the victims, are matters beyond the sphere of human pre-science. New modes of government, not generally understood, nor in certain instances approved—want of moderation and information in the people—want of abilities and rectitude in some of their rulers—a wide field open for the operations of ambition—men raised from low degrees to high stations, and rendered giddy by elevation and the extent of their views—a revolution in private property and in national attachments—laws dictated by the spirit of the times, not the spirit of justice and liberal policy—latitude in principles as well as commerce—suspension of education—fluctuations in manners, and public counsels, and moral obligations—indifference to religion, etc., etc., are circumstances that portend evils which much prudence, vigour, and circumspection are necessary to prevent or control. To me, there appears reason to expect a long storm and difficult navigation. Calm repose and the sweets of undisturbed retirement appear more distant than a peace with Britain. It gives me pleasure, however, to reflect that the period is approaching when we shall become citizens of a better-ordered state ; and the spending a few troublesome years of our eternity in doing good to this and future generations is not to be avoided nor regretted. Things will come right, and these States will be great and flourishing. The dissolution of our government threw us into a political chaos. Time, wisdom, and perseverance will reduce it into form, and give it strength, order, and harmony. In this work you are, to speak in the style of one of your professions, a master-builder ; and God grant that you may long continue a *free* and *accepted* mason.

Thus, my dear sir, I have indulged myself in thinking loud in your hearing ; it would be an Hibernicism to say in your *sight*, though in one sense true; it is more than probable I shall frequently do the like. Your letter shall be my apology, and the pleasure resulting from the converse of those we esteem, the motive.

I am, dear sir,

With perfect esteem and regard,

Your most obedient servant,

JOHN JAY.

GENERAL WASHINGTON TO JAY.

MIDDLEBROOK, April, 1779.

DEAR SIR:

In one of your former letters you intimate, that a free communication of sentiments will not be displeasing to you. If, under this sanction, I should step beyond the line you would wish to draw, and suggest ideas or ask questions which are improper to be answered, you have only to pass them by in silence. I wish you to be convinced that I do not desire to pry into measures the knowledge of which is not necessary for my government as an executive officer, or the premature discovery of which might be prejudicial to plans in contemplation.

After premising this, I beg leave to ask what are the reasons for keeping the continental frigates in port? If it is because hands cannot be obtained to man them on the present encouragement, some other plan ought to be adopted to make them useful. Had not Congress better lend them to commanders of known bravery and capacity for a limited term, at the expiration of which the vessels, if not taken or lost, to revert to the States—they and their crews, in the mean time, enjoying the exclusive benefit of all captures they make, but acting either singly or conjointly under the direction of Congress? If this or a similar plan could be fallen upon, comprehending the whole number, under some common head, a man of ability and authority commissioned to act as commodore or admiral, I think great advantages might result from it. I am not sure but at this moment, by such a collection of the naval force we have, all the British armed vessels and transports at Georgia might be taken or destroyed, and their troops ruined. Upon the present system, our ships are not only very expensive and totally useless in port, but sometimes require a land force to protect them, as happened lately at New-London.

The rumour of the camp is, that Monsieur Gerard is about to return to France; some speak confidently of its taking place. If this be a fact, the motives doubtless are powerful; as it would open a wide field for speculation, and give our enemies, whether with or without real cause, at least a handle for misrepresentation and triumph.

Will Congress suffer the Bermudian vessels, which are said to have arrived at Delaware and Chesapeake Bays, to exchange their salt for flour, as is reported to be their intention? Will they not rather order them to depart immediately? Indulging them with a supply of provisions at this time will be injurious to us in two respects: it will deprive us of what we really stand in need of for ourselves, and will contribute to the support of that swarm of privateers which resort to Bermuda, from whence they infest our coast, and, in a manner, annihilate our trade. Besides these considerations, by withholding a supply, we throw many additional mouths upon the enemy's magazines, and increase proportionably their distress. They will not and cannot let their people starve.

In the last place, though first in importance, I shall ask, is there any thing doing, or that can be done, to restore the credit of our currency? The depreciation of it is got to so alarming a point that a wagon-load of money will scarcely purchase a wagon-load of provisions.

I repeat what I before observed, that I do not wish for your reply to more of these matters than you can touch with strict propriety.

Very truly I am, dear sir,

Your most obedient and affectionate servant,

GEORGE WASHINGTON.

JAY TO GENERAL WASHINGTON.

PHILADELPHIA, 26th April, 1779.

DEAR SIR :

The questions contained in your favour of the —— April instant are as important as the manner of introducing them is delicate.

While the maritime affairs of the continent continue under the direction of a committee, they will be exposed to all the consequences of want of system, attention, and knowledge. The marine committee consists of a delegate from each State ; it fluctuates ; new members constantly coming in, and old ones going out ; three or four, indeed, have remained in it from the beginning ; and few members understand even the state of our naval affairs, or have time or inclination to attend to them. But why is not this system changed ? It is, in my opinion, convenient to the family compact. The commercial committee was equally useless. A proposition was made to appoint a commercial agent for the States under certain regulations. Opposition was made. The ostensible objections were various. The true reason was its interfering with a certain commercial agent in Europe and his connections.

You will, if I am not greatly mistaken, find Mr.

Gerard disposed to be open and communicative. He has acquired an extensive knowledge of our affairs; I have no reason to believe he will use it to our prejudice. There is as much intrigue in this State-house as in the Vatican, but as little secrecy as in a boarding-school. It mortifies me on this occasion to reflect that the rules of Congress on the subject of secrecy, which are far too general, and perhaps for that reason more frequently violated, restrains me from saying twenty things to you which have ceased to be private.

The state of our currency is really serious. When or by what means the progress of the depreciation will be prevented, is uncertain. The subject is delicate, but the conduct of some men really indicates at least great indifference about it. It will not be many days before measures having a great, though not immediate influence on this subject, will be either adopted or rejected. I shall then have an opportunity of being more particular.

> I am, my dear sir,
>> With perfect esteem and regard,
>>> Your obedient servant,
>>>> JOHN JAY.

GENERAL WASHINGTON TO JAY.

HEAD-QUARTERS, MIDDLEBOOK,
May 10th, 1779.

I seize a moment of leisure to thank you, my dear sir, for your obliging favors of the 21st and 26th of April. My friendship for you will always make me take pleasure in cultivating the esteem and confidence of which you so politely assure me. You give an affecting summary of the causes of the national evils we feel, and the still greater we have reason to apprehend. To me it appears that our affairs are in a very delicate situation ; and what is not the least to to be lamented is, that many people think they are in a very flourishing way ; and seem in a great measure insensible to the great danger with which we are threatened. If Britain should be able to make a vigorous campaign in America this summer, in the present depreciation of our money, scantiness of supplies, want of virtue and want of exertion, 't is hard to say what may be the consequence.

It is a melancholy consideration that any concerned in the conduct of public affairs should discover an indifference to the state of our currency. Nothing, in my opinion, can be more manifest, than that if something effectual be not done to restore its credit, it will in a short time either cease to circulate altogether, or circulate so feebly as to be utterly incapable of drawing out the resources of the country. This is nearly the case now.

> With every sentiment of esteem and regard,
> I am, dear sir,
> Your most obedient servant
> GEORGE WASHINGTON.

EGBERT BENSON TO JAY.[1]

DEAR SIR :

Since I had the pleasure of writing to you last the Committee [of the Continental Congress] have returned from Vermont, and they passed thro' this place when I happened unfortunately not to be at home. Altho I have not had an opportunity to converse with them yet from what has

---

[1] This letter from Judge Benson is of interest, not only as referring to the Vermont controversy, but as throwing light on the current expedients for raising war taxes, making loans, and meeting the depreciation of the currency. It is to be read in connection with Jay's letter to Governor Clinton, following.

been communicated to me by the Governor and the papers which I have seen, their embassy has not been productive of the good I both wished and expected. I am certainly exceedingly disappointed as to what I supposed was the principal object of their errand, namely information ; for I imagined these gentlemen would have taken measures for discovering the general sense of the inhabitants instead of confining themselves to a short epistolary conference with Governor Chittenden, [of Vermont] proposing questions many of them foreign to the subject and contenting themselves in almost every instance with answers either unintelligible or evasive. It would be improper to charge these gentlemen with having intentionally acted wrong, and while I disapprove of their proceedings I would not mean to impeach their integrity.—Notwithstanding the defective Manner in which they have conducted the business they have at least clearly established this fact, that Governor Chittenden *himself* is determined at all events not to reunite with us, for we may undoubtedly suppose such his determination, when with apparent Sincerity he says that his *religious* rights and privilidges would be in danger from a Union with a Government, by the fundamental [law] of which all Religions are tolerated and all Establishments expressly excluded. I am confident these sentiments do not generally prevail among the inhabitants on the Grants. I have conversed with several of them ; tho, being ignorant of the true Nature of the controversy, blindly attached to the New State, yet they all seem disposed to acquiesce in the decision of Congress. The Governor I believe spoke his mind very freely to the Committee especially with respect to their letter recommending to several · towns on the Grants as it were a temporary Submission to the new State for military purposes. He utterly refused to countenance the Measure by any orders to the Militia in that quarter, and offered to give the Committee the reasons of his refusal in writing but they declined accepting them. The assertion that Genl. J. Clinton has made a requisition of Men from Vermont you may be assured is false. The Legislature will meet early in the next Month when we shall be at our *ne plus* relative to this business unless something decisive is speedily done by Congress.

The People are much pleased that you have at last published your journals, tho' some of the proceedings are exceedingly reprehended, particularly the loan of 2,000,000 to Pennsylvania. We cannot comprehend the propriety of lending an enormous Sum to a trading State, their Government established and in full possession of all their territory. Advancing monies indefinitely to delegates without an application from their respective states is another proceeding for which Congress is censured. From what I can learn I think it more than probable you will be instructed as to both these matters. We have an idea that the politics of Pennsylvania have crept into Congress and that most of your proceedings are poisoned by their party disputes about their government and that Congress ought to remove from that State. How just this surmise is I will not determine, but it seems to be so much the opinion of many here that I should not be surprised if the Legislature were also to send instruction upon this subject.

A regulating scheme has not been attempted anywhere in the State except at Albany, and how it succeeds there I do not certainly know but can easily conjecture. It is amazing that people should still pursue a system so evidently futile and absurd. I sincerely wish the *limitation* may be *limited* to the City of Albany. I possibly am in the opposite extreme and so far from reducing prices agreeable to this plan, I think the Embargo Act ought immediately to be repealed and our farmers indulged with an opportunity of carrying their produce to the highest market. We have already by embargos and other restrictions sacrificed too much to the Common Cause; it is time we should observe a different policy, and place our subjects upon equality with those of other States. Taxation is the only *honest* and rational remedy for the depreciation of the Currency, but I fear it will be too slow in its operation to answer the present purpose and recourse must be had to other expedients. An internal *compulsory* loan appears the most eligible; and I would therefore propose that Estates to a certain Amount should be obliged to advance a certain Sum on loan to the public. Our separate effort will avail little, but I beleive if a plan of this kind was recommended by Congress and adopted by all the States very considerable sums might be raised. I could wish to be favored with your sentiments before the Legislature meets. It does not appear to me improper to take this method for cancelling our own emissions. Inclosed you have a list of the members chosen at the last Election in those instances where I have been able to procure the Names.

I congratulate you upon the Commencement of the third year of our Independence. We have at last secured a *possession* which among the lawyers is esteemed a Considerable point gained. My best respects to Mess⁵· Duane and Morris.

I am most sincerely yours

EGB^T· BENSON.

N. B. Holt in his last paper published the resolutions moved for by our delegates. We are at a loss to know where he obtained a Copy.

POUGHKEEPSIE July 6th, 1779.

JAY TO GOVERNOR CLINTON.

PHILADELPHIA, August 27, 1779.

DEAR SIR:

If New York and New Hampshire, by acts of their respective Legislatures, will authorize Congress to settle the line between them, and if New York will further, by act of their Legislature, empower Congress to adjust the disputes with the people of the Grants on equitable and liberal principles, I am well persuaded it will conduce to the interest and happiness of the State. The apprehension of interfering with your police, on the one hand, and the apparent equity as well as policy of hearing the revolters before a decision against them, on the other, are obstacles which at present embarrass Congress.

Mr. Duane was of opinion before he left us that we should forbear further proceedings on the subject in Congress till the sense of our Legislature should be known. I hope it will be one of their first objects, and that they will not be too nice and critical in their reservations and restrictions. The jurisdiction is the great point; it is of no great consequence to the State, who possess and cultivate the soil, especially as we have vacant lands enough to do justice to individuals who may suffer by a decision against them.[1]

There are many other matters about which I should write to you were it necessary ; as Mr. Morris and Mr. Duane will be with you, you will obtain more particular information from them than from my letters.

I wish the Legislature would make it a standing rule to direct the attendance of some of their delegates at every session and enter into free conference with them on the great affairs of the Continent.

---

[1] Compare Jay's letter to Governor Clinton of September 25, 1779. To understand all the allusions to the Vermont controversy in these letters, as well as in Benson's preceding, reference must be made to the literature on the subject in the histories of New York, Vermont, and New Hampshire, and in the proceedings of the Continental Congress.

Many advantages, not necessary to enumerate, would result from such a measure. In times like the present it would be imprudent to trust some things to letters which at best cannot be so satisfactory as personal interviews.

Several circumstances which have come to my knowledge lead me to suspect that pains have been taken to injure Mr. Morris in the opinion of his constituents. Justice to him, as well as regard to truth, obliges me to say that he deserves well of New York, and America in general. It has been the uniform policy of some, from the beginning of the contest, to depreciate every man of worth and abilities who refused to draw in their harness. Pennsylvania suffers severely from it at this day; many of their former faithful servants have been dismissed, and others called to office who rather receive importance from, than give weight to, the places they fill. The moment any State ceases to be ably as well as honestly represented in Congress it becomes a cypher, and its vote will no longer be directed by the interest and sentiments of the State and Union, but by the art and management of designing and plausible politicians.

I think it my duty also, upon this occasion, to assure you that Mr. Duane's industry and attention to business, and his invariable attachment to the welfare of those who sent him, deserve their commendation. Colonel Floyd's conduct while here gained him much respect; he moved on steady, uniform principles, and appeared always to judge for himself, which, in my opinion, is one very essential qualification in a delegate, and absolutely necessary to prevent his being a mere tool.

I have prevailed upon myself to make these representations, because I think them just and because I cannot suppose they will be ascribed to improper motives by any—by you I know they will not. Popularity is not among the number of my objects ; a seat in Congress I do not desire, and as ambition has in no instance drawn me into public life, I am sure it will never influence me to continue in it. Were I to consult my interest I should settle here and make a fortune ; were I guided by inclination I should now be attending to a family who, independent of other misfortunes, have suffered severely in the present contest.

It is of great importance that your delegation here do not remain long in its present situation. Whatever men you may think proper to send, let me again and again press you to send able ones. The reputation of the State is exceeding high, and it would be mortifying to see it diminish.

Permit me also to suggest to you the propriety of adopting the plan by which Massachusetts provides for the maintenance of their delegates. They have a house, and keep a table at the expense of the State, besides which an allowance is made them for the maintenance of their families, who ought not to suffer by the loss of that time which is devoted to public service. Your delegates, on the contrary, are not allowed sufficient to maintain, or rather to subsist, themselves. I have heard of two or three gentlemen proposed in your State for delegates—the Chancellor, General Schuyler, and General Scott. There is another, of whom I have heard no mention, Mr. Hobart, who, if he could be spared, would, I think, be a good member; during the winter he might remain here without great inconvenience to you.

JOHN JAY.

CIRCULAR-LETTER FROM CONGRESS TO THEIR CONSTITUENTS.[1]

FRIENDS AND FELLOW-CITIZENS :

In governments raised on the generous principles of equal liberty, where the rulers of the state are the servants of the people, and masters of those from whom they derive authority, it is their duty to inform their fellow-citizens of the state of their affairs, and by evincing the propriety of public measures lead them to unite the influence of inclination to the force of legal obligation in rendering them successful. This duty ceases not, even in times of the most perfect peace, order, and tranquillity, when the safety of the commonwealth is neither endangered by force or seduction from abroad, nor by faction, treachery, or misguided ambition from within. At this season, therefore, we find ourselves in a particular manner impressed with a sense of it, and can no longer forbear calling your attention to a subject much misrepre-

---

[1] The above letter was prepared by Mr. Jay, at the request of Congress, September 8, 1779, to accompany the resolutions of that body of the 1st and 3d inst., " for stopping the further emission of bills of credit."

sented, and respecting which dangerous as well as erroneous opinions have been held and propagated,— we mean your finances.

The ungrateful despotism and inordinate lust of domination which marked the unnatural designs of the British king and his venal Parliament to enslave the people of America, reduced you to the necessity of either asserting your rights by arms or ingloriously passing under the yoke. You nobly preferred war. Armies were then to be raised, paid, and supplied ; money became necessary for these purposes. Of your own there was but little ; and of no nation in the world could you then borrow. The little that was spread among you could be collected only by taxes, and to this end regular governments were essential ; of these you were also destitute. So circumstanced, you had no other resource but the natural value and wealth of your fertile country. Bills were issued on the credit of this bank, and your faith was pledged for their redemption. After a considerable number of these had circulated, loans were solicited, and offices for the purpose established. Thus a national debt was unavoidably created, and the amount of it is as follows :

Bills emitted and circulating $159,948,880

Moneys borrowed before the 1st of March, 1778,
    the interest of which is payable in France .   7,545,196$\frac{44}{90}$

Moneys borrowed since the 1st of March, 1778,
    the interest of which is payable here . . .   26,188,909

Money due abroad, not exactly known, the bal-
    ances not having been transmitted, supposed
    to be about   4,000,000

For your further satisfaction, we shall order a particular account of the several emissions, with the times limited for their redemption, and also of the several loans, the interest allowed on each, and the terms assigned for their payment, to be prepared and published.

The taxes have as yet brought into the treasury no more than $3,027,560 ; so that all the moneys supplied to Congress by the people of America amount to more than 36,761,665 dollars and 67-90ths, that being the sum of the loans and taxes received. Judge then of the necessity of emissions, and learn from whom and from whence that necessity arose.

We are also to inform you that on the first day of September instant we resolved, " that we would on no account whatever emit more bills of credit than to make the whole amount of such bills two hundred millions of dollars " ; and as the sum emitted and in circulation amounted to $159,948,880, and the sum of $40,051,120 remained to complete the two hundred million above mentioned, we on the third day of September instant further resolved, " that we would emit such part only of the said sum of 40,051,120 dollars as should be absolutely necessary for public exigences before adequate supplies could otherwise be obtained, relying for such supplies on the exertions of the several States."

Exclusive of the great and ordinary expenses incident to the war, the depreciation of the currency has so swelled the prices of every necessary article, and of consequence made such additions to the usual amount of expenditures, that very considerable supplies must be immediately provided by loans and taxes ; and we unanimously declare it to be essential to the welfare of these States, that the taxes already called for be paid into the Continental treasury by the time recommended for that purpose. It is also highly proper that you should extend your views beyond that period, and prepare in season as well for bringing your respective quotas of troops into the field early the next campaign, as for providing the supplies necessary in the course of it. We shall take care to apprize you from time to time of the state of the treasury, and to recommend the proper measures for supplying it. To keep your battalions full, to encourage loans, and to assess your taxes with prudence, collect them with firmness, and pay them with punctuality, is all that will be requisite on your part. Further ways and means of providing for the public exigences are now under consideration, and will soon be laid before you.

Having thus given you a short and plain state of your debt, and pointed out the necessity of punctuality in furnishing the supplies already required, we shall proceed to make a few remarks on the depreciation of the currency, to which we entreat your attention.

The depreciation of bills of credit is always either natural, or artificial, or both. The latter is our case. The moment the sum in circulation exceeded what was necessary as a medium in commerce, it began and continued to depreciate in proportion as the amount of the surplus increased ; and that proportion would hold good until the sum emitted should become so great as nearly to equal the value of the capital or stock on the credit of which the bills were issued. Supposing, therefore, that $30,000,000 was necessary for a circulating medium, and that $160,000,000 had issued, the natural depreciation is but little more than as 5 to 1 ; but the actual depreciation exceeds that proportion, and that excess is artificial. The natural depreciation is to be removed only by lessening the quantity of money in circulation. It will regain its primitive value whenever it shall be reduced to the sum necessary for a medium of commerce. This is only to be effected by loans and taxes.

The artificial depreciation is a more serious subject, and merits minute investigation. A distrust, however occasioned, entertained by the mass of the people, either in the ability or inclination of the United States, to redeem their bills, is the cause of it. Let us inquire how far reason will justify a distrust in the ability of the United States.

The ability of the United States must depend upon two things : first, the success of the present revolution ; and, secondly, on the sufficiency of the natural wealth, value, and resources of the country.

That the time has been when honest men might, without being chargeable with timidity, have doubted the success of the present revolution, we admit ; but that period is passed. The independence of America is now as fixed as fate, and the petulant efforts of

Britain to break it down are as vain and fruitless as the raging of the waves which beat against her cliffs. Let those who are still afflicted with these doubts consider the character and condition of our enemies. Let them remember that we are contending against a kingdom crumbling into pieces; a nation without public virtue, and a people sold to and betrayed by their own representatives ; against a prince governed by his passions, and a ministry without confidence or wisdom ; against armies half paid and generals half trusted ; against a government equal only to plans of plunder, conflagration, and murder—a government, by the most impious violations of the rights of religion, justice, humanity, and mankind, courting the vengeance of Heaven, and revolting from the protection of Providence. Against the fury of these enemies you made successful resistance, when single, alone, and friendless, in the days of weakness and infancy, before your hands had been taught to war or your fingers to fight. And can there be any reason to apprehend that the Divine Disposer of human events, after having separated us from the house of bondage, and led us safe through a sea of blood towards the land of liberty and promise, will leave the work of our political redemption unfinished, and either permit us to perish in a wilderness of difficulties, or suffer us to be carried back in chains to that country of oppression, from whose tyranny he hath mercifully delivered us with a stretched-out arm ?

In close alliance with one of the most powerful nations in Europe, which has generously made our cause her own, in amity with many others, and enjoying the good-will of all, what danger have we to fear from Britain ? Instead of acquiring accessions of territory by conquest, the limits of her empire daily contract; her fleets no longer rule the ocean, nor are her armies invincible by land. How many of her standards, wrested from the hands of her champions, are among your trophies, and have graced the triumphs of your troops ? And how great is the number of those who, sent to bind you in fetters, have become your captives, and received their lives at your hands ? In short, whoever considers that these States are daily increasing in power; that their armies have become veteran ; that their governments, founded in freedom, are established ; that their fertile country and their affectionate ally furnish them with ample supplies ; that the Spanish monarch, well prepared for war, with fleets and armies ready for combat, and a treasury overflowing with wealth, has entered the lists against Britain ; that the other European nations, often insulted by her pride, and alarmed at the strides of her ambition, have left her to her fate ; that Ireland, wearied with her oppressions, is panting for liberty ; and even Scotland displeased and uneasy at her edicts ;—whoever considers these things, instead of doubting the issue of the war, will rejoice in the glorious, the sure, and certain prospect of success. This point being established, the next question is, whether the natural wealth, value, and resources of the country will be equal to the payment of the debt.

Let us suppose, for the sake of argument, that, at

the conclusion of the war, the emissions should amount to 200,000,000 ; that, exclusive of supplies from taxes, which will not be inconsiderable, the loans should amount to 100,000,000, then the whole national debt of the United States would be 300,000,000. There are at present 3,000,000 of inhabitants in the thirteen States ; three hundred millions of dollars, divided among three millions of people, would give to each person one hundred dollars ; and is there an individual in America unable, in the course of eighteen or twenty years, to pay it again ? Suppose the whole debt assessed, as it ought to be, on the inhabitants in proportion to their respective estates, what then would be the share of the poorer people ? Perhaps not ten dollars. Besides, as this debt will not be payable immediately, but probably twenty years allotted for it, the number of inhabitants by that time in America will be far more than double their present amount. It is well known that the inhabitants of this country increased almost in the ratio of compound interest. By natural population they doubled every twenty years ; and how great may be the host of emigrants from other countries, cannot be ascertained. We have the highest reason to believe the number will be immense. Suppose that only ten thousand should arrive the first year after the war, what will those ten thousand, with their families, count in twenty years' time ? Probably double the number. This observation applies with proportionable force to the emigrants of every successive year. Thus, you see, great part of your debt will be payable, not merely by the present number of inhabitants, but by that number swelled and increased by the natural population of the present inhabitants, by multitudes of emigrants daily arriving from other countries, and by the natural population of those successive emigrants, so that every person's share of the debt will be constantly diminish. ing by others coming to pay a proportion of it.

These are advantages which none but young countries enjoy. The number of inhabitants in every country in Europe remains nearly the same from one century to another. No country will produce more people than it can subsist; and every country, if free and cultivated, will produce as many as it can maintain. Hence we may form some idea of the future population of these States. Extensive wildernesses, now scarcely known or explored, remain yet to be cultivated, and vast lakes and rivers, whose waters have for ages rolled in silence and obscurity to the ocean, are yet to hear the din of industry, become subservient to commerce, and boast delightful villas, gilded spires, and spacious cities rising on their banks.

Thus much for the number of persons to pay the debt. The next point is their ability. They who inquire how many millions of acres are contained only in the settled part of North America, and how much each acre is worth, will acquire very enlarged, and yet very inadequate ideas of the value of this country. But those who will carry their inquiries further, and learn that we heretofore paid an annual tax to Britain of three millions sterling in the way of trade, and still grew rich; that our commerce was then confined to her; that we were obliged to carry our commodities to her market, and consequently sell them at her price; that we were compelled to purchase foreign commodities at her stores, and on her terms, and were forbid to establish any manufactories incompatible with her views of gain; that in future the whole world will be open to us, and we shall be at liberty to purchase from those who will sell on the best terms, and to sell to those who will give the best prices; that as the country increases in number of inhabitants and cultivation, the production of the earth will be proportionably increased, and the riches of the whole proportionably greater;—whoever examines the force of these and similar observations, must smile at the ignorance of those who doubt the ability of the United States to redeem their bills.

Let it also be remembered that paper money is the only kind of money which cannot "make to itself wings and fly away." It remains with us, it will not forsake us, it is always ready and at hand for the purpose of commerce or taxes, and every industrious man can find it. On the contrary, should Britain, like Nineveh (and for the same reason), yet find mercy, and escape the storm ready to burst upon her, she will find her national debt in a very different situation. Her territory diminished, her people wasted, her commerce ruined, her monopolies gone, she must provide for the discharge of her immense debt by taxes, to be paid in specie, in gold, or silver, perhaps now buried in the mines of Mexico or Peru, or still concealed in the brooks and rivulets of Africa or Hindostan.

Having shown that there is no reason to doubt the ability of the United States to pay their debt, let us next inquire whether as much can be said for their inclination. Under this head three things are to be attended to :

1st. Whether, and in what manner, the faith of the United States has been pledged for the redemption of their bills.

2d. Whether they have put themselves in a political capacity to redeem them ; and

3d. Whether, admitting the two former propositions, there is any reason to apprehend a wanton violation of the public faith.

1st. It must be evident to every man who reads the journals of Congress, or looks at the face of one of their bills, that Congress have pledged the faith of their constituents for the redemption of them. And it must be equally evident, not only that they had authority to do so, but that their constituents have actually ratified their acts by receiving their bills, passing laws establishing their currency, and punishing those who counterfeit them. So that it may with truth be said that the people have pledged their faith for the redemption of them, not only collectively by their representatives, but individually.

2d. Whether the United States have put themselves in a political capacity to redeem their bills, is a question which calls for more full discussion.

Our enemies, as well foreign as domestic, have laboured to raise doubts on this head. They argue that the Confederation of the States remains yet to be

or explicit? It has been expressly assented to, and ratified by every State in the Union. Accordingly, for the direct support of this declaration, that is, for the support of the independence of these States, armies have been raised, and bills of credit emitted, and loans made to pay and supply them. The redemption, therefore, of these bills, the payment of these debts, and the settlement of the accounts of the several States, for expenditures or services for the common benefit, and in this common cause, are among the objects of this Confederation; and, consequently, while all or any of its objects remain unattained, it cannot, so far as it may respect such objects, be dissolved consistently with the laws of GOD or MAN.

But we are persuaded, and our enemies will find, that our Union is not to end here. They are mistaken when they suppose us kept together only by a sense of present danger. It is a fact, which they only will dispute, that the people of these States were never so cordially united as at this day. By having been obliged to mix with each other, former prejudices have worn off, and their several manners become blended. A sense of common permanent interest, mutual affection (having been brethren in affliction), the ties of consanguinity daily extending, constant reciprocity of good offices, similarity in language, in governments, and therefore in manners, the importance, weight, and splendour of the Union,—all conspire in forming a strong chain of connection, which must for ever bind us together. The United Provinces of the Netherlands, and the United Cantons of Switzerland, became free and independent under circumstances very like ours; their independence has been long established, and yet their confederacies continue in full vigour. What reason can be assigned why our Union should be less lasting? or why should the people of these States be supposed less wise than the inhabitants of those? You are not uninformed that a plan for the perpetual Confederation has been prepared, and that twelve of the thirteen States have already acceded to it. But enough has been said to show that for every purpose of the present war, and all things incident to it, there does at present exist a perfect solemn confederation, and therefore, that the States now are, and always will be, in political capacity to redeem their bills, pay their debts, and settle their accounts.

3d. Whether, admitting the ability and political capacity of the United States to redeem their bills, there is any reason to apprehend a wanton violation of the public faith?

It is with great regret and reluctance that we can prevail upon ourselves to take the least notice of a question which involves in it a doubt so injurious to the honour and dignity of America.

The enemy, aware that the strength of America lay in the union of her citizens and the wisdom and integrity of those to whom they committed the direction of their affairs, have taken unwearied pains to disunite and alarm the people, to depreciate the abilities and virtue of their rulers, and to impair the confidence reposed in them by their constituents. To this end, repeated attempts have been made to draw an absurd and fanciful line of distinction between the Congress and the people, and to create an opinion and a belief that their interests and views were different and opposed. Hence the ridiculous tales, the invidious insinuations, and the whimsical suspicions that have been forged and propagated by disguised emissaries and traitors in the garb of patriots. Hence has proceeded the notable discovery, that as the Congress made the money they also can destroy it, and that it will exist no longer than they find it convenient to permit.it. It is not surprising that in a free country, where the tongues and pens of such people are and must be licensed, such political heresies should be inculcated and diffused; but it is really astonishing that the mind of a single virtuous citizen in America should be influenced by them. It certainly cannot be necessary to remind you, that your representatives here are chosen from among yourselves; that you are, or ought to be, acquainted with their several characters; that they are sent here to speak your sentiments, and that it is constantly in your power to remove such as do not. You surely are convinced that it is no more in their power to annihilate your money than your independence, and that any act of theirs for either of those purposes would be null and void.

We should pay an ill compliment to the understanding and honour of every true American, were we to adduce many arguments to show the baseness or bad policy of violating our national faith, or omitting to pursue the measures necessary to preserve it. A bankrupt, faithless republic would be a novelty in the political world, and appear among reputable nations like a common prostitute among chaste and respectable matrons. The pride of America revolts from the idea; her citizens know for what purpose these emissions were made, and have repeatedly plighted their faith for the redemption of them; they are to be found in every man's possession, and every man is interested in their being redeemed; they must therefore entertain a high opinion of American credulity who suppose the people capable of believing, on due reflection, that all America will, against the faith, the honour, and the interest of all America, be ever prevailed upon to countenance, support, or permit so ruinous, so disgraceful a measure. We are convinced that the efforts and arts of our enemies will not be wanting to draw us into this humiliating and contemptible situation. Impelled by malice and the suggestions of chagrin and disappointment at not being able to bend our necks to their yoke, they will endeavour to force or seduce us to commit this unpardonable sin, in order to subject us to the punishment due to it, and that we may henceforth be a reproach and a byword among the nations. Apprized of these consequences, knowing the value of national character, and impressed with a due sense of the immutable laws of justice and honour, it is impossible that America should think without horror of such an execrable deed.

If, then, neither our ability nor inclination to discharge the public debt is justly questionable, let our conduct correspond with this confidence, and let us rescue our credit from its present imputations. Had the attention of America to this object been unremitted, had taxes been seasonably imposed and collected, had proper loans been made, had laws been passed and executed for punishing those who maliciously endeavoured to injure the public credit,—had these and many other things equally necessary been done, and had our currency, notwithstanding all these efforts, declined to its present degree of depreciation, our case would indeed have been deplorable. But as these exertions have not been made, we may yet experience the good effects which naturally result from them. Our former negligences, therefore, should now animate us with hope, and teach us not to despair of removing, by vigilance and application, the evils which supineness and inattention have produced.

It has been already observed, that in order to prevent the further natural depreciation of our bills, we have resolved to stop the press, and to call upon you for supplies by loans and taxes. You are in capacity to afford them, and are bound by the strongest ties to do it. Leave us not, therefore, without supplies, nor let in that flood of evils which would follow from such a neglect. It would be an event most grateful to our enemies ; and, depend upon it, they will redouble their artifices and industry to compass it. Be, therefore, upon your guard, and examine well the policy of every measure and the evidence of every report that may be proposed or mentioned to you before you adopt the one or believe the other. Recollect that it is the price of the liberty, the peace, and the safety of yourselves and posterity that now is required ; that peace, liberty, and safety, for the attainment and security of which you have so often and so solemnly declared your readiness ˙ to sacrifice your lives and fortunes. The war, though drawing fast to a successful issue, still rages. Disdain to leave the whole business of your defence to your ally. Be mindful that the brightest prospects may be clouded, and that prudence bids us be prepared for every event. Provide, therefore, for continuing your armies in the field till victory and peace shall lead them home ; and avoid the reproach of permitting the currency to depreciate in your hands when, by yielding a part to taxes and loans, the whole might have been appreciated and preserved. Humanity as well as justice makes this demand upon you. The complaints of ruined widows, and the cries of fatherless children, whose whole support has been placed in your hands and melted away, have doubtless reached you ; take care that they ascend no higher. Rouse, therefore ; strive who shall do most for his country ; rekindle that flame of patriotism which, at the mention of disgrace and slavery, blazed throughout America and animated all her citizens. Determine to finish the contest as you began it, honestly and gloriously. Let it never be said, that America had no sooner become independent than she became insolvent, or that her infant glories and growing fame were obscured and tarnished by broken contracts and violated faith, in the very hour when all the nations of the earth were admiring and almost adoring the splendour of her rising.

By the unanimous consent of Congress,

JOHN JAY, *President.*

PHILADELPHIA, Sept. 13, 1779.

JAY TO FREDERICK JAY.

PHILADELPHIA, 16th September, 1779.

DEAR FREDERICK :

I am now to inform you that I have resigned the office of chief justice [of New York] ; and if the State should incline to keep me here, I shall consent to stay, provided either you or Sir James [1] will undertake to attend constantly to our good old father and his unfortunate family : otherwise I shall at all events return for that purpose. Sir James has his doubts respecting his future destination ; and therefore his return is precarious at present. I wish to know, without delay, the result of your reflections on this subject. Should you succeed with Wadsworth, I think you would then be in capacity to serve them as well as ever : if you live on Harris' farm, you will not. Make up your mind on this matter : if you find you cannot pay necessary attention to Fishkill, prevent my election, and let me know your intention by the first opportunity. I am, dear Fredy,

Your affectionate brother,

JOHN JAY.

---

[1] Sir James Jay, elder brother of John, knighted by George III. in 1763, on the occasion of the presentation of an address from the governors of King's (Columbia) College.

JAY TO GOVERNOR CLINTON.

PHILADELPHIA, 25th September, 1779.

DEAR SIR:

Whether the resolutions of Congress of the 24th inst., providing for the settlement of all disputes between New York and her neighbours, as well as revolted citizens, will please my constituents as much as they do me is uncertain. Nor am I convinced of the prudence of committing to paper all the reasons which induce me to think them (all circumstances considered) perfectly right. Some of them, however, I shall communicate. My first object on coming here was to prevail upon Congress to interpose, though in the smallest degree; well knowing, that if they once interfered ever so little, they might with more ease be led to a further and more effectual interposition.

Soon after my arrival, I found the following objections to an interference with Vermont generally prevailing.

1st. That Congress, being instituted for the sole purpose of opposing the tyranny of Britain, and afterward of establishing our independence, had no authority to interfere in the particular quarrels of any State. Hence all their former resolutions on the subject were merely negative. 2d. That the confederation had not yet taken place, and that the business should be postponed till all the States had acceded: an event then daily expected. 3d. That it was an improper season to interfere, and that the attention of Congress ought not to be diverted from the general objects of the war. 4th. That harsh measures against Vermont might induce them to join the enemy and increase their force. 5th. That they possessed a strong country, were numerous, warlike, and determined; and that more force would be required to reduce them, than could be spared from the general defence.

These were some of the ostensible objections. Besides which I had reason to suspect the following private ones:

1st. That divers persons of some consequence in Congress and New England expected to advance their fortunes by lands in Vermont. 2d. That Vermont, acquiring strength by time, would become actually independent, and afterward acknowledged to be so. 3d. That being settled by New England people, and raised into consequence by New England politics, it would be a fifth New England State, and become a valuable accession of strength both in and out of Congress. 4th. That ancient animosities between New York and New England naturally inclining the former to side with the middle and southern States, the less formidable she was the better, and therefore the loss or separation of that territory was rather to be wished for than opposed. These and many other considerations of the like nature induced me to postpone bringing on the matter till I could have an opportunity of preparing the way for it by acquiring a knowledge of the characters then in Congress, etc.

It is also proper to observe that the House was for the greater part of the winter so heated by divisions on points of general importance, that it would have been improper and imprudent to have called upon them to decide on this delicate business till more temper and calmness had taken place. When these began to appear the subject was introduced, and you have had a copy of the resolutions proposed by New York on that occasion. Against them all objections before mentioned operated, with this additional one, that it would be highly unjust and impolitic to determine against Vermont, without previous inquiry into the merits of their claims, and giving them an opportunity of being heard. This objection, so far as it respected their claim to independence, was absurd though plausible; but it was not to be overcome; and though we might have carried a resolution against it by a slender majority, that majority would have consisted of southern members against a violent opposition from New England and their adherents. A resolution carried under such circumstances would rather have encouraged than disheartened Vermont, and was, therefore, ineligible.

Hence I conceived it to be expedient to promote the measure of appointing a committee of inquiry; knowing that if Congress proceeded to inquire, it would be a ground for pressing them to go further and determine, especially as I was apprised that the result of these inquiries would be in our favour.

The committee, you know, never had a formal meeting; it, nevertheless, had its use. The individual reports of the members who composed it advanced our cause; and even Mr. Witherspoon, who was and is suspected by New York, made representations in our favour.

Your last resolutions were of infinite service, by evincing the moderation, justice, and liberality, and, at the same time, the spirit of the State. On the other hand, the law of Vermont for whipping, cropping, and branding your magistrates made an impression greatly to their disadvantage. Before these emotions should have time to subside, as well in observance of our instructions, I pressed Congress from day to day to adopt such measures as the public exigencies called for, and thereby prevent the flames of civil war from raging. It would not, I believe, have been difficult to have obtained what some among you would call very spirited and pointed resolutions, but which, in my opinion, would have been very imprudent ones ; because, among other reasons, they would not have been unanimous. You will find the recitals and particular resolutions numbered in the margin of the copy herewith enclosed, from 1 to 13. I shall trouble you with a few explanatory remarks on each of them, under heads numbered in like manner.

1st and 2d. These recitals were inserted to show the reason why Congress now proceed without the report of the committee, after having resolved to postpone the further consideration of the subject till their report should be made.

3d. This recital justifies the facts set forth in your representations, and in case an appeal to the public should become necessary, may be used with advantage to New York.

4th. This recital destroys the doctrine that the

Union (independent of the articles of confederation) had no other object than security against foreign invasions.

5th. This recital is calculated to impress the people with an opinion of the reasonableness and policy of the requisition or recommendation which follows, and therefore will the more readily induce those States to adopt the measures recommended to them.

6th. You may inquire for what reason I consented to this recital, as it puts Massachusetts and New Hampshire on a footing with New York; whereas I well knew that New York alone had a right to claim jurisdiction over Vermont. My reasons were these: Vermont extends over Connecticut River into the acknowledged jurisdiction of New Hampshire; as to Massachusetts, the recital admits only her *claims*, not her *title;* and it is as impossible to deny the existence of claims when made, as it is to prevent them. Their delegates pointedly asserted and insisted on the claim .of Massachusetts; and it appeared to me expedient to provide for a speedy determination of all claims against us, however ill-founded. You may further ask why Vermont is made a party? The reason is this: that by being allowed a hearing, the candour and moderation of Congress may be rescued from aspersions; and that these people, after having been fully heard, may have nothing to say or complain of, in case the decision of Congress be against them, of which I have no doubt.

7th. It is true that by this resolution the merits of former settlements with these States will be again the subject of inquiry, discussion, and decision ; and therefore it may at first sight appear improper ; but these settlements will still remain strong evidence of our rights, however objectionable they may be represented to be by those States. Nor will Congress be easily prevailed upon to annul them, because in that case all their boundaries would be afloat. Besides, in my opinion, it is much better for New York to gain a permanent peace with their neighbours by submitting to these inconveniences, than by an impolitic adherence to strict rights, and a rigid observance of the dictates of dignity and pride, remain exposed to perpetual dissensions and encroachment. Peace and established boundaries, under our circumstances, are, I think, almost inestimable.

8th. The reason of this is assigned in the last sentence under the 6th head.

9th. For the same purpose of preserving the appearance of equality in claims, whatever difference there may be in titles, the three States are mentioned in this recommendation, The object of it is a settlement of all disputes respecting interfering grants, in case Vermont should be abolished, and that district in part, or in the whole, adjudged to either of the three States.

10th. I am sure you will admit my prudence in giving your voice for this resolution.

11th. As it was not absolutely certain that New Hampshire and Massachusetts would pass the laws in question, and as I was sure that New York would, it appeared to me highly expedient to provide, by this resolution, that the dispute between New York and

Vermont should be determined, whether the other two States came in or no; and, lest the former guarantee contained in the tenth resolution might be construed to be contingent, and to depend on the event of all the three States adopting the measures recommended to them, it is here repeated. You will observe that neither of the three States are to vote on the decision.

12th. On the plan of hearing Vermont, this resolution, however inconvenient, became indispensable. Care, however, has been taken in it to exempt all persons from their jurisdiction who profess allegiance to either of the three States. But you will say, Why to the *three* States? Why not to New York only; from whom they revolted, and under whose actual jurisdiction they last were? Because it would have clashed with the equality of claims before mentioned, and the least opposition to which would have prevented these resolutions from being unanimous; a circumstance, in my opinion, infinitely more valuable than the preservation of useless etiquette. And, further, because the district is here so described as to extend over the river and affect New Hampshire. In a word, the necessity of the resolution was so obvious that there was no avoiding it. These inconveniences will be temporary, and, if the principles laid down in it are observed, will not be very great; especially as Congress have determined a violation of it to be a breach of the peace of the confederacy, and have declared their resolution to maintain it.

13th. This resolution needs no comment, the policy and justice of it being extremely evident. Anxious to avoid a moment's delay in sending you these resolutions, I have not time by this opportunity of adding any thing further than that upon this occasion I have acted according to the best of my judgment, after having maturely considered and well weighed the force and tendency of every consideration and circumstance affecting the business in question. When I first received my special commission, I did not apprehend that this matter was in a more particular manner confided to me than to my colleagues, though some of them considered it in that light. The commission vested me with no further power than what any other of your delegates possessed; nor was any matter given more particularly in charge to me than to the others by the Legislature. Their late instructions, however, speak a different language. I am satisfied to be viewed in that light, that is, to be the responsible man; and, provided the measures I adopt are not thwarted, I am confident that I shall be able to bring all these matters to a happy conclusion. I hope, however, that this will not be considered as a hint for my being continued in the delegation; I assure you, nothing but an adherence to the resolutions and principles of action I adopted and professed at the commencement of the war would induce me to remain here at the expense of health as well as property; for though I shall always be ready to serve my country when called upon, I shall always be happy to find it consistent with my duty to remain a private citizen. I am, sir,

Your most obedient servant, JOHN JAY.

JAY TO THE PRESIDENT OF CONGRESS.[1]

PHILADELPHIA, 4th October, 1779.

SIR,

It gives me very sensible pleasure to find, from the act of Congress enclosed in your Excellency's polite favour of the 1st inst., that my conduct in the chair and the execution of public business has been honoured by the approbation of Congress. The testimony given of it by this act demands my warmest acknowledgments. Be pleased, sir, to assure the Congress, that my happiness is inseparable from the welfare and esteem of my country, and that my endeavours to promote the one and merit the other, shall continue unremitted.

I have the honour to be,
With great respect and esteem,
Your excellency's most obedient servant,
JOHN JAY.

ROBERT R. LIVINGSTON TO JAY.

KINGSTON, 6th October, 1779.

DEAR JOHN:

I have just now heard that you are upon the point of leaving us. I might have expected to have received this intelligence from yourself, rather than from loose report, since there is scarce a transaction in the world in which I

---

[1] This letter refers to another important step in Jay's official career as noticed in the Preface. On or about September 28, 1779, Congress appointed him "minister plenipotentiary to negotiate a treaty of amity and commerce and of alliance" between the United States and Spain. He resigned the presidency of Congress on the 28th, and was succeeded in that office by Samuel Huntington, of Connecticut. The "act of Congress" referred to above included the usual resolutions complimentary to the retiring president. See letters following from Livingston, Washington, and Pendleton.

feel myself more interested. I rejoice at it as it advances your fortune and reputation. I lament it, as it adds to the losses I have already felt in the course of this war, that of a friend whom I had sense enough to value, even before age had ripened my judgment, and whom an after acquaintance with the world has taught me to think inestimable. I call it a loss, for I have but little prospect of seeing you here again. You will now move in a more enlarged sphere, and will hardly think of recrossing the Atlantic, till the blood runs too slowly in our veins to keep up the ardour of friendship. I was going to give you a long detail of State politics, but they are now unworthy your attention. Besides that, I by no means feel myself disposed at this moment to view them in any other than the most contemptible light, or to execrate them for detaining me here, when I so ardently wish to receive your last adieu. When do you embark, and where? If from Boston, tell me when to meet you at Fishkill, and perhaps (if the Legislature adjourn) to accompany you. If this pleasure is denied me, believe that you and yours are attended by every tender wish which the sincerest friendship can dictate. I will not wrong you so much as to ask you to omit no occasion of lessening the pain I feel in your absence, by writing to me by every conveyance; your own heart has and will for ever suggest that thought. Adieu, my dear John.

May you be as happy as I wish you,

ROBERT R. LIVINGSTON.

GENERAL WASHINGTON TO JAY.

WEST-POINT, October 7, 1779.

DEAR SIR:

Among the number of your friends, permit me also to congratulate you, and my country, on your late honourable and important appointment. Be assured, sir, that my pleasure on this occasion, though it may be equalled, cannot be exceeded by that of any other.

I do most sincerely wish you a pleasant and agreeable passage, the most perfect and honourable accomplishment of your ministry, and a safe return to the bosom of a grateful country.

With the greatest regard, and sincerest personal attachment, I have the honour to be,

Your most obedient and
Affectionate humble servant,
GEORGE WASHINGTON.

EDMUND PENDLETON TO JAY.

EDMUNSBURY, October 11, 1779.

DEAR SIR:

I congratulate you, sir, upon your appointment to represent the American States at the court of Madrid ; the just testimony of that confidence which the honourable body you have presided over, have in your abilities and integrity. May health, success, and every felicity accompany you ; but, while I am sensible of the advantages we shall reap from your eminent services there, I have my fears that they will be missed, importantly, where you now are ; and that the spirit of party, almost laid to sleep, will revive upon your absence. I cordially wish you may be able to heal the new-made breach between Spain and Britain since France appears disposed to peace, and I am mistaken if the court of London are not ready to make up with us, if nothing respecting our allies hinders it. Indeed we want an honourable peace ; but I hope there lives not a wretch who wishes it upon terms of dishonour to our noble allies.

I am, sir, with unfeigned regard,

Your most obliged and obedient servant,
EDMUND PENDLETON.

JAY TO GENERAL WASHINGTON.

PHILADELPHIA, 14th October, 1779.

My Dear Sir :

Your very kind letter of the 7th inst., gave me all that pleasure which accompanies marks of cordial esteem and attachment from those whose commendation is praise, and whose friendship is discriminate.

Among the objects of my mission are some which, however just, will not be easily attained, and therefore its success will be precarious, and probably partial. The only satisfaction I promise myself from this appointment, will flow from the rectitude with which the duties of it will be discharged, and not from a prospect of general approbation.

God grant that the time may not be far distant when peace and liberty shall lead you from the field, to enjoy, in silence and retirement, the luxury of reflecting that you had saved your country.

Adieu, my dear sir,

With sincere affection and esteem,

I am your friend and servant,

JOHN JAY.

INSTRUCTIONS TO JAY AS MINISTER TO SPAIN.[1]

Sir,

By the treaties subsisting between his most Christian Majesty and the United States of America, a power is reserved to his Catholic Majesty to accede to the said treaties and to participate in their stipulations at such time

---

[1] Jay's instructions, preserved among his own papers, differ from the form as given in Sparks' " Diplomatic Correspondence," vol. vii., p. 169, in containing the additional clause at the end respecting trade with the Tortugas and Honduras, and being of later date.

as he shall judge proper, it being well understood nevertheless, that if any of the stipulations of the said treaties are
not agreeable to the King of Spain, his Catholic Majesty
may propose other conditions analogous to the principal aim
of the alliance and conformable to the rules of equality,
reciprocity and friendship. Congress is sensible of the
friendly regard to these States manifested by his most
Christian Majesty and these United States ; and therefore
that nothing may be wanting on their part to facilitate the
views of his most Christian Majesty and to obtain a treaty
of alliance and of amity and commerce with his Catholic
Majesty, have thought proper to anticipate any propositions
which his Catholic Majesty might make on that subject by
yielding up to him those objects which they conclude he may
have principally in view, and for that purpose have come to
the following resolution,

" That if his Catholic Majesty shall accede to the said treaties
and in concurrence with France and the United States of America continue the present war with Great Britain for the purpose
expressed in the treaties aforesaid, he shall not thereby be pre-
cluded from securing to himself the Floridas ; on the contrary if
he shall obtain the Floridas from Great Britain, these United
States will guaranty the same to his Catholic Majesty ; provided
always that the United States shall enjoy the free navigation of
the river Mississippi into and from the Sea."

You are therefore to communicate to his most Christian
Majesty the desire of Congress to enter into a treaty of
alliance and of amity and commerce with his Catholic
Majesty and to request his favourable interposition for that
purpose ; at the same time you are to make such proposals
to his Catholic Majesty as in your judgment, from circumstances, will be proper for obtaining for the United States
of America equal advantages with those which are secured
to them by the treaties with his most Christian Majesty,
observing always the resolution aforesaid as the ultimatum
of these United States. You are particularly to endeavour

to obtain some convenient port or ports below the 31st degree of north latitude on the river Mississippi free for all merchant vessels, goods, wares and merchandize, belonging to the inhabitants of these States.

The distressed state of our finances and the great depreciation of our paper money incline Congress to hope that his Catholic Majesty, if he shall conclude a treaty with these States, will be induced to lend them money; you are therefore to represent to him the great distress of these States on that account, and to solicit a loan of five million of dollars upon the best terms in your power not exceeding six per centum per annum, effectually to enable them to co-operate with the allies against the common enemy. But before you make any proposition to his Catholic Majesty for a loan, you are to endeavour to obtain a subsidy in consideration of the guaranty aforesaid.

You are to use your utmost endeavours for obtaining permission for the citizens and inhabitants of these States to lade and take on board their vessels salt at the island of Salt Tortuga; and also to cut, load and bring away logwood and mahogany in and from the bay of Honduras and its rivers, and to build on its shores storehouses and magazines for the woodcutters and their families in the extent ceded to his Britannic Majesty by the seventeenth article of the definitive treaty concluded at Paris the tenth day of February, 1763, or in as great extent as can be obtained.

Given at Philadelphia this Sixteenth day of October in the year of our Lord one thousand seven hundred and seventy nine and in the fourth year of our Independence, by the Congress of the United States of America.

SAML. HUNTINGTON, President.

Attest,   Chas. Thompson, Secy.

The honble. John Jay, Minister Plenipotentiary appointed to negotiate a treaty of amity and commerce and of alliance with his Catholic Majesty.

Will it not be painful to my dear mamma to imagine to herself the situation of her children at that time? Her children did I say? Rather let her imagine the dangerous situation of more than three hundred souls, tossed about in the midst of the ocean in a vessel dismasted and under no command, at a season too that threatened approaching inclemency of weather. And would you for a moment suppose me capable of regretting that I had for a time bid adieu to my native land, in order to accompany my beloved friend? Would you have despaired of ever embracing your affectionate children? or would you have again recommended them to HIM who appointed to the waters their bounds—WHO saith unto the waves thus far shalt thou go, and to the winds, peace, be still! Mamma's known piety and fortitude sufficiently suggest the answer to the two latter queries; and to the former it becomes me to reply. I assure you that in no period of our distress, though ever so alarming, did I once repine, but incited by his amiable example, I gave fear to the winds, and cheerfully resigned myself to the disposal of the ALMIGHTY.

After our misfortunes of the 7th and 8th of November (the memorable era from which we now date all events relative to ourselves), a council of the officers was held to consider where it was most expedient to bend our course. It was unanimously concluded that it would be impossible to reach Europe at this season with a ship in the condition that ours was. They were likewise united in opinion that the southern direction was the only one that offered a prospect of safety; and of the islands, Martinico was the most eligible, for its commodious harbour, and the probability of being supplied with materials to refit. Accordingly, the first fair wind that offered (which was not till near three weeks from the above-mentioned era), was embraced in pursuance of the advice given by the officers; and, after having passed through very squally latitudes, we are now in smooth seas, having the advantage of trade-winds which blow directly for the islands ; nor are we, if the calculations made are just, more than 200 miles distant from the destined port.

SIR : MARTINICO, ST. PIERRE, 25th December, 1779.

I have done what, perhaps, I shall be blamed for ; but my pride as an American, and my feelings as a man, were not on this occasion to be resisted. The officers of the *Confederacy* were here without money, or the means of getting any. The idea of our officers being obliged to sneak, as they phrase it, from the company of French officers for fear of running in debt with them for a bottle of wine, or a bowl of punch, because not able to pay for their share of the reckoning, was too humiliating to be tolerable, and too destructive to that pride and opinion of independent equality which I wish to see influence all our officers. Besides, some of them wanted necessaries too much to be comfortable, or in this country decent. In a word, I have drawn on the fund pointed out for the payment of part of my salary, for one hundred guineas in their favour, to be divided among them according to their respective ranks. Indeed, it would have given me pleasure to have done something towards covering the nakedness of the crew, but the expense I have been put to by coming here, and the preparations for another voyage would not admit of it.

I have the honor to be, sir,

With great esteem and personal regard,

Your excellency's most obedient and humble Servant,

JOHN JAY.

JAY TO BENJAMIN FRANKLIN.

DEAR SIR :   CADIZ, 26th January, 1780.

You have doubtless been amused this month or two past with various conjectures about the fate of the *Confederacy*. She left Chester (on the Delaware) the 18th [26th ?] October bound for France ; was dismasted and split her rudder the 7th November off the banks of Newfoundland. On the 23d following, the officers of the ship being all of opinion that the condition of her rudder forbid our proceeding to Europe, we steered for Martinico and arrived there the 18th December. We sailed from thence the 28th following in the *Aurora*, and I expected to have proceeded with her to Toulon, but on arriving here, the 22d inst., we heard of the success of the enemy in the Mediterranean and of several cruisers near the coast which we had fortunately escaped. The further prosecution of my voyage having thus become improper, I gave notice of my appointment and arrival to Don Joseph De Galvez, the Secretary of State for the Department of the Indies. . . .

Although I had letters with me to gentlemen in other parts of Spain, yet it unluckily happened that I had none for any person here. You may imagine therefore that I was at first a little embarrassed in the article of money, but it gives me pleasure to inform you that the polite and unsolicited offer of Chevalier Roche and Mr. Ponet have made me easy on that head for the present.

American credit suffers exceedingly in this place from reports that our loan office bills payable in

France have not been duly honoured but have been delayed payment under various *pretexts*, one of which is that it was necessary for a whole lot of bills to arrive before the money would be paid. How far you may be in capacity to answer the demands upon you I cannot determine, but many considerations induce me to entreat you by all means punctually to pay the bill in question. Private honour forbids that these gentlemen should by an act of kindness to me expose their friends to inconvenience, and public credit demands that the reputation of Congress be not destroyed by the protests of bills drawn under their immediate authority for the necessary subsistence of their servants. I might also add that if this bill should fail there will be an end put to my credit, and on the consequences of such an event it is neither necessary or pleasant to dwell.

I have in my possession several letters or rather packets directed to you and am much at a loss what to do with them. Be pleased to direct me. There are many things I wish to say to you but you must, my dear sir, excuse my postponing them to another opportunity. I have been so confined since my arrival by preparing letters for Madrid, France, and America, that I have not yet been two hours out my chamber.

God bless you, my dear sir, and long continue you the blessing of health and cheerfulness. Believe me to be with sincere regard and esteem,

Your most obedient servant,

His Excellency,   JOHN JAY.
   Benjamin Franklin, Esq.

P. S.—Be pleased to present my compliments to Mr. Adams. I shall do myself the pleasure of writing to him by the next opportunity. When we left Philadelphia Mr. and Mrs. Bache with their children (which are really fine ones) were in perfect health.

JAY TO COUNT DE VERGENNES.[1]

CADIZ, 27th January, 1780.

SIR:

It is with very sensible pleasure that I commence a correspondence with a Minister, of whose disposition and abilities to promote the happiness of my country we have received repeated proofs, and on a subject that affords His Most Christian Majesty an opportunity of perceiving the desire and endeavours of the United States to become cordial and steadfast friends and allies to an illustrious branch of his royal house.

By the treaties subsisting between His Most Christian Majesty and the United States of America, His Most Christian Majesty, in consequence of his intimate union with the King of Spain, did expressly reserve to his Catholic Majesty the power of acceding to the said treaties, and to participate in their stipulations at such time as he should judge proper. It being well understood, nevertheless, that if any of the said stipulations should not be agreeable to the King of Spain, his Catholic Majesty might propose other conditions analogous to the principal aim of the alliance, and conformable to the rules of equity, reciprocity, and friendship. And the Deputy

---

[1] Minister of Foreign Affairs at the French Court.

of the said States, empowered to treat with Spain, did promise to sign, *on the first requisition* of his Catholic Majesty, the act or acts necessary to communicate to him the stipulations of the treaties above mentioned, and to endeavor in good faith the adjustment of the points in which the King of Spain might propose any alteration, conformable to the principles of equality, reciprocity, and perfect amity.

But as the above reservation has always been no less agreeable to the United States than to their great and good ally, both considerations conspired in inducing them to make the first advances towards attaining the object of it. And, therefore, instead of waiting till the requisitions mentioned in the said article should be made, they have thought proper to assure his Majesty, not only of their readiness to comply with the terms of it, but of their desire to obtain his confidence and alliance, by carrying it immediately into execution on the most liberal principles. Trusting also that the same wise reasons which induced his most Christian Majesty to give birth to the said article would lead him to facilitate the endeavours of his allies to execute it, they resolved that their desire to enter into the said treaties should be communicated to his Majesty, and that his favorable interposition should be requested.

The more fully to effect these purposes, the Congress were pleased, in September last, to do me the honour of appointing me their Minister Plenipotentiary, and, in pursuance of this appointment, I sailed from America for France on the 26th of October last, with

M. Gerard, who was so obliging as to wait till I could embark in the frigate assigned for his service. After being thirteen days at sea, the frigate was dismasted, and her rudder so much damaged that it was thought imprudent to proceed on our voyage. We therefore steered for Martinique, and arrived there on the 18th of December. I cannot on this occasion forbear expressing my warmest acknowledgments for the very polite attention and hospitality with which we were received and treated, both by the officers of government and many respectable inhabitants of that island. We left Martinique on the 28th day of the same month in the *Aurora*, in which I expected to have gone to Toulon, but on touching at this place, it appeared that the further prosecution of our voyage had become impracticable without running risks that could not be justified.

Thus circumstanced, the respect due to his Most Catholic Majesty demanded an immediate communication of my appointment and arrival, which I had the honour to make in a letter to his Excellency, Don Joseph Galvez, of the Council of his Catholic Majesty, and general Secretary of State for the Department of the Indies, of which the enclosed is a copy.

Will you therefore, sir, be so obliging as to lay this circumstance before his Most Christian Majesty, and permit me, through your Excellency, to assure him of the desire of Congress to enter into a treaty of alliance and of amity and commerce with his Catholic Majesty, and to request his favourable interposition for that purpose?

I am happy in being able to assure you that the

United States consider a cordial union between France, Spain, and them as a very desirable and most important object, and they view the provision which his Most Christian Majesty has made for it by the above-mentioned article, not only as evincive of his attention to his royal ally, but of his regard to them.

Under these views and these impressions, they are most sincerely disposed, by the liberality and candour of their conduct, to render the proposed treaties speedy in their accomplishment and perpetual in their duration.

Your Excellency will receive this letter by M. Gerard, who is so obliging as to take charge of it, and to whom the Congress have been pleased to give such ample testimonies of their esteem and confidence, as to enable him to exert his talents with great advantage on every occasion interesting to them.

I cannot conclude without indulging myself in the pleasure of acknowledging how much we are indebted to the politeness and attention of the Marquis de La Flolte, and the other officers of the *Aurora*, during the course of our voyage.

With great respect and esteem, I have the honour to be, etc., JOHN JAY.

JAY TO DON JOSEPH GALVEZ.[1]

SIR : CADIZ, 27th January, 1780.

Permit me through your Excellency to have the honour of representing to His Most Catholic Majesty,

[1] Jay understood from the French Minister, M. Gerard, that Galvez was the proper court official at Madrid to whom his despatches should be addressed. This proved to be a mistake, Count de Florida Blanca, with whom he subsequently communicated, being the secretary charged with colonial affairs.

that on the sixth day of February, 1778, the respective Plenipotentiaries of His Most Christian Majesty, and the United States of America, by whom the treaties now subsisting between them were concluded, did make and subscribe a secret article in the words following, viz. :

" The Most Christian King declares, in consequence of the intimate union which subsists between him and the King of Spain, that in concluding with the United States of America this treaty of amity and commerce, and that of eventual and defensive alliance, his Majesty had intended, and intends to reserve expressly, as he reserves by this present separate and secret act, to his Catholic Majesty, the power of acceding to the said treaties and to participate in their stipulations, at such time as he shall judge proper. It being well understood, nevertheless, that if any of the stipulations of the said treaties are not agreeable to the King of Spain, his Catholic Majesty may propose other conditions analogous to the principal aim of the alliance, and conformable to the rules of equality, reciprocity, and friendship. The deputies of the United States, in the name of their constituents, accept the present declaration to its full extent ; and the deputy of the said States, who is fully empowered to treat with Spain, promises to sign, on the first requisition of his Catholic Majesty, the act or acts necessary to communicate to him the stipulations of the treaties above written. And the said deputy shall endeavour, in good faith, the adjustment of the points in which the King of Spain may propose any alteration, conformable to the principles of equality, reciprocity, and perfect amity ; he the said deputy not doubting but the person or persons, empowered by his Catholic Majesty to treat with the United States, will do the same with regard to any alterations of the same kind, that may be thought necessary by the said Plenipotentiary of the United States."

The Congress, willing to manifest their readiness fully to comply with an article, which they have reason to believe particularly agreeable to their great and good ally, and being desirous of establishing perpetual amity and harmony with a prince and nation whom they greatly respect, and with whom various circumstances lead them to wish for the most cordial and permanent friendship, have thought proper to request his most Catholic Majesty to accede to the said treaties, and thereby preclude the necessity of that measure's originating in the manner specified in the article. For this purpose they have done me the honour to appoint me Minister Plenipotentiary, and directed me to communicate to his most Catholic Majesty the desire of Congress on this subject, and to request his favourable interposition. They also made it my duty to give his most Catholic Majesty the fullest assurances of their sincere disposition to cultivate his friendship and confidence; and authorized me, in their behalf, to enter into such treaties of alliance, amity, and commerce, as would become the foundations of perpetual peace to Spain and the United States, and the source of extensive advantages to both.

Thus commissioned, I embarked without delay on board the frigate, which had been appointed to carry the Sieur Gerard to France, and sailed with him for that kingdom, from Pennsylvania, on the 26th day of October last.

But after having been thirteen days at sea, the frigate was dismasted, and her rudder so greatly injured as to oblige us to alter our course and steer for Martinique. We arrived there on the 18th day of December last; and sailed from thence on the 28th day of the same month in a French frigate which was bound to Toulon, but had orders to touch at this port for intelligence. We arrived here the 22d instant, and received information of recent events, which rendered the further prosecution of our voyage too hazardous to be prudent.

Providence having thus been pleased to bring me directly to Spain, the respect due to his Most Catholic Majesty forbids me to postpone communicating to him my appointment and arrival; and the same motive will induce me to remain here till he shall be pleased to signify to me his pleasure. For although nothing would afford me more sensible pleasure, than the honour of presenting to his Majesty the despatches, which I am charged by Congress to deliver to him, yet on this, as on every other occasion, it shall be my study to execute the trust reposed in me in the manner most pleasing to his Majesty, agreeable to the true intent and meaning of the article above mentioned.

And that his most Christian Majesty may have the highest evidence of the intention and desire of Congress fully and faithfully to execute this article, I shall immediately do myself the honour of communicating the same, together with my appointment and arrival; and I flatter myself that the request of Congress for his favourable interposition will meet with the same friendly attention which he has uniformly extended to all their concerns, and of which I am too sensible not to derive the highest satisfaction from acknowledging it on every occasion.

Mr. Carmichael, my secretary, will have the honour of delivering this despatch to your Excellency, as well as of giving every information in his power to afford. This gentleman was a member of Congress at the time of his appointment, and will be able more fully to express the ardour with which the United States desire to establish a union with France and Spain, on principles productive of such mutual attachment and reciprocal benefits as to secure to each the blessings of uninterrupted tranquillity.

I have the honour to be, with great consideration and respect, &c.

JOHN JAY.

P. S.—I do myself the honour of transmitting to your Excellency, herewith enclosed, a copy of my letter to his Excellency the Count de Vergennes.

JAY TO THE PRESIDENT OF CONGRESS.

CADIZ, 27th January, 1780.

SIR:

This morning M. Gerard set out from this city for France, and Mr. Carmichael, charged with despatches from me to the Spanish Ministry, accompanies him as far as Madrid.

We arrived here the 22d inst., and I have been so much engaged ever since in preparing letters, etc., as not to have an opportunity of writing circumstantially to your Excellency by Captain Proctor, who I am told is to sail early in the morning for the Delaware or Chesapeake.

We left Martinique on the 28th of December, in the *Aurora* frigate, bound to Toulon. On touching here for intelligence we were informed that the enemy had acquired a decided superiority in the Mediterranean, and that the coast was infested by their cruisers, all of whom we had fortunately escaped. Hence it became improper for me to proceed to France by water, and it would in my opinion have been indelicate, and therefore imprudent, to have passed silently through this kingdom to that for the purpose of making a communication to his most Christian Majesty, which could be fully conveyed by paper. On this subject I shall take the liberty of making a few further remarks in a future letter.

Congress will be enabled to judge of the propriety and plan of my conduct from the papers herewith enclosed, viz., a copy of a letter to M. Galvez, the Spanish Minister; a copy of a letter to the Count de Vergennes; of both these I have sent copies to Dr. Franklin; a copy of a letter to Mr. Arthur Lee; and a copy of my instructions to Mr. Carmichael.

It is in pursuance of what appears to me to be my duty, that I shall render frequent, particular, and confidential accounts of my proceedings to Congress. I flatter myself care will be taken to prevent the return of them to Europe.

I have the honor to be, &c.

JOHN JAY.

JAY'S INSTRUCTIONS TO WILLIAM CARMICHAEL.[1]

CADIZ, January 27th, 1780.

You will proceed to Madrid with convenient expedition, and if M. Gerard, with whom you set out, should travel too deliberately, I advise you to go on before him. The propriety of this, however, will depend much on circumstances, and must be determined by your own discretion.

On delivering my letter to M. Galvez, it would be proper to intimate, that I presumed it would be more agreeable to him to receive my despatches from you, who could give him information on many matters about which he might choose to inquire, than in the ordinary modes of conveyance. And it may not be amiss to let him know, that his not receiving notice of our arrival from me by M. Gerard's courier, was owing to a mistake between that gentleman and me.

Treat the French Ambassador with great attention and candour, and that degree of confidence only which prudence and the alliance between us may prescribe. In your conversations with people about the Court, impress them with an idea of our strong attachment to France; yet, so as to avoid permitting them to imbibe an opinion of our being under the *direction* of any counsels but our own. The former will induce them to think well of our constancy and good faith; the latter, of our independence and self-respect.

Discover, if possible, whether the Courts of Madrid and Versailles entertain, in any degree, the same

---

[1] Jay's Secretary of Legation.

mutual disgusts, which we are told prevail at present between the two nations, and be cautious when you tread on this delicate ground. It would also be useful to know who are the King's principal confidants, and the trains leading to each.

To treat prudently with any nation, it is essential to know the state of its revenues. Turn your attention, therefore, to this object, and endeavour to learn whether the public expenditures consume their annual income, or whether there be any, and what overplus or deficiency, and the manner in which the former is disposed of, or the latter supplied.

If an opportunity should offer, inform yourself as to the regulations of the press at Madrid, and, indeed, throughout the kingdom ; and the particular character of the person at the head of that department. Endeavour to find some person of adequate abilities and knowledge in the two languages, to translate English into Spanish with propriety, and, if possible, elegance. I wish also to know which of the religious orders, and the individuals of it, are most esteemed and favoured at Court.

Mention, as matter of intelligence, rather than in the way of argument, the cruelties of the enemy, and the influence of that conduct on the passions of Americans. This will be the more necessary, as it seems we are suspected of retaining our former attachments to Britain.

In speaking of American affairs, remember to do justice to Virginia, and the western country near the Mississippi. Recount their achievements against the savages, their growing numbers, extensive settlements, and aversion to Britain for attempting to involve them in the horrors of an Indian war. Let it appear also from your representations, that ages will be necessary to settle those extensive regions.

Let it be inferred from your conversation that the expectations of America, as to my reception and success, are sanguine ; that they have been rendered the more so by the suggestions of persons generally supposed to speak from authority, and that a disappointment would be no less unwelcome than unexpected.

I am persuaded that pains will be taken to delay my receiving a decided answer as to my reception, until the sentiments of France shall be known. Attempts will also be made to suspend the acknowledgment of our independence, on the condition of our acceding to *certain* terms of treaty. Do nothing to cherish either of these ideas ; but, without being explicit, treat the latter in a manner expressive of regret and apprehension, and seem to consider my reception as a measure which we hoped would be immediately taken, although the business of the negotiation might be postponed till France could have an opportunity of taking the steps she might think proper on the occasion.

You will offer to transmit to me any despatches which M. Galvez may think proper to confide to you ; or to return with them yourself, if more agreeable to him.

You will be attentive to all other objects of useful information, such as the characters, views, and connections of important individuals ; the plan of operations for the next campaign; whether any and what secret overtures have been made by Britain to France or Spain, or by either of them to her, or each other; whether any of the other powers have manifested a disposition to take a part in the war; and whether it is probable that any, and which of them, will become mediators for a general peace, and on what plan. If the war should continue, it would be advantageous to know whether Spain means to carry on any serious operations for possessing herself of the Floridas and banks of the Mississippi, etc., etc., etc.

Although I have confidence in your prudence, yet permit me to recommend to you the greatest circumspection. Command yourself under every circumstance; on the one hand, avoid being suspected of servility, and on the other, let your temper be always even and your attention unremitted.

You will oblige me by being very regular and circumstantial in your correspondence, and commit nothing of a private nature to paper unless in cipher.

JOHN JAY.

WILLIAM CARMICHAEL TO JAY.

MADRID, February 15, 1780.

DEAR SIR:

I arrived in this city late in the evening of the 11th, after a tedious and disagreeable journey. The next day, though much indisposed, I waited on the French Ambassador, who had, by a message over night, requested M. Gerard to engage me to dinner. I was received by him and all his family in the most friendly manner, and was offered every service in his power to render us, without those personal professions, which give birth to many unmeaning words and more suspicion. Indeed, I have neither expressions nor time to

represent the apparent candor and liberality of his sentiments. He entered fully into the good disposition of his
Court, and informed me, that the King, as a further proof
of his friendship for us, had agreed to pay us annually the
additional sum of three millions of livres during the continuance of the war, in order to enable us to purchase the
necessaries for our army, &c. &c. and that his Majesty had
also determined to send a considerable marine and land
force early in the year to America, to be at the disposition
and under the direction of our General. Seventeen sail of
the line, and four thousand troops, are also to be sent to
the West Indies, if they have not already sailed. Judge
after this, if attention, candor, and apparent unreservedness,
were not the more necessary on my part.

On inquiring, I found that M. Galvez was at the Pardo,
about two leagues from Madrid, where the King resides at
present, and in the course of conversation discovered, that
the proper channel of address ought to have been through
the Count de Florida Blanca.

The Ambassador offered to introduce me, but as this
could not be done with propriety without previous application, he undertook to make it the day following, and to fix
the time for my reception by both, and I think the manner
will be the sole difficulty.

Among other circumstances, which induce this conclusion,
is the certain knowledge I have obtained, that M. Mirales
received instructions several months past to enter into
engagements with Congress, to take into pay a body of
troops to assist in the conquest of Florida. Your own
good sense will point out the use which may be made of
this intelligence. It answers to one point of the instructions which I had the honor to receive from you. The
short time I have been in this city has not hitherto given
me an opportunity of writing so circumstantially as I could
wish, in the matters abovementioned, and much less of
giving a decided opinion on many objects contained in

your instructions. I find, however, hitherto no difficulty in acquiring in time a knowledge on most of the subjects recommended to my attention.

I have reason to believe, that the same disgusts do not subsist between the Crowns as between the nations, but the most perfect harmony and good understanding.

I have been positively assured, and from good authority, that no overtures have been made for peace.

The Dutch are arming, which is a circumstance in our favor, as their preparations originate from their discontent with England, on account of the late affair of the convoy.

Mr. Harrison is here, and proposes to proceed to Cadiz next week, which will furnish me a good opportunity of writing to you. I enclose you the last paper received from America; the people were in high spirits, and everything in a good state in the beginning of January.

I cannot conclude without mentioning the very polite manner in which the French Ambassador offered his personal civilities in everything, that depended on him, to be useful to you in this place.

M. Gerard will write to you himself, yet I must do him the justice to mention his personal kindness to me, and the candid representations he has made in every public company here of the prosperous situation of our affairs.

I have the honor to be, &c.
WILLIAM CARMICHAEL.

BENJAMIN FRANKLIN TO JAY.

PASSY, Feb. 22d, 1780.

SIR :

It gives me infinite pleasure to hear of your Excellency's safe arrival in Spain. Knowing that the *Confederacy* had Sailed the 28th of Octr. we began to despair of ever hearing more of her.

I received your advice of the bill drawn on me for four thousand and seventy-nine livres tournóis, at sixty days date, which I order'd to be immediately paid as you desired. I have also lodged a credit for you at Madrid of 24,000 Livres, deducting this bill. You will be so good as to furnish Mr. Carmichael with 1800 livres of it, which he has desired of me.

I enclose a letter of introduction to the Marquis d'Yranda with whom the credit is placed, and whose acquaintance and friendship may be otherwise of use to you.

With great esteem and respect

I have the honor to be

Your Excellency's most

obedient and most humble

Servant,

B. FRANKLIN.

JOHN ADAMS TO JAY.

PARIS, HOTEL DE VALOIS, Feby. 22^d, 1780.

DEAR SIR:

I most sincerely congratulate you on your happy arrival in Europe, which must be the more agreeable to you for the terrible voyages you have had. Every good American in Europe I believe suffered a great anxiety from the length of time that passed between the day when it was known the *Confederacy* sailed, and the time when the news arrived of your being at Cadiz. I too have had my hair breadth escapes, and after my arrival, a very tedious journey in the worst season of the year by land. Happy, however, shall we be if all our hazards and fatigues should contribute to lay the foundation of a free and a prosperous people.

I hope no accident or disagreeable circumstance has happened to your family, to whom I shall be obliged to you to present my respects.

From what I saw and heard in Spain, from the strong assurances I received of the good will of the Court and nation, and from the great attention and respect that were paid to me by officers of government of the highest rank in the provinces through which I passed, I am persuaded yon will meet with the most distinguished reception, and I hope will soon have the honor and satisfaction of concluding a treaty with Spain.

You will have the advantage of more frequent and speedy intelligence from home than we can have; at least you will have it in your power. There are vessels oftener arriving from America at Bilboa and Cadiz, I think, than in France. Many of these vessels come from Boston and Newbury Port, perhaps the most of them; so that by directing your correspondents to send their letters that way you will have them much sooner than we can commonly obtain them, and by transmitting yours to Messrs. Gardoqui and Co. at Bilboa, and M. Montgomery or some other at Cadiz, your dispatches will go more speedily and more safely than ours. We find it almost impossible to get a letter across the Bay of Biscay from France in a merchant vessel there are so many privateers in the route, the danger from whom is avoided chiefly by vessels from Bilboa keeping near the coast and running into harbour in case of danger, and wholly by those from Cadiz.

We have nothing new here at present, but what you must have had before. Pray what think you of Peace? It seems to be the will of Heaven that the English should have success enough to lead them on to final destruction. They are quite intoxicated with their late advantages, altho' a poor compensation for what they cost.

My respects to Mr. Carmichael, and believe me to be, with respect and esteem, sir,

Your most obedient humble Servant,

JOHN ADAMS.

FLORIDA BLANCA[1] TO JAY.

[Translation.]

PARDO, February 28th, 1780.

SIR:

Having received by the hands of Don Joseph de Galvez the letter which your Excellency sent by Mr. Carmichael, and having communicated the contents to his Majesty, I have it in command to inform you, that his Majesty highly approves the choice, which the American Congress have made of you to the trust mentioned in your letter, as well on account of the high estimation in which his Majesty holds the members who made the choice, as the information he has received of your probity, talents, and abilities. His Majesty also received with pleasure the information of the desire which the Colonies have to form a connexion with Spain, of whose good disposition they have already received strong proofs. Nevertheless, his Majesty thinks it necessary in the first place, that the manner, the forms, and the mutual correspondence should be settled, upon which that Union must be founded, which the United States of America desire to establish with this monarchy. For this purpose there is no obstacle to your Excellency's coming to this Court, in order to explain your intentions and those of the Congress, and to hear those of his Majesty, and by that means settling a basis upon which a perfect friendship may be established, and also its extent and consequences.

His Majesty thinks, that until these points are settled, as he hopes they will be, it is not proper for your Excellency to assume a formal character, which must depend on a public acknowledgment and future treaty. But your Excellency may be assured of the sincerity and good dispositions of his Majesty towards the United States, and of his earnest desire to remove every difficulty, for the mutual

---

[1] Spanish Secretary of State for the Indies.

happiness of them and of this monarchy. This has been intimated to Mr. Carmichael, who can communicate the same to your Excellency, to whom I beg leave to make a tender of my service, being, &c.

COUNT DE FLORIDA BLANCA.

JAY TO THE PRESIDENT OF CONGRESS.

SIR :   CADIZ, 3d March, 1780.

Captain Morgan being still here, waiting for a fair wind, I have an opportunity of transmitting to your Excellency a copy of a letter just come to hand from the Count de Florida Blanca, in answer to mine to M. Galvez.

Being apprehensive that if present I should probably be amused with verbal answers capable of being explained away if necessary, until the two courts could have time to consult and decide on their measures, I thought it more prudent that my first application should be by letter rather than in person.

The answer in question, divested of the gloss which its politeness spreads over it, gives us, I think, to understand, that our independence shall be acknowledged, provided we accede to certain terms of treaty, but not otherwise ; so that the acknowledgment is not to be made because we are independent, which would be candid and liberal, but because of the previous considerations we are to give for it, which is consistent with the principles on which nations usually act.

I shall proceed immediately to Madrid. There are many reasons (hereafter to be explained) which induce me to suspect that France is determined to manage between us, so as to make us debtors to their influence and good correspondence with Spain for every concession on her part, and to make Spain hold herself obligated to their influence and good correspondence with us for every concession on our part. Though this may puzzle the business, I think it also promotes it.

M. Gerard has often endeavoured to persuade me that a certain resolution of Congress would, if persisted in, ruin the business, which, however, he did not appear much inclined to believe, but, on the contrary, that if every other matter was adjusted you would not part on that point. I assured him that ground had, in my opinion, been taken with too much deliberation now to be quitted, and that expectations of that kind would certainly deceive those who trusted them. And, indeed, as affairs are now circumstanced, it would, in my opinion, be better for America to have no treaty with Spain than to purchase one on such servile terms. There was a time when it might have been proper to have given that country something for their making common cause with us, but that day is now past. Spain is at war with Britain.

I do not like the cipher in which I write, and shall therefore defer further particulars till Mr. Thompson shall receive the one now sent him.

I have the honour to be, with great respect and esteem, your Excellency's most obedient servant,

JOHN JAY.

JAY TO FLORIDA BLANCA.

SIR :   CADIZ, March 6, 1780.

I have been honoured with your Excellency's favour of the 24th ultimo, which did not come to my hands till some time after its arrival.

The sentiments which his Majesty is pleased to entertain of me, together with the polite manner in which your Excellency has been so obliging as to express them, demand my warmest acknowledgments, and give additional force to the many motives which render me desirous of a permanent union between his Majesty and the United States.

The honour and probity, which have ever characterized the conduct of Spain, together with the exalted reputation his Majesty has acquired by being an eminent example of both, have induced the people of the United States to repose the highest confidence in the proofs they have received of his friendly disposition towards them ; and to consider every engagement with this monarchy as guaranteed by that faith, and secured by that ingenuousness which have so gloriously distinguished his Majesty and this kingdom among the other princes and nations of the earth.

Permit me to request the favour of your Excellency to assure his Majesty that the people of the United States are convinced that virtue alone can animate and support their governments ; and that they can in no other way establish and perpetuate a national character, honourable to themselves and their posterity, than by an unshaken adherence to the rules which religion, morality, and treaties may prescribe for their conduct. His royal mind may also be persuaded, that gratitude will never cease to add the influence of inclination to the power of dignity, in rendering them solicitous for the happiness and prosperity of those generous nations, who nobly strengthened their opposition to a torrent of oppression, and kindly aided in freeing them from the bondage of a nation, whose arrogance and injustice had become destructive of the rights of mankind, and dangerous to the peace and tranquillity of Christendom.

Having, therefore, the most perfect conviction that the candour and benignity of his Majesty's intentions are equal to the uprightness and sincerity of those of Congress, I shall set out in a few days for Madrid, with the pleasing expectation that there will be little delay or difficulty in adjusting the terms of a union between a magnanimous monarch and a virtuous people, who wish to obtain, by an alliance with each other, only reciprocal benefits and mutual advantages.

I have the honour to be, with perfect respect and consideration, your Excellency's most obedient and most humble servant,

JOHN JAY.

FLORIDA BLANCA TO JAY.

[Translation.]

PARDO, March 9th, 1780.

Before entering into a discussion with Mr. Jay or Mr. Carmichael, jointly or separately, on the subject of the affairs of the United States of North America, and their mutual interest with respect to Spain, it is judged indispensable at Madrid, that the Catholic King should be exactly informed of the civil and military state of the American Provinces, and of their resources to continue the present war, not only for the defence of their own liberty, but also with respect to the aid and succors they may be able to afford to Spain in its operations, in case hereafter this Crown should become the ally of America. The *Civil Affairs* ought to comprehend:

1st. A true account of the population and form of government of each Province of the Union, and the resolution of the inhabitants to continue the war with vigor, as long as it is necessary.

2dly. Whether there is any powerful party in favor of England, and what consequences are to be apprehended from it; whether the heads of this party suffer themselves to be seduced by the great promises of the British government.

3dly. A statement of the revenues of these Provinces, and of their ability to contribute to the general expense; to which may be added, whether they will be able long to support this burthen, and even to increase it should it be judged necessary.

4thly. A statement of the public debts, and of the particular debts of each State, taken collectively or separately, of their resources to lessen them, and the possibility of their being able to support their credit in all the operations of government, in the commerce of their inhabitants, and above all in the protection of national industry.

5thly. By what means, or with what branches of commerce will the States of America have it in their power to indemnify Spain, whenever this power may second the views and operations of the Americans; and particularly the Court wishes to know, whether it may be convenient for the said States to furnish ships of war of the best construction for the Spanish marine, and likewise timber and other articles for the King's arsenals, and the whole without loss of time, and fixing the terms on which they would make an agreement of this nature, and who would be commissioned to bring the vessels and these naval stores to Spain.

With respect to the *Military State* of America, it is necessary to be informed first, of the number and strength of the different bodies of troops armed by the Provinces, and of their present situation, in order to judge whether they are sufficient to oppose the enemy wherever they may go, and particularly in Carolina and Georgia.

Further, it may be expedient to know the means of augmenting the American Army in case it is necessary, or to keep it always on the same footing, notwithstanding its daily losses. In what condition their clothing and arms are at present; whether they are partly in want of those articles, and how much it would require to remedy these defects.

The subsistence of an army being an object of the greatest consequence, the Court desires to know if proper measures have been taken for that purpose, that it may be ascertained whether it can act everywhere, if necessary, even in the above mentioned Provinces, without danger of being in want of necessaries.

It is highly essential for the Provinces of America to keep a marine to act against the common enemy, and to secure their own possessions during the present war. The Spanish Minister therefore is desirous of knowing its strength, including the armed vessels belonging to individuals, and by what means it may be augmented, and what succors will be necessary for that purpose.

The Court of Spain, desirous of information on these subjects with all possible frankness and precision, does not pretend to dive into matters which Mr. Jay or Mr. Carmichael may regard as reserved to themselves. Its only aim is to be acquainted with the present state of the American forces, their resources, and ability to continue the war, so that if it was in consideration for new allies to supply them with succors of any kind, the former might be able to plan on solid grounds their operations convenient for the common cause, and for the particular advantage of these States, without running the risk of being misled by false calculations for want of foresight and proper information.

COUNT DE VERGENNES TO JAY.

VERSAILLES, March 13th, 1780.

SIR:

I have received your favor of the 27th of January, and I am fully sensible of the confidence you have reposed in me, by communicating to me the object of your mission. You know too well the attachment of his Majesty to the United States not to feel assured that he sincerely wishes you success, and will be eager to contribute to it. The Count de Montmorin[1] has received instructions accordant with this disposition, and I do not doubt that your confidence in him will enable him to fulfil them to your entire satisfaction.

I have the honor to be, &c.,

DE VERGENNES.

JAY TO FLORIDA BLANCA.

MADRID, April 25th, 1780.

SIR:

Mr. Carmichael has delivered to me a paper he had the honour of receiving from your Excellency before my arrival here, containing heads of many important inquiries,[2] respecting which it was thought

---

[1] French Minister at the Court of Spain.
[2] See letter from Florida Blanca, of March 9, 1780.

necessary that his Catholic Majesty should be exactly informed, before entering into a discussion with me and Mr. Carmichael, jointly or separately, on the subject of the affairs of the United States of North America, and their mutual interest with respect to Spain ; but that the court, though desirous of information on these several articles, with all possible frankness and precision, did not mean to dive into matters which Mr. Carmichael and myself might regard as reserved to ourselves only. . . .

The inquiries in question are numerous and important. They do honour to the sagacity which suggested them, and, if fully answered, would produce a very interesting history of the present condition of the American States. On some of the subjects proposed, I can give your Excellency full and positive intelligence ; on others, only general and by no means precise information. On all, however, I shall write with candour.

Such is the nature of the American governments and confederacy, that the Congress, and all other rulers of the people, are responsible to them for their conduct, and cannot withhold from their constituents a knowledge of their true situation without subjecting themselves to all the evils which they experience who substitute cunning in the place of wisdom. Hence it is that a knowledge of their affairs is easily attainable by all who will be at the trouble of collecting it ; and as it is neither the policy nor inclination of America to draw a veil over any part of their affairs, your Excellency may be persuaded that every consideration forbids their servants, by a suppression or misrepresentation of facts, to deceive or mislead those whose amity they so sincerely endeavour to cultivate as they do that of Spain.

I.—THE CIVIL STATE OF NORTH AMERICA.

Your Excellency has, with great propriety, arranged the subjects of your inquiry under two heads—the *civil* and *military* states of North America. The first of these is again branched into several subdivisions, at the head of which is the

Population of each State.

The exact number of inhabitants in the United States has not, I believe, been ascertained by an actual census in more than two or three of them. The only computation made by Congress was on the 29th of July, 1775, the manner and occasion of which exclude every suspicion of its exceeding the true number. Congress had emitted bills of credit to a very considerable amount, and were apprized of the necessity of emitting more. Justice demanded that this debt should be apportioned among the States according to their respective abilities ; an equitable rule whereby to determine that ability became indispensable. After much consideration, Congress resolved " that the proportion or quota of each colony should be determined according to the number of the inhabitants of all ages (including negroes and mulattoes) in each colony " ; but as that could not *then* be ascertained *exactly*, they were obliged to judge of

and compute the number from circumstantial evidence.
The delegates gave to Congress an account of the
population of their respective colonies, made from
the best materials then in their power, and so great
was their confidence in each other that from those
accounts that computation was principally formed.
Your Excellency will readily perceive that the delegates were far from being under any temptations to
exaggerate the number of their constituents ; they
were not ignorant that, by such exaggerations, they
would increase their portion of aids, both of men and
money, and that whatever errors they might commit
could not be rectified by an actual numeration during
the war.   The computation then formed was as follows :

New Hampshire. . .	124,069 and a half
Massachusetts Bay . .	434,244
Rhode Island . . .	71,959 and a half
Connecticut	248,139
New York	248,139
New Jersey	161,290 and a half
Pennsylvania	372,208 and a half
Delaware	37,219 and a half
Maryland	310,174 and a half
Virginia	496,278
North Carolina . . .	248,139
South Carolina . . .	248,139

3,000,000

Exclusive of the inhabitants of Georgia, who were
not at that time represented in Congress, and of

whose numbers I have no information that I can confide in.

The form of government of each state.

In the pamphlets I have now the honour of transmitting to your Excellency, viz., No. 1, No. 2, No. 3, No. 4, and No. 5, you will find the constitutions of New York, New Jersey, Pennsylvania, Delaware, and South Carolina. The others I have not with me. The great outlines of them all are very similar. By the last accounts from America it appears that Massachusetts Bay had not as yet agreed upon their constitution, but had it then under consideration.

It cannot be necessary to observe to your Excellency that these new modes of government were formed by persons named and authorized by the people for that express purpose ; that they were, in general, instituted with great temper and deliberation, upon such just and liberal principles, as, on the one hand, to give effectual security to civil and religious liberty, and, on the other, make ample provision for the rights of justice and the due exercise of the necessary powers of government.

The articles of confederation agreed upon by Congress, and approved by every State in the Union except Maryland, provide for the general government of the confederacy, and the ordering of all matters essential to the prosperity and preservation of the Union in peace and war. I ought also to inform your Excellency, that the reasons why Maryland has as yet withheld her assent to those articles, do not arise from any disaffection to the common cause, but merely from their not having adopted certain principles respecting the disposition of certain lands.

The union and resolution of the inhabitants to continue the war with vigour as long as may be necessary.

On this subject, I can give your Excellency certain and positive information ; the storm of tyranny and oppression, which had for some years been constantly growing more black and more terrible, began to burst with violence on the people of North America in the year 1774. It was seen and felt and deprecated by all, except those who expected to gather spoils in the ruins it was designed to occasion. These were those who enjoyed, or expected emoluments from Great Britain, together with their immediate dependants and connections ; such as the officers of government throughout the colonies, but with some very distinguished exceptions ; those of the clergy of the Church of England almost without exception, who received annual salaries from the society established in England for Propagating the Gospel in Foreign Parts ; foreign adventurers, buyers and sellers, who, being no further attached to the country than as it afforded the means of gain, soon prepared to speculate in confiscations, and courted the notice of their sovereign by intemperate zeal for the ruin of his subjects. With these exceptions, the great body of the people moved together, and united in such firm and considerate measures for the common safety, and conducted their affairs with such regularity, order, and system as to leave no room to suppose them to be the work of only a prevailing party, as our enemies have always represented and affected to consider them.

There was, it is true, another class of persons not much less dangerous, though far more contemptible than those I first mentioned; persons who, in every revolution, like floating weeds in every storm, obey the strongest wind, and pass from side to side as that happens to change. I mean the *neutrals*, a pusillanimous race, who, having balanced in their minds the advantages and disadvantages, the gains and dangers of joining either side, are seduced by their fears to form a thousand pretexts for joining neither; who, to manifest their loyalty to their king, when his armies were successful, gave them every aid in their power, except drawing their swords against their country; and who, when their countrymen prevailed, were ready to render them all possible service, except taking arms against their prince.

The auxiliaries, whom the British measures and forces found in the country, consisted of persons from these classes. And although, when these first appeared in and wounded the bosom of America, she was obliged to extend her arms to repel the assaults of a foreign enemy, yet such was the union and spirit of her inhabitants, that she was soon enabled not only to put them under her feet, but on the ruins of her former governments to erect new ones in the midst of invasions from without and treacherous combinations from within. Being able to obtain no other terms of peace than unconditional obedience, she had sufficient courage to declare herself independent in the face of one of the best appointed armies Britain could ever boast of ; as well as sufficient strength to limit its operations, and reduce its numbers.

It may perhaps be observed, that the first object of the war was a redress of grievances ; that the present object is *independence ;* and it may be asked whether the people are as much united with respect to the last as they were with respect to the first.

I am certain that the people of America never were so well united as they are at present, in that of their independence. Exclusive of actual observation on the spot, I think so because :

1st. The Declaration of Independence was made by Congress at a time when the great body of their constituents called for it.

2dly. Because that declaration was immediately recognized by the general assemblies and legislatures of the several States, without exception.

3dly. Because the successful army under General Burgoyne was defeated and captured by a great collection of the neighbouring militia, to whom he had offered peace and tranquillity on their remaining at home ; terms which it was natural to suppose a great many of them would have accepted, had the Declaration of Independence been disagreeable to them.

4thly. Because the Congress, consisting of members annually elected, have repeatedly, expressly, and unanimously declared their determination to support it at every hazard.

5thly. Because their internal enemies have been either expelled or reduced, and their estates, to a very great amount in some of the States, confiscated and actually sold.

6thly. Because constitutions and forms of government have since been instituted and completely organized, in which the people participate, from which they have experienced essential advantages, and to which they have of consequence become greatly attached.

7thly. Because Congress unanimously refused to enter into treaty with the British commissioners on any terms short of independence ; and because every State, though afterward separately solicited, refused to treat otherwise than collectively by their delegates in Congress.

8thly. Because the inhuman and very barbarous manner in which the war has been conducted by the enemy has so alienated the affections of the people from the king and government of Britain, and filled their hearts with such deep-rooted and just resentments, as render a cordial reconciliation, much less a dependence on them, utterly impossible.

9thly. Because the doctrine propagated in America by the servants of the King of Great Britain, that no faith was to be kept with Americans in arms against him, and the uniformity with which they have adhered to it, in their practice as well as professions, have destroyed all confidence, and leave the Americans no room to doubt but that, should they again become subjects of the King of Britain on certain terms, those terms would as little impede the progress of future oppression, as the capitulation of Limerick, in 1691, did with respect to Ireland.

10thly. Because the treaty with France, and consequently virtue, honour, and every obligation due to the reputation of a rising nation, whose fame is unsullied by violated compacts, forbid it.

11thly. Because it is the evident and well-known interest of North America to remain independent.

12thly. Because the history of mankind, from the earliest ages, with a loud voice calls upon those who draw their swords against a prince, deaf to the supplication of his people, to throw away the scabbard.

13thly. Because they do not consider the support of their independence as difficult. The country is very defensible and fertile ; the people are all soldiers, who with reason consider their liberty and lives as the most valuable of the possessions left them, and which they are determined shall neither be wrested nor purchased from them but with blood.

14thly. Because, for the support of their independence, they have expressly, by a most solemn act, pledged to each other their lives, their fortunes, and their sacred honour ; so that their bond of union, for this very purpose, thus formed of all the ties of common interest, common safety, mutual affection, general resentments, and the great obligations of virtue, honour, patriotism, and religion, may with reason be deemed equal to the importance of that great object.

Whether there is any powerful party in favour of England, and what consequences are to be apprehended from it ? Whether the heads of this party suffer themselves to be seduced by the promises of the British Government ?

What has been already said on the subject of the union of the people in North America will, I imagine, in a great measure, answer these questions.

If by a party in favour of England is meant a party for relinquishing the independence of the United States, and returning to the dominion of Britain, on any terms whatever, I answer, there is no such party in North America ; all the open adherents of the crown of Great Britain having either voluntarily quitted or been expelled from the country.

That Britain has emissaries and masked adherents in America, industrious in their little spheres to perplex the public measures, and disturb the public tranquillity, is a fact of which I have not the most distant doubt; and it is equally true, that some of these wicked men are by a few weak ones thought to be patriots, but they cannot with any propriety be called a party, or even a faction. The chief mischief they do, is collecting and transmitting intelligence, raising false reports, and spreading calumnies of public men and measures ; such characters will be found in every country so circumstanced, and America has not been negligent in providing laws for their punishment.

The obvious policy of the court of London has induced them to boast perpetually of their party in

America; but where is it? of whom composed? what
has it done, or is doing? are questions to which they
constantly give evasive answers. Much also have
they said of the numbers that have joined their arms
in America. The truth is, that at Boston, Rhode
Island, New York, and Philadelphia, they gleaned
some of that refuse of mankind to be found and purchased by anybody in all commercial cities. It is also
true, that some men of weight and influence in the
country, who joined the enemy on their first successes,
did draw away with them several of their immediate
dependants, whom they persuaded or otherwise influenced to enlist in their service. To these may also
be added the prisoners, who at different times they
forced into their service by famine, and other severities
too numerous as well as barbarous to be here particularized. But I have no reason to believe, that all
these aids put together ever exceeded three thousand
men. This business, however (except with respect
to prisoners), has long been over, and before I left
America, many of those deluded people had returned
and implored the pardon of their country.

In America, as in all other popular governments,
your Excellency knows there must and ever will be
parties for and against particular measures and particular men. The enemy, adverting to this circumstance, have had address enough to ascribe differences
and temporary heats arising from this source, in which
they were not interested, to causes much higher, and
more flattering to their importance; and this they
have done with so much art, as to have imposed in

some instances on the credulity of men high in reputation for sagacity and discernment.

If your Excellency will be pleased to peruse a pamphlet marked No. 6, which you will find enclosed with the other papers I herewith transmit, and entitled "Observations on the American Revolution," you will perceive that nothing is to be apprehended from this supposed party in North America.

A statement of the revenues of the States, and of their ability to contribute to the general expense; whether they will be able long to support this burden, and increase it if necessary.

The confederated States have no fixed revenues, nor are such revenues necessary, because all the private property in the country is at the public service. The only restriction imposed by the people is, that it be taken from them with wisdom and justice: or, to be more explicit, that the sums required be proportionate to the public exigences, and assessed on the individuals in proportion to their respective abilities.

A nation can seldom be destitute of the means of continuing a war, while they remain unsubdued in the field, and cheerfully devote their all to that service. They may indeed experience great distress, but no distress being equal to that of subjection to exasperated oppressors, whose most tender mercies are cruel, the Americans had little difficulty in making their election.

A statement of the public debts.

This subject your Excellency will find fully discussed in an address of Congress to their constituents, in which they compute their debts, and mention the means they had taken to preserve the public credit. It is also herewith enclosed, and marked No. 7.

A statement of the debts of each particular State.

Although exact accounts of these debts are contained in the public printed acts of each State, yet as I neither have any of those acts or extracts from them with me, and my general knowledge on this head is very imperfect, I am deterred from giving your Excellency any information respecting it, by the very great risk I should run of misleading you on this point.

The resources to lessen these debts.

Taxes ; foreign and domestic loans ; sales of confiscated estates, and ungranted lands.

The possibility of their supporting their credit in all the operations of government, in the commerce of their inhabitants, and, above all, in the protection of national industry.

As to the possibility of supporting their credit in the cases mentioned, there is no doubt it is very *possible.* How far it is *probable*, is a question less easy to answer. If the taxes called for by Congress last fall be duly paid, all will be safe. But whether they have been paid or not I am wholly uninformed, except that I find in a public paper that Virginia had make good her first payment. As I daily expect to receive advices from America on this subject, I shall postpone saying any thing further on it at present; but your Excellency may rely on my communicating to you a full state of what intelligence I may have respecting it.

As to supporting their credit in *commerce*, it is attended with considerable though not insurmountable difficulties. They are of two kinds—the want of sufficient commodities for remittances, and the risk of transporting them. North America abounds in valuable commodities, such as fish, oil, lumber, provisions of flesh and corn, iron, tobacco, and naval stores; peltry, indigo, potash, and other articles—all of which have greatly diminished since the war. The labourers formerly employed in producing them having been often called to the field, and by other effects of the war been prevented from regularly following their usual occupations. Of some of these articles, America still produces more than is necessary for her own consumption, but the risk of transporting them to Europe renders her remittances very uncertain. The asylum, which all British armed vessels find in the ports of Portugal, enables them to cruise very conveniently and with great advantage off the western islands, and other situations proper for annoying vessels from thence to France, Spain, or the Mediterranean. Hence it is that the trade from America to St. Eustatia has of late so greatly increased, it being carried on principally in small, fast-sailing vessels that draw but little water, and that the chief remittances to Europe have been in bills of exchange instead of produce.

With respect to the protection of *national industry*, I take it for granted that it will always flourish where it is lucrative and not discouraged, which was the case in North America when I left it : every man being then at liberty, by the law, to cultivate the earth as he pleased, to raise what he pleased, to manufacture as he pleased, and to sell the produce of his labour to whom he pleased, and for the best prices, without any duties or impositions whatsoever. I have indeed no apprehensions whatever on this subject. I believe there are no people more industrious than those of America, and whoever recurs to their population, their former exports, and their present productions amid the horrors of fire and sword, will be convinced of it.

By what means, or what branches of commerce, will the States of America have it in their power to indemnify Spain, whenever this power may second the views and operations of the Americans?

America will indemnify Spain in two ways—by fighting the enemy of Spain, and by commerce. Your Excellency will be pleased to remark that Spain, as well as America, is now at war with Britain, and therefore that it is the interest of both to support and assist each other against the common enemy. It cannot be a question whether Britain will be more or less formidable if defeated or victorious in America ;

and there can be no doubt but that every nation interested in the reduction of her power will be compensated for any aids they may afford America by the immediate application of those aids to that express purpose at the expense of American blood.

Your Excellency's well-known talents save me the necessity of observing, that it is the interest of all Europe to join in breaking down the exorbitant power of a nation which arrogantly claims the ocean as her birthright, and considers every advantage in commerce, however acquired by violence or used with cruelty, as a tribute justly due to her boasted superiority in arts and in arms.

By establishing the independence of America, the empire of Britain will be divided, and the sinews of her power cut. Americans, situated in another hemisphere, intent only on the cultivation of a country more than sufficient to satisfy their desires, will remain unconnected with European politics, and, not being interested in their objects, will not partake in their dissensions. Happy in having for their neighbours a people distinguished for love of justice and of peace, they will have nothing to fear, but may flatter themselves that they and their posterity will long enjoy all the blessings of that peace, liberty, and safety for which alone they patiently endure the calamities incident to the cruel contest they sustain.

While the war continues the commerce of America will be inconsiderable, but on the restoration of peace it will soon become very valuable and extensive. So great is the extent of country in North America yet to be cultivated, and so inviting to settlers, that labour will very long remain too dear to admit of considerable manufactures. Reason and experience tell us that, when the poor have it in their power to gain affluence by tilling the earth, they will refuse the scanty earnings which manufacturers may offer them. From this circumstance it is evident that the exports from America will consist of raw materials, which other nations will be able to manufacture for them at a cheaper rate than they can themselves. To those who consider the future and progressive population of that country, the demands it will have for the manufactures and productions of Europe, as well to satisfy their wants as to gratify their luxury, will appear immense, and far more than any one kingdom in it can supply. Instead of paying money for fish and many other articles, as heretofore, Spain will then have an opportunity of obtaining them in exchange for her cloth, silks, wines, and fruits ; notwithstanding which it is proper to observe that the commerce of the American States will for ever procure them such *actual wealth* as to enable them punctually to repay whatever sums they may borrow.

How far it may be convenient for these States to furnish ships of war, timber, and other articles for the king's arsenals, without delay ; and, if in their power, on what terms ?

I am much at a loss to determine at present, and therefore will by no means give your Excellency my conjectures for intelligence.

It is certain, that in ordinary times, America can build ships as good, and cheaper than any other people, because the materials cost them less. The ships of war now in her service, as to strength and construction, are not exceeded by any on the ocean. On this subject I will write to America for information, and give your Excellency the earliest notice of it. Naval stores, and particularly masts and spars, may certainly be had there, and of the best quality ; and I doubt not but that the Americans would carry them to the Havannah or New Orleans, though I suspect, their being in a manner destitute of proper convoys for the European trade, would render them backward in bringing them to Spain, on terms equal to the risk of capture on the one hand, and the expectations of purchasers on the other.

II.—THE MILITARY STATE OF NORTH AMERICA.

The number and strength of the American troops ; their present situation, and ability to oppose the enemy, especially in Georgia and Carolina.

Six months have elapsed since I left America, and I had not seen a return of the army for some time before that period. It did not, I am certain, amount to its full complement, and, in my opinion, did not in the whole exceed thirty or thirty-five thousand men ; I mean regular troops.

The commander-in-chief, whose abilities, as well as integrity, merit the highest confidence, was authorized to conduct all the military operations in the United

States at his discretion ; subject, nevertheless, to such orders as the Congress might think proper from time to time to give. It is impossible, therefore, for me (not having received a single letter from America on these subjects since my arrival) to decide in what manner or proportions these troops are employed or stationed, though I am confident it has been done in the best manner.

All the men of proper age in America are liable to do military duty in certain cases, and, with a few exceptions, in all cases. The militia is for the most part divided into a certain number of classes, and whenever reinforcements to the main army, or any detachment of it, are wanting, they are supplied by these classes in rotation. These reinforcements, while in the field, are subject to the like regulations with the regular troops, and with them submit to the severest discipline and duty. Hence it is, that the people of America have become soldiers, and that the enemy have never been able to make a deep impression in the country, or long hold any considerable lodgments at a distance from their fleets. Georgia and South Carolina, indeed, enjoy these advantages in a less degree than the other States, their own militia not being very numerous, and speedy reinforcements from their neighbours of North Carolina and Virginia rendered difficult by the length of the way. They have, nevertheless, given proofs of their spirit by various and great exertions ; and I have reason to believe, that all possible care has been taken to provide for their safety, by furnishing them with a proper body of troops under Major-General Lincoln, a very good officer, as well as a very good man.

Arms are still wanting in America, many of those imported proving unfit for use, and the number of inhabitants who were without proper arms at the beginning of the war, calling for great supplies. The army, and a considerable part of the militia, especially in the Northern States, have in general good arms.

The article of clothing has been, and still is, a very interesting one to the American army. It is impossible to describe, and, indeed, almost impossible to believe, the hardships they have endured for want of it. There have been instances, and I speak from the most undoubted authority, of considerable detachments marching barefooted over rugged tracts of ice and snow, and marking the route they took by the blood that issued from their feet ; but neither these terrible extremities, nor the alluring offers of the enemy, could prevail on them to quit their standard or relax their ardour. Their condition, however, has of late been much bettered by supplies from France and Spain, and American privateers ; but adequate provision has not yet been made for the ensuing winter, and I cannot conceal from your Excellency my anxiety on that head. A supply of clothing for twenty thousand men, added to what is engaged for them in France, would make that army and all America happy.

I foresee no other difficulties in providing subsisttence for the American armies in every station in which they may be placed, than those which may attend the transportation of it. But when I reflect on the obstacles of this kind which they have already met with and surmounted, I have little uneasiness about future ones. The last crops in America promised to be plentiful when I left it, but whether there would be any and what considerable overplus for exportation, was then undetermined; the damages done the wheat in Maryland, Virginia, and North Carolina by a fly, which infested those countries, not being to my knowledge at that time ascertained.

How many ships of war belong to Congress, is a question I cannot answer with certainty. I think there are not more than ten or twelve in the whole. Of privateers, there are a great number, but how many exactly has not been computed. In my opinion, they exceed one hundred, several of them very fine ships. The Governor of Martinique told me, that in that island alone, the American privateers had brought and sold above five thousand African slaves, which they had taken from the enemy. Nine tenths at least of all the rum and sugar used in North America, these three years past, have been obtained in the same way, and to their successes have the public been indebted for the most seasonable and valuable supplies of military stores which they have received. I left several vessels on the stocks at Philadelphia, and heard of more in other parts.

Upon the whole, his Majesty may rest perfectly assured, that the Americans are determined, though forsaken by all mankind, to maintain their independence, and to part with it only with their lives; the desolations and distresses of war being too familiar to them to excite any other passions than indignation and resentment.

That the country will supply its inhabitants with provisions, some clothing, and some articles of commerce.

That there is no party in America in favour of returning under the dominion of Britain, on any terms whatever.

That the King of France is very popular in America, being in all parts of it styled the protector of the rights of mankind, and that they will hold the treaty made with him inviolate.

That the people in America have very high ideas of the honour and integrity of the Spanish nation, and of his Catholic Majesty especially, and that this respect and esteem unite with their interest in rendering them so desirous of his friendship and alliance.

That the greatest difficulty under which America labours arises from the great depreciation of her bills of credit, owing principally to a greater sum having been emitted than was necessary for a medium of commerce, and to the impossibility of remedying it by taxes before regular governments are established.

That great attempts, seconded by the general voice of the people, have been made to retrieve the credit of those bills by taxation, the issue of which was as yet uncertain, but if unsuccessful, a recurrence to taxes in kind was still left, and would be practised, though it is an expedient which nothing but necessity can render eligible.

That if France and Spain were to unite their endeavours to conquer Britain in America, by furnishing the latter with the necessary aids of ammunition, clothing, and some money, there is reason to believe, that the House of Bourbon would find it the most certain and least expensive method of reducing the power of their irreconcilable enemy, and not · only command the gratitude and perpetual attachment of America, but the general approbation of all who wish well to the tranquillity of Europe and the rights of mankind. Thus would that illustrious house erect lasting and glorious monuments to their virtues in the hearts of a whole people.

I fear your Excellency will consider the intelligence here given less full and precise than you expected. I regret that it is not in my power to render it more so, but it is not. I hope, however, that it will be thought sufficient to open a way to those further discussions which must precede the measures necessary to bind America to Spain, as well as to France, and thereby complete the division, and consequently the humiliation, of the British Empire; a work too glorious and laudable not to merit the notice of so magnanimous a prince as his Majesty, and engage the attention of a minister of such acknowledged abilities as your Excellency.

I flatter myself that the importance of the subject will apologize for my trespassing so long on your Excellency's patience so soon after your return to Aranjues.

I have the honour to be, etc.,

JOHN JAY.

JAY TO JOHN ADAMS.

MADRID, 26 April, 1780.

DEAR SIR:

I have at length had the pleasure of receiving your very friendly letter of the 22d February last. It has been very long on the road. Accept my thanks for your kind congratulations, and permit me to assure you that I sincerely rejoice in your having safely reached the place of your destination on a business which declares the confidence of America, and for an object in the attainment of which I am persuaded you will acquire honour to yourself and advantages to her.

The circumstances you mention as indications of the disposition of Spain undoubtedly bear the construction you give them. [1] (I found the same at Cadiz, although there were pains taken there and here to prevent any conduct towards me that might savour of an admission or knowledge of our independence. Considering the object of our treaty, I thought this extraordinary. I do not, however, ascribe it to any malevolence with respect to us, but merely to a design in that gentleman [?] or his instructors so to manage the proposed treaties here as that both Spain and America may hold themselves indebted for the attainment of their respective objects to the influence and good offices of their common ally.

The acknowledged integrity of his Catholic Majesty, and respected abilities and candour of his minister, are

---

[1] The portions of the letter in parentheses are erased in Jay's original draft, and do not appear in the copy printed in Adams' "Writings."

very flattering circumstances ; and I have too much
confidence in our friends, the French, to believe that
they wish to keep Spain and America longer asunder,
although a design of squeezing a little reputation out
of the business may embarrass the measures for a
junction. As the Count de Florida Blanca is, I am
told, a man of abilities, he doubtless will see and
probably recommend the policy of making a deep
impression on the hearts of the Americans by a seasonable acknowledgment of their independence, and by
affording them such immediate aids as their circumstances and the obvious interest of Spain demand.
Such measures at this period would turn the respect
of America for Spain into lasting attachment and in
that way give strength to every treaty they may
form).

Sir John Dalrymple[1] is here ; he came from Portugal
for the benefit of his Lady's health (as is said). He
is now at Aranjues. He has seen the Imperial Embassador, the Governor of the City, Signor Cam-
pomanes, the Duke of Alva, and several others, named
to him I suppose by Lord Grantham, who I find was
much respected here. He will return through France
to Britain. I shall go to Aranjues the day after to-
morrow and will form some judgment of that gentleman's success, by the conduct of the Court toward
America.

I am much obliged by your remarks on the most
proper route for letter and intelligence to and from

---

[1] See Sparks' " Diplomatic Correspondence," vol. vii., pp. 266–67 ; also
Lord Rochford's project to prevent the war, p. 268.

America, and shall profit by them. You may rely on receiving the earliest accounts of whatever interesting information I may obtain, and that I shall be happy in every opportunity of evincing the esteem with which I am, dear sir,

Your most obedient servant,

JOHN JAY.

JAY TO FLORIDA BLANCA.

MADRID, 27th April, 1780.

Mr. Jay presents his most respectful compliments to his Excellency the Count de Florida Blanca, and has the honour of transmitting the enclosed extract of a letter from an American gentleman, lately arrived at Bourdeaux, to Mr. Carmichael, who is well acquainted with him, and represents him to me as worthy of credit.

Mr. Jay also transmits a copy of the Constitution of North Carolina, and will, with great pleasure, endeavour to complete his Excellency's collection of the American forms of government.

EXTRACTS OF A LETTER FROM BOURDEAUX, DATED MARCH THE 30TH, TO WM. CARMICHAEL, ESQ.

"I arrived here the 28th inst. in the *Buckskins*, Johns, from Baltimore, which place I left the latter end of December, but the ship having been frozen up in the Patuxent for near two months we did not leave that river till the latter end of February, and finally got to sea the 2d inst. The winter proved the severest known in America, far exceeding that of the year 1740. At Philadelphia the cold was two degrees greater than ever remembered. The snows were so great and the cold so intense as to prevent travelling in almost any manner. This calamity added to the circumstance of a Commissary General's being either displaced or having resigned, and leaving the magazines very poorly furnished, reduced our army to very hard straights. They were ten days without bread, and in a letter which I saw from a member of Congress were these words : ' Our army was four days on half a herring and a gill of rice a man per day.' Our Assembly, viz, that of Maryland was sitting. The President received a letter from his Excellency, General Washington, informing him of the State of the army, and urging a speedy supply of provisions. They immediately made an Act authorizing the Executive power to seize on all stores and provisions they could find any where in the State, which was accordingly put in execution, and large supplies of all sorts were quickly collected and forwarded to camp, where as great plenty reigned before we came away as could be wished for.

"A fleet of 166 sail of transports &c, left Sandy Hook the 24th of December with 6000 troops on board, some say Genl. Clinton also, and thence conjectured that they were destined for Carolina. However that might be, it was impossible for them to keep our coast for many days, a dreadful hurricane which continued fifteen days without interruption having begun on the 1st of the year. There was no account of them the 20th of February when my last letter came from thence.

"The North Carolina and Virginia troops marched to the Southward, as also Baylor's Light Dragoons. I understood that the army at Head Quarters [1] consisted of ten battalions each of 1500

---

[1] Reference is made here to the Morristown, N. J., encampment, winter of 1779–80, when the sufferings of the troops were more intense than at Valley Forge in 1777–78. The following extract from a letter to Jay from Kitty Livingston, his sister-in-law, dated, Phila., Dec. 26, '79, gives interesting details :

"Genl. Washington's quarters are at the widow Ford's house on the road from Morris[town] to Persippiney. Genl. Green's at Arnold's, Genl. Knox at Mr. Duyckings, Lord Sterling at Baskenridge, Genl. Smallwood at Mr. Kembles, Genl. Sullivan at Chatham, two Jersey Brigades at Elizabethtown. The Virginia Brigades have passed thro' town on the way to Charlestown [S. C.] with Colo. Washington's Squadron. We have never had so many troops in winter quarters as at present, and they are exceedingly well situated—good water & fuel all around them. As the Genl. does not meet Mrs. Washington here she sets out early to-morrow for camp. We had yesterday a Christmas dinner in compliment to her at the Chevaliers [Luzerne]. Next Thursday he gives a ball to thirty Ladies ; to-morrow evening we have a Second at Mrs.

men ; the times of many of the Virginia and Maryland troops had just expired but I heard with much pleasure that they were re-enlisting with alacrity. No enterprise of any note had been attempted by either army.

" Our trade is of late become securer than it hath been during the war. Philadelphia, you know, hath some privateers out, and their Letters of Marque and those from Baltimore going out always in small fleets, are not only able to resist, but to overcome any thing that they have met with of late in those seas. Eleven sail came out of Baltimore when we did. They mounted about 120 guns and carried near 2000 hogsheads of tobacco.

" We had accounts that the Spaniards had taken Pensacola and were advancing towards St. Augustine."

JAY TO DE NEUFVILLE & SON.[1]

MADRID, April 27, 1780.

GENTLEMEN :

I have had the pleasure of receiving your favour of the 6th inst., and am much obliged by your kind congratulations on my arrival in Europe.

Holkers. His Excellency intends having concerts once a week at his house— he entertains very generally and with Elegance. I have seen him wear a suit of cloathes of the Countess du la Luzerne's work, which does that Lady great honor. Last Thursday the assemblies commenced, & there are private dances, one a week ; to-morrow Evening there is one at the City tavern. Dr. Cadwallader's death has prevented the young Ladies returning as soon as they intended ; they are expected soon with Mrs. Dickinson to keep house at the Genl's in Second Street. The Genl. has a Son. Mrs. Peters has lost her mother. There has been a death in many families of my most intimate acquaintance. . . . Col. Laurens having resigned his appointment to France the choice of another is now in agitation. Several gentlemen are nominated— Mr. Govr. Morris among the number ; he continues here tho' out of Congress. Mr. Penn is returned to Congress & with him a Mr. Jones in the place of Mr. Hewes [of North Carolina] who died shortly after you left America. I had very good reason to suppose the Lady in the bush had made a conquest of him. He had—poor man—amassed a great fortune in the Southern clime, but paid the price of his health & life without any enjoyment of it."

[1] A firm at Amsterdam, which shipped goods and military stores to America during the war.

The letters you mention to have written to Congress had been received before I left Philadelphia, and referred to a committee. This mark of attention was justly due to the interest you take in the American cause, and the disposition you manifest to serve it. I presume that the committee soon made a report, and that answers to your letters have been written, although perhaps the many hazards to which letters from America are exposed may have prevented their reaching you.

When the rulers of your republic recollect in what manner and on what occasion they became free, I am persuaded they cannot but wish duration to our independence, nor forbear considering it as an event no less interesting to every commercial nation in Europe than important to America. These and similar considerations, added to the injustice they daily experience from England, will, I hope, induce them to call to mind that spirit of their forefathers, which acquired a glorious participation in the empire of the ocean, and laid the foundation of the commerce, affluence, and consideration they transmitted to their posterity.

Permit me to assure you that I shall consider your correspondence as a favour, and that I am, with great respect, etc., JOHN JAY.

JAY TO BENJAMIN FRANKLIN.

MADRID, April 27, 1780.

DEAR SIR :

I am much obliged by the readiness with which my bills were accepted, and am happy to find that the reports respecting the state of others are as false as they have been injurious. At Martinico the Loan Office Bills sold at a considerable discount, and indeed it was no easy matter to sell them at all. I shall take the earliest opportunity of setting them and others right about that matter.

On my return from Aranjues, where I propose to go to-morrow, I shall transmit the papers you mention, with some others equally interesting. I can easily believe that your difficulties have been great and various. They were often the subject of conversation in America, and I am sure your friends, as well as country, will rejoice in the late important success of your negotiations. The French Court, by continuing steady and true to the objects of their treaty with us, will obtain those which induced them to make it. Their conduct towards us hitherto has, I confess, attached me to the whole nation in a degree that I could not have thought myself capable of ten years ago. In my opinion Britain is to be conquered in America, and that it would be more for the interest of her enemies to confine their offensive operations to that point than enfeeble their efforts by attention to many lesser objects. Let America be supplied with money, clothes, and ammunition, and she will, by expelling her enemies and establishing independence, do more essential injury to those imperious islanders than they have sustained for centuries.

What aid this court may be pleased to afford us is not yet ascertained. I hope they will be such as may be proportioned to the common interest, their dignity, and our wants. The minister, I am told, is able, and the King honest. On this ground I place much dependence, for I can hardly suppose that either of them will omit embracing this golden opportunity of acquiring glory to themselves and honour and advantage to their nation by completing the division and ruin of the British Empire, and that by measures which will in so great a degree conciliate the affections as well as esteem of America.

Mrs. Jay has enjoyed more health within this fortnight than she has been blessed with for three months past. She presents her respects to you, and begs that your next letter to me may enclose for her one of the best prints of yourself, which we are told have been published in France, but are not yet to be had here. I believe there is no man of your age in Europe so much a favourite with the ladies.

I am, dear sir, with great esteem and regard,

Your most obedient servant,

JOHN JAY.

JAY TO FLORIDA BLANCA.

ARANJUES, April 29, 1780.

SIR :

By the address of Congress to their constituents on the subject of their finances, which I had the honour of transmitting to your Excellency, you have doubtless observed, that in September last Congress came to a resolution of emitting no more bills than, with those already emitted and in circulation, would amount to 200,000,000 of dollars that, about the same time they called upon their constituents to raise money by taxes, and assigned the first day of January last for the first payment, at which day it was supposed that the bills to be emitted would be nearly expended.

Congress perceiving that at once to stop the great channel of supplies, that had been open ever since the war, and to substitute another equally productive, was not one of those measures which operate almost insensibly without hazard or difficulty ; and well knowing that if the first payment of these taxes should be delayed beyond the limited time, the treasury would be without money, and the public operations obstructed by all the evils consequent to it, they were of opinion that collateral and auxiliary measures were necessary to ensure success to the great system for retrieving and supporting the public credit. So early, therefore, as the 23d day of November last, they took this subject into their most serious consideration, and although they had the highest reason to confide in the exertions of their constituents, yet having received repeated assurances of his Majesty's friendly disposition towards them, and being well persuaded that they could avail themselves of his Majesty's friendship on no occasion more agreeable to him and advantageous to them, than on one so interesting to the United States, and important to the common cause, they adopted a measure which, but for these considerations, might appear extraordinary, viz., to draw bills upon me for £100,000 sterling, payable at six months' sight.

The drawing bills previous to notice of obtaining

money to satisfy them may at first view appear indelicate, but when it is considered that the whole success of this measure depended on its taking place between the 23d of November and the 1st of January last, in which period it was impossible to make the application, his Majesty's magnanimity will I am persuaded readily excuse it.

As I shall always consider it my duty to give your Excellency all the information in my power, that may enable his Majesty from time to time to form a true judgment of the state of American affairs, it is proper, that I should inform your Excellency that Congress, having reasons to believe that a loan might be obtained in Holland, did shortly after my leaving America take measures for that purpose, and on the 23d of November last resolved to draw bills on Mr. Henry Laurens, to whom that business had been committed, for the sum of £100,000 sterling.

I greatly regret that it was not in my power to advise your Excellency of these matters sooner ; but it was not until the 27th instant, at Madrid, that I received the letter which informed me of them.

As further remarks would draw this letter into greater length, than the opinion I have of your Excellency's discernment will permit me to think necessary, I forbear longer to engage your time and attention, than to request the favour of your Excellency to lay it before his Majesty.

The eyes of America are now drawn towards him by their opinion of his virtues, and the situation of their affairs ; and I flatter myself it will not be long before their hearts and affections will also be engaged by such marks of his Majesty's friendship, as his wisdom and liberality may prompt, and their occasions render expedient.

With great respect and esteem, I have the honour to be, etc.

JOHN JAY.

JAY TO GOVERNOR CLINTON.

ARANJUES, 21 MILES FROM MADRID,
6th May, 1780.

DEAR SIR :

As I have not my papers with me, I cannot ascertain the number or dates of my letters to you since I left America. I have often done myself the pleasure of writing to you ; and am in daily expectation of receiving a few lines from you.

The last accounts from America were of the 10th March, contained in two or three Boston newspapers, brought to Bilboa from Newbury. They give us reason, indeed, to expect that your namesake's fleet has been thoroughly dispersed, and his designs on South Carolina thereby defeated. I am anxious for a confirmation of this intelligence ; it would operate in Europe as much to our advantage, though perhaps not so much to our glory, as a victory. As long as you can maintain your importance, and appear neither to want friends or fear foes, you will enjoy respectability on this side of the water, and reap all the advantages resulting from it. By her power, justice, commerce, and consequence, America must expect to gain and keep friends. The equity of her cause is with many only a secondary consideration.

It is said, you have again adopted the system of regulating prices ; I expect no good·from it. What has been done with Vermont ? It would give me pain to hear that things remained in the state I left them. Delay is a trump card that ought not to be permitted to remain in hand.

An English paper contains what they call, but I can hardly believe to be, your confiscation act. If truly printed, New York is disgraced by injustice too palpable to admit even of palliation. I feel for the honour of my country, and therefore beg the favour of you to send me a true copy of it ; that if the other be false, I may, by publishing yours, remove the prejudices against you, occasioned by the former.

I wish to know who are your members in Congress. I find Livingston is one, and am glad of it. What has become of Morris ? Don't let his enemies in or out of the State run him down.

When you write to me, recollect that it is ten to one but your letter will be inspected in its way to me through the post-offices of France or Spain. Write, therefore, under this impression. When you see my old friends, remember me affectionately to them. You know who they are.

> Very sincerely
>> Your most obedient servant,
>>> JOHN JAY.

JAY'S NOTES OF CONFERENCE WITH FLORIDA BLANCA.[1]

ARANJUES, May 11, 1780.

Mr. Jay having waited on the Count de Florida Blanca, in consequence of a message received on the evening of the 10th, the latter commenced the conversation by observing that he was sorry that his ignorance of the English language prevented him from speaking with that ease and frankness with which he wished to speak in his conferences with Mr. Jay, and which corresponded with his own disposition and character.

---

[1] The history of Jay's Spanish Mission appears in full in vols. vii. and viii. of Sparks' "Diplomatic Correspondence." In the present work those portions alone are republished which refer immediately to the points at issue, or which throw Jay's politic management of American interests into relief. The above notes are extracted from his elaborate report to Congress of his attempts at negotiation at the Spanish Court down to May 26, 1780.—See "Diplomatic Correspondence," vol. vii., pp. 220–282. Other reports followed.

Under his instructions and the friendly attitude of France, Jay hoped, first, to secure a treaty of alliance and commerce with Spain, and, second, to obtain from that power the loan of a substantial sum of money and military supplies. After experiencing for more than two years what Sparks describes as "innumerable embarrassments, vexatious delays, cold treatment, and a provoking indifference that would have exhausted the patience, if not ruffled the temper of most men," he met with no success in the former object and very little in the latter. "The Spanish Court," continues Sparks, "seemed nowise inclined to recognize the independence of the United States, or to show them any substantial marks of friendship, and yet there was evidently a willingness to keep on terms, and be prepared to act according to the issue of events. Tardy promises of money were made by the Minister, which he was reluctant to fulfil, and it was with extreme difficulty at last, that Mr. Jay succeeded in procuring from his Catholic Majesty the pitiful loan of one hundred and fifty thousand dollars. He was never received in his public capacity, nor in any other character, than that of a private gentleman empowered to act as Agent for the United States." Jay, moreover, was hampered by the action of Congress. Assuming that Spain would grant the desired loan that body authorized its creditors to draw bills upon Jay before the money was forthcoming and far in excess of the small sums he was able to obtain from time to time. On this point see "Life of Jay," vol. i., pp. 107–110.

He observed that he intended to speak on two points. The first related to the letter Mr. Jay had written to him, on the subject of bills of exchange drawn on him by Congress, that being an affair the most pressing and more immediately necessary to enter upon. He said that the last year he should have found no difficulty on that head, but that at present, although Spain had money, she was in the situation of Tantalus, who, with water in view, could not make use of it; alluding to the revenue arising from their possessions in America, which they were not able to draw from thence. That their expenses had been so great in the year 1779, particularly for the marine, as to oblige them to make large loans, which they were negotiating at present. He entered into a summary of those expenses, and particularized the enormous expense of supporting thirty-five ships of the line and frigates in French ports. He observed, that to do this they had prepared a very expensive and numerous convoy at Ferrol and other ports of Spain, loaded with provisions, naval stores, and every other article necessary for the squadron before mentioned, which convoy did not arrive at Brest until the day on which the Spanish fleet sailed from thence. That the supplies so sent had emptied their magazines at Cadiz, Ferrol, and other ports, and had frequently obliged them to buy at enormous prices the necessary stores to supply the fleet under the admirals Cardova and Gaston, on their arrival in the ports of Spain. That they had been forced to sell these stores thus sent to France, and others purchased for the same purpose at Bordeaux, Nantes, and elsewhere, at half price ; and added, that their loss on this occasion could scarce be calculated. This, joined to the other expenses, and the great losses they had sustained .in their marine and commerce, but chiefly in the former, and the great expenses they were at in consequence thereof, rendered it difficult for the King to do for America what he could have done easily the last year, and which he declared repeatedly, and in the strongest manner, it was his intention to do, as might be judged from his conduct heretofore ; touching slightly on the succours sent us from Spain, the Havana, and Louisiana, but dwelling on his conduct in the negotiation last year with Great Britain, in which he would on no account be brought to sacrifice the interests of America.

Such being his Majesty's disposition and intentions previous to the war, Mr. Jay might easily judge that he was not less determined at present to support their interests, whether formally connected with America by treaty or not. That, notwithstanding the losses and misfortunes sustained, the King's resolution, courage, and fortitude induced him to continue the war, and therefore they were obliged to incur much expense in order to fill their magazines and make necessary preparations for this campaign and the next, yet that it was his Majesty's intention to give America all the assistance in his power. That it was as much his inclination as duty to second these dispositions, and that he had received the King's orders to confer with his colleagues thereon. He observed, however, that, although he was First Secretary of State, he must first confer with them on this subject; and from his own personal inclinations to second the King's intentions and to serve America, he was desirous of concerting with Mr. Jay measures in such a manner as would prevent him from meeting with opposition from his colleagues, and therefore he spoke to him not as a minister, but as an individual.

In order to facilitate this, he said it was necessary to make some overtures for a contract, in case Mr. Jay was not absolutely empowered to make one; and then he pointed out the object most essential to the interests of Spain at the present conjuncture. He said that for their marine they wanted light frigates, cutters, or swift sailing-vessels of that size. That for ships-of-the-line, they could procure them themselves; that if America could furnish them with the former, they might be sent to their ports in Biscay, loaded with tobacco or other produce, and, discharging their cargoes, be left at the disposition of Spain. He also mentioned timber for vessels, but said that was an article not so immediately necessary, though it might be an object of consequence in future. He observed that he mentioned this at present in order that Mr. Jay might turn his thoughts on that subject as soon as possible, and that he would, in order to explain himself with more precision, send him, either on Saturday or Sunday next, notes containing his ideas on this subject, and adding that he hoped that the one, viz., Jay, would assist the other, meaning himself, to manage matters in such a way as to procure the means of obtaining for America present aid.

With respect to the bills of exchange which might be presented, he said that at the end of the present year, or in the beginning of the next, he would have it in his power to advance twenty-five, thirty, or forty thousand pounds sterling, and in the meantime, should these bills be presented for payment, he would take such measures as would satisfy the owners of them, viz., by engaging, in the name of his Majesty, to pay them, observing that the King's good faith and credit were so well known that he did not imagine this would be a difficult matter. He also said that, in consequence of what Mr. Jay had written with respect to clothing for the American army, it might be in his power to send supplies of cloth, etc., which he would endeavour to do.

Mr. Jay, in answer, assured him of his high sense of the frankness and candour with which he had been so obliging as to communicate the King's intentions and his own sentiments, and gave him the strongest assurances that he should, for his part, with the same frankness and candour, give him all the assistance and information in his power to forward his generous intentions in favour of his country, and that he might depend that in doing this he would neither deceive him in his information nor mislead him by ill-grounded expectations.

The Count then expressed his confidence in these assurances, said he had been well informed of the characters both of Mr. Jay and Mr. Carmichael (who was present at the conference), and said that he considered them as *les hommes honnêtes,* and that no consideration could have prevailed upon him to have treated with men who did not sustain that reputation.

The Count then proceeded to the second point, viz., with respect to the treaty in contemplation between Spain and America. He began by observing that he now spoke as a Minister, and as such that he would be as candid and frank as he had just been speaking as a private man ; and that it was always his disposition to do so with those from whom he expected the same conduct. He then proceeded to observe that there was but one obstacle from which he apprehended any great difficulty in forming a treaty with America, and plainly intimated that this arose from the pretensions of America to the navigation of the Mississippi. He repeated the information which the Court had received from M. Miralles, that Congress had at one time relinquished that object ; that he also knew from the same source that afterwards they had made it an essential point of the treaty. He expressed his uneasiness on this subject, and entered largely into the views of Spain with respect to the boundaries. He mentioned Cape Antonio and Cape ———, and expressed their resolution, if possible, of excluding the English entirely from the Gulf of Mexico. They wished to fix them by a treaty, which he hoped would be perpetual between the two countries. He spoke amply of the King's anxiety, resolution, and firmness on this point, and insinuated a wish that some method might be fallen upon to remove this obstacle. He observed that the King had received all his impressions with respect to the necessity of this measure previous to his being in place, and appeared to regard it as a point from which his Majesty would never recede, repeating that still, however, he was disposed to give America all the aid in his power, consistent with the situation of his affairs, to distress the common enemy ; that this point being insisted on, it would be necessary for the Court of Spain to obtain the most accurate knowledge of local circumstances, with which he supposed Mr. Jay and his constituents were more fully apprised than his Majesty's Ministers could be. That for this purpose he had already written to the Havana and Louisiana, in order to obtain all the necessary information, which he gave reason to believe they had not yet received. He dwelt on the necessity of this information previous to any treaty, and expressed his own regret that ways and means could not be found to obviate or overcome this impediment.

Mr. Jay here took an opportunity to mention that many of the States were bounded by that river, and were highly interested in its navigation, but observed that they were equally inclined to enter into any amicable regulations which might prevent any inconveniences with respect to contraband or other objects, which might excite the uneasiness of Spain.

The Count still, however, appeared to be fully of opinion that this was an object that the King had so much at heart that he would never relinquish it, adding, however, that he hoped some middle way might be hit on which would pave the way to get over this difficulty, and desired Mr. Jay to turn his thoughts and attention to the subject, in which, he assured him, he was as well disposed to assist him as in the means of procuring the assistance and succours for America before-mentioned ; always repeating the King's favourable disposition, his inviolable regard to his promises, etc., etc. On this subject he also subjoined that whenever Mr. Jay chose to go to Madrid he desired to have previous notice of it ; for in those cases he would leave his sentiments in writing for him with Mr. Carmichael ; or, if he should also go to Madrid, that he would then write to Mr. Jay there, to which he might return an answer by the *Parle* (a post which goes to and from Madrid) to Aranjues, every twenty-four hours.

Mr. Jay expressed his full confidence in what the Count had done him the honour to communicate to him, and assured him of his satisfaction and happiness in having the good-fortune to transact a business so important to both countries, with a Minister so liberal and candid in his manner of thinking and acting.

The conference ended with much civility on the one part and on the other, and with an intimation from the Count, that he should take an opportunity of having the pleasure of Mr. Jay's company at dinner, and of being on that friendly footing on which he wished to be with him.

What passed in the course of this conference needs no comment, though it calls for information and instructions. If Congress remains firm, as I have no reason to doubt, respecting the Mississippi, I think Spain will finally be content with equitable regulations, and I wish to know whether Congress would consider any regulations necessary to prevent contraband, as inconsistent with their ideas of free navigation. I wish that as little as possible may be left to my discretion, and that as I am determined to adhere strictly to their sentiments and directions, I may be favoured with them fully, and in season.

The Count de Florida Blanca had upon all occasions treated me with so much fairness, candour, and frankness, that between the confidence due to him and the footing I was and ought to be on with the French Ambassador, I was embarrassed exceedingly, especially as there is little reason to doubt of their being on confidential terms with each other. I was reduced to the necessity, therefore, of acting with exquisite duplicity, a conduct which I detest as immoral, and disapprove as impolitic, or of mentioning my difficulties to the Count, and obtaining his answers. I preferred the latter, and wrote the following letter to the Count de Florida Blanca:

ARANJUES, May 12, 1780.

SIR :

It is with the utmost reluctance, that I can prevail upon myself to draw your Excellency's attention from the great objects that perpetually engage it. But the liberality, frankness, and candour, which distinguished your conduct towards me the last evening, have impressed me with such sentiments of correspondent delicacy, as to place me in a most disagreeable situation.

Deeply sensible of the benefits received by my country from their illustrious ally, prompted by duty and inclination to act not only with the highest integrity, but the greatest frankness towards him and his Minister, and influenced by the good opinion I have imbibed of the talents, attachment, and prudence of the Count de Montmorin, I have given him and his Court assurances that he should receive from me all that confidence, which these considerations dictate. These assurances were sincere ; I have most strictly conformed to them, and as no circumstances of delicacy forbid it, I have communicated to him the information I gave your Excellency relative to American affairs, and the resolution of Congress for drawing bills upon me, these being the only transactions within my knowledge and department, which related to that proposed connection between Spain and America, for the accomplishment of which, the King of France has been pleased to interpose his kind offices with his Catholic Majesty.

But, Sir, my feelings will not allow me to permit the confidence due to one gentleman to interfere with that which may be due to another. Honour prescribes limits to each, which no consideration can tempt me to violate. You spoke to me the last evening in the character of a private gentleman, as well as of a public Minister, and in both without reserve. Let me entreat your Excellency therefore to inform me, whether I am to consider your conferences with me, either in the whole or in part, as confidential. I am apprised of the delicacy of this question. I wish I could know your sentiments without putting it. I assure you my esteem and respect are too sincere and too great not to make me regret every measure that can give you an uneasy sensation. On this occasion I am urged by justice to you as well as to myself, and that must be my apology.

Unpractised in the ways of courts, I rejoice in finding that I am to transact the business committed to me with a gentleman, who adorns his exalted station with virtues as well as talents, and looks down on that system of finesse and chicanery which, however prevalent, wisdom rejects and probity disapproves.

With sentiments of attachment and esteem, I have the honour to be, etc.

JOHN JAY.

To this I received the following answer :

[Translation.]

ARANJUES, May 14, 1780.

SIR :

Sensible of the favorable opinion you are pleased to entertain of my conduct, both as a minister and a private gentleman, I have the honor to assure you that, on every occasion, you shall experience nothing but frankness and candour on my part. Besides that my own principles are invariable on these points, I am certain thereby to follow the example and good intentions of the King my master.

The delicacy, which induced you to doubt, whether there would be any impropriety in communicating to the Ambassador of France the explanation we had in the course of our late conference, accords well with the idea I first formed of your character, and I am pleased with this mark of your attention. Besides, it appears to me that you may do it freely, especially as those explanations are founded on principles of equity and wisdom, for the benefit of the common cause. But if, hereafter, circumstances demand a more pointed reserve, by accidents we cannot now foresee, we shall always have time to agree upon those points which it may be necessary to keep secret.

I am, Sir, with the most sincere attachment, and the most perfect consideration, your most humble and most obedient servant,

COUNT DE FLORIDA BLANCA.

JAY ON THE NAVIGATION OF THE MISSISSIPPI.[1]

Mr. Gerard had [in 1778] intimated to Congress the propriety of their taking speedy measures for drawing Spain into the general cause. He often enlarged on the policy and objects of that Court, one of which was to regain the Floridas, and to become possessed of the exclusive navigation of the Gulf of Mexico, and, of course, the Mississippi. He said he was confident that if these were ceded to her, it would not be difficult to induce her to join us ; and especially as the Family Compact, and the refusal of Britain to accept her mediation, would afford a good pretext. He further insinuated, that we might reasonably ex-pect to obtain from that court a considerable sum of

---

[1] The above is an extract from what is described in his "Life," vol. i., p. 95, as " Jay's History of his Spanish Mission "—a paper he appears not to have completed. Its reference to the navigation of the Mississippi gives it an inter-est here in connection with Florida Blanca's first mention of the subject in conference with Jay, as reported in preceding document.

money, which, considering the state of our finances, was a desirable object.

Though Congress was desirous of an alliance with Spain, and ready to take measures for the purpose, yet whom to employ became a serious question. Mr. Lee's connections insisted that he ought to be the man; while others, who had neither a predilection for nor aversion to him, thought it inexpedient to commit that business to one respecting whom America at present entertained doubts, and who had become disagreeable to France, and, consequently, in a certain degree, to Spain. By these unfortunate circumstances nearly a year was wasted in fruitless altercation, and the opportunity of obtaining loans from Spain lost, by her having entered into war, and having occasion for all her money to defray the expense of it.

Some time prior to my appointment to Spain, suspicions of it prevailed, and both Mr. Gerard and Mr. Miralles expressed much satisfaction at the prospect of that event. On my coming to Congress in the fall of 1778, and constantly after, both Mr. Gerard and Mr. Miralles, the Spanish agent, had shown me every mark of civility and attention, though I have reason to think that both of them entertained higher opinions of my docility than were well founded.

As a member of Congress, it appeared to me very improper to make their proceedings a topic of conversation out-of-doors; and I made it an invariable rule not to speak of their debates, or of any matters before them, to any who were not members. Mr. Gerard used very frequently to spend an evening with me, and sometimes sat up very late. As the evening advanced, he often became more open, and spoke without reserve on the subject of the views of Spain, and the interest of America with respect to her. He pressed our quitting to her the Floridas and Mississippi as indispensable prerequisites to a treaty, and urged a variety of reasons to support his opinions; disclaiming, at the same time, his having any instructions on that head, and intimating that his friendship for the United States was his sole motive to declaring his opinion at any time relative to her concerns.

I soon found that he conversed in like manner with many others, and that he was seriously endeavoring to carry these points in Congress.

I was early convinced that provided we could ob-obtain independence and a speedy peace, we could not justify protracting the war, and hazarding the event of it, for the sake of conquering the Floridas, to which we had no title, or retaining the navigation of the Mississippi, which we should not want this age, and of which we might probably acquire a partial use with the consent of Spain. It was therefore my opinion that we should quit all claim to the Floridas, and grant Spain the navigation of her river below our territories, on her giving us a convenient free port on it, under regulations to be specified in a treaty, provided they would acknowledge our independence, defend it with their arms, and grant us either a proper sum of money, or an annual subsidy for a certain number of years. Such, then, was the situation of things as to induce me to think that a conduct so decided and spirited on the part of Spain would speedily bring about a peace, and that Great Britain, rather than hazard the loss of Canada, Nova Scotia, and the islands by continuing the war, would yield the Floridas to Spain, and independence to us. But when Spain afterwards declared war for objects that did not include ours, and in a manner not very civil to our independence, I became persuaded that we ought not to cede to her any of our rights, and of course that we should retain and insist upon our right to the navigation of the Mississippi.

JOHN ADAMS TO JAY.

PARIS, May 13th, 1780.

DEAR SIR:

I had two days ago the pleasure of yours of the 26th of April, and am very happy to have at last received from your hand an account of your safe arrival in that Capital.

The Count de F. Blanca is agreed to be a man of abilities, but somehow or other, there is something in the European understanding different from that we have been more used to. Men of the greatest abilities, and the most experience, are with great difficulty brought to see, what appears to us as clear as day. It is habit, it is education, prejudice, what you will, but so it is. I can state a very short argument, that appears to me a demonstration, upon French and Spanish principles alone, that it is more for their interest to employ their naval force in America than in Europe, yet it is in vain that you state this to a minister of state; he cannot see it, or feel it, at least in its full force, and until the proper point of time is past and it is too late. So I think it may be demonstrated, that it is in the interest of France and Spain to furnish America with an handsome loan of money, or even to grant them subsidies, because a sum of money thus expended would advance the common cause, and even their particular interests, by enabling the Americans to make greater exertions, than the same sums employed in any other way. But it is in vain to reason in this manner with an European minister of state. He cannot understand you. It is not within the compass of those ideas that he has been accustomed to. I am happy, however, that at length we have a Minister at Madrid. I am persuaded that this will contribute vastly to opening the eyes both of France and Spain. I shall be obliged to you for intelligence, especially concerning your progress in your affair.

I am with much Esteem,
Dear Sir, your Servant,
JOHN ADAMS.

JOHN ADAMS TO JAY.

PARIS, May 15th, 1780.

DEAR SIR:

I shall not always stand upon ceremony nor wait for answers to letters, because useful hints may be given which would be lost if one were to wait returns of posts.

The Channel fleet is reckoned this year at from thirty to thirty-seven ships of the Line, but it is well known that they depend upon seamen to be pressed from their first West Indian fleet in order to make up this computation, without which they cannot man thirty. It is therefore of great importance that this first West India fleet should be intercepted. It will come home the latter end of June or beginning of July, certainly not before the middle of June. A ship or two of the Line with a fifty gun ship or two and five or six frigates, would have a great probability of intercepting this fleet. Is there any service upon which such a number of vessels could be better employed than in cruising pretty far in the Bay of Biscay and somewhat north of Cape Clear with this view. It is really astonishing that France and Spain should be so inattentive to the English convoys. The safest, easiest, surest way of reducing the power and the spirits of the English is to intercept their trade. It is every year exposed, yet every year escapes; by which means they get spirits to indulge their passions, money to raise millions and men to man their ships.

Pray is it not necessary to think a little of Portugal? Should not Spain, France and America too, use their influence with Portugal to shut her ports against the armed vessels of all nations at war, or else freely admit the armed vessels of all? Under her present system of neutrality as they call it, the ports of Portugal are as advantageous to England as any of her own, and more injurious to the trade of Spain and America, if not of France, while they are of no use at all to France, Spain or America. This little impotent morsel of a State ought not to do so much mischief so unjustly. If she is neutral, let her be neutral—not say she is neutral and be otherwise. Would it not be proper for Congress to evince some sensibility to the injuries the United States receive from these States, such as Denmark and Portugal? I think they should remonstrate coolly and with dignity—not go to war, nor be in a passion about it, but show that they understand their behaviour. Denmark restored Jones's and Landais' prizes to England without knowing why. Why would it not do to remonstrate, then prohibit any productions of Portugal from being consumed in America?

The prospect brightens in the West Indies. De Giuchen has arrived. De la Motte Piquet has defended himself very well, secured his convoys, fought the English even with inferior force and got the better. De Giuchen's appearance dissipated all thoughts of their expedition, and threw the English Islands into great consternation. But you will see in the public prints all the news which the two Courts have received, Versailles and London. The force from Brest which sailed the 2nd and that from Cadiz, which I hope sailed as soon or sooner, will not diminish the terror and confusion of the English in America and the Islands.

J. A.

JAY TO HIS FATHER.

MADRID, 23d May, 1780.

DEAR SIR :

Various have been the scenes through which I have passed since last we bid each other farewell. Some of them have been dangerous, and many of them disagreeable. Providence has, however, been pleased to bring me safe through them all to the place of my destination, and I hope will restore me to my country and friends as soon as the business committed to me shall be completed. Then I shall have the pleasure of entertaining you with the recital of many interesting matters which the risk to which all my letters are exposed forbids me to commit to paper.

I will, nevertheless, give you some little account of our journey from Cadiz to Madrid, because as the manner of travelling here differs entirely from that of our country it may afford you some amusement. The distance is between three and four hundred English miles. We were told at Cadiz that it would be necessary to take with us beds, hams, tea, sugar, chocolate, and other articles of provision, as well as kitchen utensils for dressing them, for that we should seldom find either on the road. We were further informed that these journeys were usually performed in carriages resembling a coach and drawn by six mules, the hire of which was from a hundred and thirty to a hundred and fifty dollars, and that they would carry near a thousand weight of baggage. We accordingly made the necessary provision for eating and sleeping comfortably by the way. We crossed the bay of Port St. Mary's in very pleasant weather and in a handsome boat which the brother of the Minister of Indies was so kind as to lend us. We staid a night in that place waiting for carriages, and were very hospitably entertained by Count O'Reilly, the same who established the Spanish government at New Orleans at the end of the last war. He is a man of excellent abilities and great knowledge of men as well as of things. He has risen to be Inspector and Lieutenant-General of the armies of Spain, into which he introduced a degree of discipline to which they had long been stangers, and Captain-Governor of Andalusia, etc.

.   .   .   .   .   .

We travelled at the rate of between twenty and thirty miles a day, and the same mules brought us to Madrid that we set out with from Cadiz, at which they had arrived from Madrid only a day before we left it. We stopped but once in the course of the day. At the end of the journey they appeared to be in as much flesh and spirits as when we set out. The manner of driving them is in my opinion greatly to their disadvantage, very fast up and down hill and slow on plain ground. I had no idea of there being animals of this kind in the world so fine. I am convinced that they are stronger as well as more durable than horses, though not so handsome. One reason perhaps why the mules of this country exceed those of others, is that the generality of their horses are better. The Andalusian horses, of which you have often heard. are noble animals, handsome, sprightly, and well-tempered. It is more than probable that when I return home I shall take a couple of mules with me ; I am more than satisfied that two very good mules are worth three very good horses.

The Poradas or inns are more tolerable than had been represented to us. Many of them had very good rooms, but swarming with fleas and bugs. The mules were generally lodged under the same roof, and my bedroom has frequently been divided from them by only a common partition. The innkeepers gave themselves little trouble about their guests further than to exact as much from them as possible. . . . At one tavern we dined late, and, except the Colonel, went to bed without supper. We took breakfast in the morning. Our servants, four in number, ate of the provisions they brought, except a little bread and milk, and we all slept in our own beds. When the reckoning was called it amounted to 477 reals, that is, £9 10s. 9d. York money. They charged us for fourteen beds, though our number, including servants, amounted only to eight. On observing this to them, we were told that there were many beds in the rooms in which we had slept and in others communicating with them, and that we might have used them all if we pleased. We remarked that it was impossible for eight persons to use fourteen beds; they replied, that was not their fault. There was no remedy, and I paid after taking an account of the particulars with a receipt at the foot of it, which I keep as a curiosity.

I am told that these impositions arise from this circumstance: The houses in which these Poradas are kept generally belong to great men, who for rent and license to keep tavern demand from the poor wretches much more than they can honestly get by that business, and thence they are driven to make up the deficiency by the iniquitous practices. The landlords know this, and to enjoy their high rents support their tenants against travellers and take care that the latter be losers by all disputes with innkeepers. Besides, as travellers cannot remain long enough at one place to prosecute and abide the event of such litigations, they generally put up with the first loss.

On the subject of politics, I make it a rule to write to none but Congress.

Love to all the family, I am, dear sir,

Your dutiful and affectionate son.

P. S.—I bought a very fine negro boy of fifteen years old at Martinico.

JAY TO FLORIDA BLANCA.

Mr. Jay presents his most respectful compliments to his Excellency, Count de Florida Blanca, and has the honour of informing his Excellency that his health is so far re-established as to enable him now to attend to the papers which his Excellency was so polite as to postpone sending him on that account; and that Mr. Jay purposes to be at Aranjues next Wednesday, unless, contrary to his expectations, his fever should return.

MADRID, 24th May, 1780.

JAY TO THE PRESIDENT OF CONGRESS.[1]

MADRID, May 26, 1780.

SIR:

The house of Gardoqui at Bilboa are rich, in favour with the ministry, and friends to America. The Navy Board have sent to them for goods for the use of the navy, and have remitted to them only an inconsiderable part of the sum to which they will amount, desiring the residue on credit, and promising speedy payment. One of the house now here spoke to me on the subject; I advised him to complete the orders. It is of the utmost consequence that the Navy Board be punctual in their remittances. American credit is not high, and ought to be higher. I am the more anxious on this subject, as that house is exceedingly well disposed, and a disappointment would not only be injurious to them, but much more so to us. Perhaps it would be a good rule if the United States were to contract debt only with governments, and never with individuals abroad.

I received a letter last week from a Captain Haw-

---

[1] This is the closing portion of Jay's official communication to Congress, mentioned in note to " Jay's Notes of Conference " etc., May 11th *ante*.

kins at Cadiz, informing me that the Americans, who had escaped from captivity and were collected there, were fitting out a vessel for America, which they were arming, and wished to be enabled to act offensively and defensively on their way home, by having a proper commission from me for that purpose. As I had neither blank commissions nor authority to grant them, I referred him to Dr. Franklin.

Congress will be pleased to consider how far it may be proper to remove these obstacles, by sending me both. This leads me again to remind your Excellency of several letters I wrote you from Cadiz, respecting American seamen coming to Spain from captivity at Gibraltar and other places. As copies of these letters have been sent by different vessels, I presume some of them have reached you. It certainly is necessary that provision be made for these people, and in a regular established manner. I am very desirous of instructions on this subject.

The credit given me by Congress on Dr. Franklin is expended, and I am without other means of obtaining supplies than by private credit, which I am at a loss to satisfy. To apply to, and be maintained by, the Court, is, in my opinion, too humiliating to be for the public good ; and as yet I have neither received nor heard of remittances from America. It would give me pleasure to know in what manner Congress mean I should be supplied, and whether any measures have been taken for that purpose.

I am much embarrassed for the means of conveying and receiving intelligence. Being at a great distance from the sea, all my letters to and from thence here must either be conveyed by private couriers or the public post. All my letters by the latter, whether in France or Spain, are opened. By that conveyance, therefore, it would not always be proper to write either to Congress, to Dr. Franklin, Mr. Adams, or others, with that freedom which would often be useful, and sometimes necessary. The salary allowed me, so far from admitting the expense of private couriers, is inadequate for the common purposes for which it was given. This is a delicate subject, and I wish it was not my duty to say any thing respecting it. This place is the dearest in Europe. The Court is never stationary, passing part of the year in no less than five different places, viz., Madrid, Pardo, Aranjues, St. Ildefonso, and the Escurial; hence considerable expenses arise. I forbear enumerating particulars, my design being only to mention this matter to Congress, not to press it upon them. I shall always live agreeably to my circumstances; and if, from their being too narrow, inconveniences result to the public, they ought to be informed of it. I hope what I have said will be viewed in this light only; so far as I am personally interested, I am content.

Mr. Harrison, a gentleman of Maryland, now here, will be the bearer of this letter to Cadiz. I therefore embrace this good and unusual opportunity of being so minute and explicit in it.

The family of Galvez is numerous and of weight. The one on the Mississippi has written favourably of the Americans to his brothers here, three of whom are in office. It would be well to cultivate this disposition whenever opportunities of doing it offer.

The resolution providing for Spanish prisoners at New York was well judged.

Dr. Franklin is more advantageously circumstanced than I am to gain and transmit to Congress intelligence of the disposition of Holland and of the Northern Powers.

From the conduct of their Ministers here, I have no reason to predict much to our advantage. They are cold, and I have received nothing more than common civility from any of them, except the Ministers of Holland and Sweden, and indeed not much more from them. Perhaps they have been rendered unusually cautious by an extract of a letter from Madrid in the Leyden paper, mentioning the precious reception Mr. Carmichael met with here, and the attentions he received from the foreign Ministers. You have probably seen it in the *Courier de l'Europe.*

From what I hear of the character of the Empress of Russia, I cannot but think that a prudent agent there would be very useful. They say she is sensible, proud, and ambitious. Hence I infer that such a mark of attention would be grateful, and consequently useful.

I should have given your Excellency seasonable intelligence of the Spanish fleet and armament, which lately sailed from Cadiz, as I believe to the Havana, and whose objects I suspect to be the Floridas or Jamaica, or probably both, but I omitted writing on that subject previous to the departure of the fleet, from a persuasion that any letters by the post containing such advices would not be permitted to proceed, and therefore I thought it unnecessary ; nor will I now swell the pages of this letter, already very voluminous, by entering into particulars relative to it, especially as that armament will probably have begun its operations before this letter will come to your Excellency's hands.

The reports of dissensions in Congress, which prevailed here prior to my arrival, and the causes to which they were ascribed, had filled this Court with apprehensions ; and it gives me pleasure to assure you that the present appearance of union in Congress is attended here with very happy effects.

The people in this country are in almost total darkness about us. Scarce any American publications have reached them, nor are they informed of the most recent and important events in that country. The affairs of Stony Point, Paulus Hook, etc., etc., had never been heard of here, except perhaps by the great officers of state, and they could scarcely believe that the Roman Catholic religion was even tolerated there.

There are violent prejudices among them against us. Many of them have even serious doubts of our being civilized, and mention a strange story of a ship driven into Virginia by distress, about thirty years ago, that was plundered by the inhabitants, and some of the crew killed in a manner and under circumstances which, if true, certainly indicate barbarity. The King and Ministry are warm, yet I have reason to believe that the bulk of the nation is cold, toward us ; they appear to me to like the English, hate the French, and to have prejudices against us.

I mention these things to show in a stronger light the necessity of punctuality in sending me from time to time all American intelligence of importance, and observing such conduct towards Spaniards in general as may tend to impress them with more favourable sentiments of us. There was a little uneasiness among the mercantile people at Cadiz respecting the capture of some Spanish vessels by privateers. I hope the former have had ample justice done them ; it certainly is of great importance that they should have reason to be satisfied.

Your Excellency may observe that I have written very particularly. Both this Court and that of France have very particular information respecting the proceedings of Congress.

Want of prudence, rather than virtue, I believe to be the cause. I nevertheless think it my duty to give Congress from time to time full information of their affairs here, and shall not be restrained by the apprehension of any consequences that may result from want of secrecy there. I make it a rule to write on these subjects only to Congress, and to them very particularly.

I have the honour to be, etc.,

JOHN JAY.

P. S.—Congress may think it extraordinary that Mr. Carmichael's handwriting does not appear in this letter. He is, with my approbation, now at

Aranjues, and I must do him the justice to say that he is always ready and willing to do his duty as Secretary.

J. J.

ARANJUES, 4 June, 1780.

DEAR SIR :

There is a distinction between ceremony and attention which is not always observed though often useful. Of the former I hope there will be little between us ; of the latter much. Public as well as personal considerations dictate this conduct on my part, and I am happy to find that you mean not to be punctilious. The hints contained in your letter correspond much with my own sentiments, and I shall endeavor to diffuse them.

This Court seems to have great respect for the old adage *festina lente*, at least as applied to our independence. The Count D' Florida Blanca has hitherto pleased me. I have found in him a degree of frankness and candour which indicates probity. His reputation for talents is high. The acknowledgment of independence is retarded by delays which in my opinion ought not to affect it. The influence of that measure on the sentiments and conduct of our enemy, as well as the neutral nations, makes it an object very important to the common cause. Its suspension I cannot think is necessary to the adjustment of the articles of treaties ; they might just as well be settled afterwards. As America is and will be independent in fact, the being so in name can be of no real moment to her individually. But Britain derives hopes from the hesitation of Spain very injurious to the common cause, and I am a little surprised that the policy of destroying these hopes does not appear more evident. If the delay proceeds from expectations that may affect the source of treaty, it is not probable they will be realized. America is to be attacked by candour, generosity, confidence, and good offices; a contrary conduct will not conciliate or persuade.

But whatever may be the cause of the mistakes on this subject, I must do them the justice to say that the general assurances given me by the Count D'Florida Blanca argue a very friendly disposition in the Court towards us, and I hope events will prove them to have been sincere. They certainly must be convinced that the power of the United States, added to that of Britain and under her direction, would enable her to give law to the Western World, and that Spanish America and the Islands would then be at her mercy. Our country is at present so well disposed to Spain, and such cordial enemies to Britain, that it would be a pity this disposition should not be cherished. Now is the time for France and Spain to gain the affections of that extensive country; such an opportunity may never offer.

France has acted wisely. I wish similar councils may prevail here. Would it not be a little extraordinary if Britain should be before Spain in acknowledging our independence? If she had wisdom left she would do it ; she may yet have a lucid interval, though she has been very long out of her senses. Spain will be our neighbor ; we both have territory enough to prevent our coveting each other, and I should be happy to see that perfect amity and cordial affection established between us which would ensure perpetual peace and harmony to both.·

I cannot write you particulars, but nothing here appears to be certain as yet. I shall in all my letters advise Congress to rely principally on themselves ; to fight out their own cause at any hazard, with spirit, and not to rely too much on the expectation of events which may never happen.

Have you received any late letters from America ? Mrs. Jay received one from her sister of the 10th of April, which mentioned several having been sent home by the way of France. I hear of many letters but receive scarce any.

I am, dear sir,

Your most obedient servant,

JOHN JAY.

P. S.—My compliments to Mr. Dana.

FLORIDA BLANCA TO JAY.[1]

[Translation.]

ARANJUES, June 7, 1780.

His Catholic Majesty would be very glad to be able to furnish, at the present crisis, funds for the payment of the one hundred thousand pounds sterling, proposed to be ad-

---

[1] On November 6, 1780, Jay transmitted to Congress his second elaborate report of proceedings at Madrid, which appears in " Diplomatic Correspond-

dressed to Mr. Jay, in order to evince the concern which the King takes in the prosperity and relief of the United States of North America, as well as in the personal satisfaction of the above mentioned gentleman. But the demands of the present war, and the great difficulty there would be to transport hither the treasures of the King's possessions in that part of the world, render it impracticable to furnish here the said sum in specie, as could be wished. Some expedient, however, may be found to remedy this inconvenience. For example; if the owners of the bills of exchange would be content with the security or responsibility of his Catholic Majesty, to pay the sum already mentioned in the term of two years. The King will readily agree to such an arrangement, even if it should be found necessary to add a moderate interest. This security, given by such a sovereign as the King of Spain, would induce the owners of those bills of exchange, and the creditors of Congress to consent to a measure so advantageous, and would equally serve to sustain the credit and good faith of the same body.

Mr. Jay, therefore, is entreated to reflect on the idea just stated to him, and in answer to inform us what measures he thinks suitable to this scheme, in order that they may be laid before the King, and his orders taken thereon. If the expedient in question should be adopted, it will at the same time be necessary to take measures in concert to reimburse to the King this considerable sum, as well as others already expended in favor of the United States. The first idea which offers for reciprocal convenience is, that Congress should engage to build without delay some

---

ence," vol. iii., pp. 306–389, the first report being referred to in note under date of May 11, 1780. In the November report, he introduces " Notes " of further conferences with Florida Blanca or his representatives. The above letter followed an unimportant interview held June 2d. Other conferences, which resulted in little more than the expressions of " assurances " on the part of Spain, were held on July 5th and September 22d.

handsome frigates and other smaller vessels of war, fixing
the price of each, and the time when they will be finished.

This point once settled, it will be proper immediately to
take measures to equip these vessels as fast as they are
ready; to point out what articles will be necessary to send
from Spain for this purpose, and in what port they will
have notice to receive them. After this it is expedient to
be informed, whether the Americans themselves will engage to come to the ports of Bilboa, St. Ander, Ferrol, or
Cadiz, for the said articles, which they will find ready, and
.fterwards transport them in their own vessels of war or
letters of marque to America. On this supposition it is
conjectured, that it would be easy to find hands enough in
America to man these new built vessels, which will sail
under Spanish colors. There are certainly among the
subjects of the said United States many who have made
the voyage, and are acquainted with the usual route of the
ships of the English East India Company, and who know
perfectly well the ports and places at which they stop.
This fact established, it is proposed to equip in the ports of
the United States four good frigates, and some other lighter
vessels, with the effects which shall be sent from hence
on account of Spain. This small squadron, under Spanish
colors, shall be employed to intercept the convoys of the
said Company by cruising in the proper latitudes. The
measures just pointed out appear to be the most proper to
reimburse, in some shape, the expenses already incurred by
his Catholic Majesty, and to answer for such security as has
been proposed to be given in this memoir. It being always
understood, that a share of the prizes taken from the English
by this small squadron shall be given to the crews, and
even to Congress, in proportion to the assistance which
they shall furnish for the equipment of the vessel.

A speedy and decisive answer to all the points here
enumerated is requested, and Mr. Jay is too enlightened not
to perceive that the common cause is interested therein.

JAY TO FLORIDA BLANCA.

ARANJUES, June 9, 1780.

SIR :

The propositions which your Excellency did me the honour to send on the 7th inst., have been considered with all the attention which their great importance demands.

The evidence they contain of his Majesty's friendly disposition towards the United States will, I am persuaded, make correspondent impressions on the citizens of America ; and permit me to assure you that his Majesty's desire of contributing to my personal satisfaction, by measures conducive to the welfare of my country, has excited my warmest acknowledgments and attachment.

The enlarged ideas my constituents entertain of the power, wealth, and resources of Spain are equal to those they have imbibed of the wisdom and probity of his Catholic Majesty, and of that noble and generous system of policy which has induced him to patronize their cause, and, by completing their separation from Great Britain, effectually to disarm the latter. Such wise and liberal designs, followed by such great and extensive consequences, would add a bright page to the annals of a reign already signalized by important events. It is, therefore, with deep regret that Congress would receive information that the aid they solicit, small when compared with their ideas of the resources of Spain, has been rendered impracticable by the expenses of a war, which, on the part of Spain, is of a recent date. Nor will their disappointment be less than their regret, when they find their credit diminished by the failure of a measure, from the success of which they expected to raise it.

The kind disposition of his Majesty to become responsible at the expiration of two years for the amount of the bills in question, and that even with interest, is a proof of his goodness, by which I am confident the United States will consider themselves greatly obliged. But when it is considered that bills of exchange, immediately on being drawn or sold, become a medium in commerce, and pass through various hands in satisfaction of various mercantile contracts ; that the drawer and every endorser become responsible for their credit at every transfer ; and that the object of the merchants last holding the bills, as well as of all other merchants, is money in hand or actively employed in trade, and not money lying still, at an interest greatly inferior to the usual profits to be gained in commerce ; I say, on considering these things, it appears to me that, although no objection can be made to the good faith of his Majesty, which is acknowledged by all the world, yet that the last holders of the bills will prefer recovering the amount of them, with the usual damages on protests, to delay of payment for two years with interest.

Should these bills, therefore, meet with this fate, his Majesty will readily perceive its influence on the credit, operations, and feelings of the United States ; on the common cause ; on the hopes and spirits of the enemy. The necessity or prudence which detains his

Majesty's treasure in his American dominions is an unfortunate circumstance at a time when it might be so usefully employed. There is, nevertheless, room to hope that the great superiority of the allied fleets and armaments in the American seas will, in the course of a year or eighteen months, render its transportation safe and easy, and that the greater part of it may arrive before the bills in question would become payable. This will appear more probable, when the time necessary to sell these bills, and the time which will be consumed in their passage from America, and the time which will be employed in their journey from different ports of Europe to this place, are all added to the half a year which is allotted for the payment of them after they have been presented. I am authorized and ready to engage and pledge the faith of the United States for the punctual repayment, with interest, and within a reasonable term, of any sums of money which his Majesty may be so kind as to lend them.

As to the aids heretofore supplied to the United States, I am without information relative to the precise terms on which they were furnished, as well as their amount. When I left Congress, they appeared to me not to possess full and positive intelligence on these points. I ascribe this, not to omissions in their commissioner, who then had the direction of these affairs, but to those miscarriages and accidents to which the communication of intelligence to a distant country is liable in time of war. If it should appear proper to your Excellency, in order that I may be furnished with an accurate and full statement of these transactions, I will do myself the honour of transmitting them immediately to Congress ; and, as they happened prior to my appointment, I shall request particular instructions on the subject.

With respect to the plan proposed for the repayment of such sums as Spain may lend to the United States, viz., by the latter furnishing the former with frigates, etc., etc., I beg leave to submit the following remarks to your Excellency's consideration. In the United States there are timber, iron, masts, shipwrights, pitch, tar, and turpentine ; and Spain can furnish the other requisites. But neither the timber, the iron, the masts, nor the other articles can be procured without money. The Congress are in great want of money for the immediate purposes of self-defence, for the maintenance of their armies and vessels of war, and for all the other expenses incident to military operations. The Congress, pressed by their necessities, have emitted bills of credit, till the depreciation of them forbids further emissions. They have made loans from their great and good ally, and, in aid of the system of gaining supplies by taxation and domestic loans, they have, for the reasons which I have already had the honour of explaining to your Excellency, drawn upon me the bills before mentioned. These bills will be sold in the United States for paper money, and that money will be immediately wanted for the purposes I have enumerated. If, therefore, this money was to be turned into frigates, the obvious ends of drawing those bills would not be attained. The war against the United States has raged without intermission for six years already, and it will not be in their power to pay their debts during its further continuance, nor until the return of peace and uninterrupted commerce shall furnish them with the means of doing it.

That excellent frigates and other vessels may be built in America cheaper than in Europe, I am persuaded. And I know, that Congress will cheerfully give every aid in their power to facilitate the execution of any plan of that kind which his Majesty may adopt, but, Sir, their necessities will not permit them to supply money to those purposes, and I should deceive your Excellency with delusive expectations were I to lead you to think otherwise. I would rather, that the United States should be without money than without good faith ; and, therefore, neither my own principles of action, nor the respect due to his Majesty and reputation of my country, will ever suffer me (if my authority extended so far) to enter into any contracts which I had not the highest reason to believe would be fully, fairly, and punctually performed on the part of my constituents. Nor, in case his Majesty should think proper to cause frigates to be built in America, can I encourage your Excellency to expect that they could be easily manned there for cruises. The fact is, that the American frigates often find difficulties in completing their complements, principally because the seamen prefer going in privateers, which are numerous, and too useful to be discouraged.

invaded, will be more fluctuating than those of Spain, and measures in which they might conveniently embark at one period may shortly after be rendered impracticable by the vicissitudes of war. It is further to be observed, that a people, rising amidst such terrible struggles, with an extensive country to defend, and that country invaded, and, as it were, on fire in several places at once, are not in good condition for foreign enterprises ; but, on the contrary, that it must generally be their interest, and of course their policy, to keep their forces and strength at home, till the expulsion of their enemies shall afford them leisure and opportunities for distant and offensive operations.

Whenever this period shall arrive, his Majesty may be assured, that the United States will not remain idle, but that, impelled by resentments too deep and too just to be transitory, as well as by unshaken attachment to their friends, they will persevere with firmness and constancy in the common cause, and cheerfully unite their efforts with those of France and Spain, in compelling the common enemy to accept of reasonable terms of peace. I can, also, with great confidence, assure your Excellency that the United States will be happy in every opportunity, which may offer during the war, of joining their arms to those of Spain, and in co-operating with them in any expeditions, which circumstances may render expedient against the Floridas, or other objects. The Americans would most cheerfully fight by the side of the Spaniards, and by spilling their blood in the same cause, and on the same occasion, convince them of their ardent desire to become their faithful friends and steadfast allies.

I cannot prevail upon myself to conclude, without expressing to your Excellency my apprehension of the anxiety and painful concern with which Congress would receive intelligence of the failure of their bills, and especially after the expectations they have been induced to conceive of the successful issue of their affairs here. What conclusions the enemy would draw from the inability of Spain to advance the sum in question, even to men actually in arms against Great Britain, I forbear to mention, nor would it become me to point out the several evil consequences flowing from such an event, to those who enjoy from nature and experience more discernment than I am blessed with.

I still flatter myself that some expedients may be devised to surmount the present difficulties, and that the harvest of laurels now ripening for his Majesty in America will not be permitted to wither for want of watering.

Influenced by this hope, I shall delay transmitting any intelligence respecting this matter to Congress, till your Excellency shall be pleased to communicate to me his Majesty's further pleasure on the subject.

I have the honour to be, etc.,

JOHN JAY.

BENJAMIN FRANKLIN TO JAY.

PASSY, June 13th, 1780.

DEAR SIR:

Yesterday, and not before, is come to hand your favour of April 14th, with the packets and despatches from Congress, etc., which you sent me by a French gentleman to Nantes.

Several of them appear to have been opened, the paper around the seals being smoked and burnt, as with the flame of a candle used to soften the wax, and the impression defaced. The curiosity of people in this time of war is unbounded. Some of them only want to see news, but others want to find (through interested views) what chance there is of a speedy peace. Mr. Ross has undertaken to forward the letters to England. I have not seen them ; but he tells me they have all been opened. I am glad, however, to receive the despatches from Congress, as they communicate to me Mr. Adams's instructions, and other particulars of which I have been long ignorant.

I am very sensible of the weight of your observation, " that a constant interchange of intelligence and attentions between the public servants at the different courts, is necessary to procure to their constituents all the advantages capable of being derived from their appointment." I shall endeavour to perform my part with you, as well as to have the pleasure of your correspondence, as from a sense of duty. But my time is more taken up with matters extraneous to the functions of a minister, than you can possibly imagine. I have written often to the Congress to establish consuls in the ports, and ease me of what relates to maritime and mercantile affairs ; but no notice has yet been taken of my request.

A number of bills of exchange, said to be drawn by order of Congress on Mr. Laurens, are arrived in Holland. A merchant there has desired to know of me, whether, if he accepts them, I will engage to reimburse him. I have no orders or advice about them from Congress ; do you know to what amount they have drawn ? I doubt I cannot safely meddle with them. . . .

Mrs. Jay does me much honour in desiring to have one of the prints that have been made here of her countryman. I send what is said to be the best of five or six engraved by different hands, from different paintings. The verses at the bottom are truly extravagant. But you must know that the desire of pleasing by a perpetual rise of compliments in this polite nation, has so used up all the common expressions of approbation, that they are become flat and insipid, and to use them almost implies censure. Hence music, that formerly might be sufficiently praised when it was called *bonne*, to go a little farther they called it *excellente*, then *superbe*, *magnifique*, *exquise*, *celeste*, all which, being in their turns worn out, there only remains *divine ;* and when that is grown as insignificant as its predecessors, I think they must return to common speech and common sense ; as from vying with one another in fine and costly paintings on their coaches, since I first knew the country, not being able to go farther in that way, they have returned lately to plain carriages, painted without arms or figures, in one uniform colour.

The league of neutral nations to protect their commerce is now established. Holland, offended by fresh insults from England, is arming vigorously. That nation has madly brought itself into the greatest distress, and has not a friend in the world.

With great and sincere esteem,
    I am, dear sir,
        Your most obedient and most humble servant,
            BENJAMIN FRANKLIN.

JAY TO LEWIS LITTLEPAGE.[1]

DEAR SIR :   MADRID, 16th June, 1780.

Your favour of the 30th ult. has been delivered to me. It gives me pleasure to hear you are in a French gentleman's family, as you will there have an oppor-

---

[1] Littlepage, a young gentleman from Virginia placed by his uncle under Jay's care in Spain. Some years later he attempted to injure his patron's reputation by false accusations. See correspondence between them in Jay's " Life," vol. i., pp. 204-228.

tunity of learning . pronunciation as well as grammar. As you will doubtless read French books, I think it would be well to choose such as would teach you things as well as languages, and of things there are few more useful than those which lead to a knowledge of mankind. History and memoirs are of this class ; of the latter, the memoirs of the late Marshal Duke D'Noialles merit attention ; they respect recent and important transactions.

I am, dear sir,
Your most obedient servant,
JOHN JAY.

JAY TO FLORIDA BLANCA.

SIR : MADRID, June 22, 1780.

I received the note your Excellency did me the honour to write on the 20th instant, and I take the earliest opportunity of expressing my thanks for your Excellency's permission to accept the bills mentioned in it, which I have accordingly done.

Agreeably to your Excellency's recommendation in the first conference, I have turned my thoughts very seriously to the objects which were the subjects of it, relative to the bills drawn upon me ; they were two.

1st. The means of paying these bills.

2dly. The proposed contract with America for light vessels, etc.

With respect to the *first*, it appeared to me that the principal difficulty was removed by your Excellency's informing me, "*that at the end of the present year it would be in your power to advance twenty-five, thirty, or forty thousand pounds sterling.*" Hence I inferred that as much time would be taken up in the sale, negotiation, and transmission of those bills, and as so long a space as six months was assigned for their payment, after being presented, the sums which it would be in your Excellency's power to advance at the end of the year would probably be equal to the amount of the bills which would then become payable; and that in the meantime such further means might be provided as would obviate difficulties with respect to those that might afterwards become due. When I reflected that I was a stranger to the resources of Spain, and that your Excellency's acknowledged abilities comprehended all the objects and combinations necessary in determining what supplies they were capable of affording, and the manner and means most proper for the purpose, it appeared to me in the light of presumption to hazard to your Excellency any propositions on the subject.

2dly. On considering the proposed contract, it became important to distinguish between the building these vessels with the money of the United States, or with that of Spain. The latter was very practicable, and I gave your Excellency that opinion in my letter of the 9th instant. The former, on the contrary, appeared to me not to be within the power of the United States, and candour obliged me to make this known to your Excellency in the same letter.

I knew it to be impossible for Congress, consistent with good faith, to contract; that, notwithstanding their great want of money, the injuries of a six years' war, and their being actually invaded, they would repay immediately the monies lent them, either in ships or otherwise. It is not uncommon for ancient and opulent nations to find it necessary to borrow money in time of war, but I believe it very seldom happens that they find it convenient to pay those debts till the return of peace. If this be the case with powerful and long-established nations, more cannot be expected from a young nation brought forth by oppression, and rising amidst every species of violence and devastation which fire, sword, and malice can furnish for their destruction.

If attentive only to obtaining payment of these bills, and thereby relieving my country from the complicated evils which must result from their being protested, I had entered into the proposed engagements for immediate repayment, by building vessels, etc.,—if I had done this, notwithstanding a full conviction that the contract so made could not be fulfilled, my conduct, however convenient in its immediate consequences, would have been highly reprehensible. This reflection, therefore, will I hope convince your Excellency of the purity of my intentions, and induce you to ascribe my objections to the contract to want of ability, and not to want of inclination, in the United States to perform it. No consideration will ever prevail upon me to practise deception, and I am happy in a persuasion that although truths may sometimes not please, yet that when delivered with decency and respect they will never offend either his Majesty or your Excellency.

Believe me, sir, the United States will not be able

to pay their debts during the war, and therefore any
plan whatever calculated on a contrary position must
be fruitless. I am ready to pledge their faith for
repaying to his Majesty, within a reasonable term
after the war, and with a reasonable interest, any
sums he may be so kind as to lend them. What
more can I offer? What more can they do? If
there be any services they can do to his Majesty, consistent with their safety and defence, they are ready
and will be happy to render them. They respect the
King and the nation, and at the very time they are
requesting his aid, they are soliciting to be united to
him by bonds of perpetual amity and alliance. Against
his enemies as well as their own they are now in
arms ; and the supplies they ask are not for the purpose of luxury or aggrandizement, but for the sole
and express purpose of annoying those enemies, and
enabling France, Spain, and themselves to obtain a
peace honourable and advantageous to each.

Of his Majesty's kind disposition towards them,
they had received not only professions but proofs.
Hence they became inspired not only with gratitude,
but with confidence in his friendship. Impelled by
this confidence, and a particular concurrence of exigencies already explained to your Excellency, they
drew the bills in question. The issue of this measure
will be highly critical, and followed by a train of consequences very important and extensive. The single
circumstance of your Excellency having permitted
me to accept the first of these bills will be considered
by our enemies as an unfortunate omen. By pre-

dicting from it further aids, their ideas of the resources of Spain and the resistance of America will naturally be raised, and their hopes of subduing the one, or reducing the power of the other, will naturally be diminished. They will impute these aids to a plan of the House of Bourbon, wisely concerted and firmly persisted in, to secure themselves and all Europe against the ambition of Britain, by completing the division of her empire, and they will cease to flatter themselves that America thus aided will become destitute of resources to carry on the war. On the other hand, America will derive fresh vigour from this mark of friendship, and their attachment to his Majesty become proportionably more strong. By mutual good offices, friendship between nations, as between individuals, is only to be established ; and it is always a happy circumstance when it subsists between those whom nature has placed contiguous to each other. But your Excellency's time is of too great importance to be engaged by such obvious reflections.

Permit me, Sir, still to indulge the pleasing expectation of being enabled to inform Congress, that his Majesty's magnanimity and friendship have prompted him, though inconvenient to his own affairs, to secure the credit of their bills ; and I am persuaded that the benevolence of your Excellency's disposition will be gratified in being instrumental in a measure which would make such agreeable impressions on the hearts and minds of so great a number of steadfast friends to the Spanish monarchy.

I have the honour to be, sir, etc.

JOHN JAY.

JAY TO EGBERT BENSON.

ARANJUEZ, June, 1780.

DEAR BENSON :

When shall we again, by a cheerful fire, or under a shady tree, recapitulate our juvenile pursuits or pleasures, or look back on the extensive field of politics we once have trodden? Our plans of life have, within these few years past, been strangely changed. Our country, I hope, will be the better for the alterations. How far we, individually, may be benefited, is more questionable. Personal considerations, however, must give way to public ones, and the consciousness of having done our duty to our country and posterity, must recompense us for all the evils we experience in their cause.

I wrote to you from Martinico. I have been four months in this kingdom without receiving more than three letters from America, and those not very interesting, being of old dates, and not particular. You are among those from whom I wish often to hear, as well because I am interested in what concerns yourself, as on account of the intelligence respecting the affairs of our State, which I hope you will sometimes favour me with. Write nothing, nevertheless, that you would wish to be entirely private ; your letters may be inspected before they reach me, that practice being general in the post-offices of France and Spain.

I flatter myself you sometimes visit your Fishkill friends. I know they esteem you, and always derive pleasure from your company. What arrangements have been made in your official departments? Are your taxes paid? Do the people continue firm? A few more glorious exertions will give them peace, liberty, and safety. What says Vermont?

Tell me how your mother and brothers do. Remember me to them and my other friends. God bless you, my friend.

I am sincerely yours,

JOHN JAY.

WILLIAM BINGHAM [1] TO JAY.

PHILAD., July 1, 1780.

DEAR SIR:

With great difficulty & repeated solicitations I procured permission from Congress to return here, and arrived in the frigate *Confedaracy* the beginning of May. Previous to my departure, I addressed you several letters from Martinico which I hope you have received. It has given me peculiar pleasure to hear of your safe arrival at Cadiz, and of the favorable reception you are like to meet with at the court of Madrid.

The sentiments of the people of this country I found surprisingly altered since I left it; they were no longer governed by that pure, disinterested patriotism, which distinguished the Infancy of the contest; private Interest seemed to predominate over every Consideration that regarded the public weal. It was necessary that they should experience some signal misfortune to rouse them into activity. The loss of Charleston and its important garrison has in a great measure had that effect, and I am happy to see the spirit of the people begin to rise on the discovery of their danger and actual situation. But what was near to prove of very fatal consequence was the state of our finances, which by not being properly organized and established on a

---

[1] Agent of Continental Congress at Martinique.

solid footing, were incorporated to the purpose of furnishing the necessary supplies for the Army. At an alarming moment when the treasury was exhausted and the Army suffering and threatening to disband for the want of provisions, the virtue of individuals was roused, which warded off the impending blow. A bank was established on private credit under the Auspices of gentlemen of the first fortune in this City. It was to raise the sum of three hundred thousand pounds in specie, or its Value, for supplying the Army with provisions for a certain time. The subscription was filled up in a few days and much larger sums might have been procured.

The direction of this bank is committed to the Care of gentlemen of known abilities and integrity and inspectors of equal reputation are appointed by the subscribers for supertending its affairs. The purchases will be made on the most advantageous terms, and the public will soon discover the immense difference that will arrise in their favor by the supplies of the Army furnished by such men or by a band of commissaries, quarter masters, *et id genus omne*. If the same public spirited establishments take place in every State, we shall derive the greatest and most essential advantages from them.

The flame of patriotism has not confined itself altogether to our sex. The ladies caught the enlivening warmth. A subscription was set on foot by them for the purpose of relieving the Army and very liberal sums have been collected.

Altho' the loss of Charleston is a very serious matter, yet I am in great hopes that we shall more than counterballance its bad effect by our success before the campaign is over. But the reliance is in a great measure founded on the exertions of the French forces, which are daily expected here to our Assistance. Until they arrive, we must remain altogether on the defensive, and endeavor to prevent the enemy from penetrating into the country and carrying devastation throughout it.

General Gates is appointed to the command of the Southern Army and I believe will soon be able to collect a very respectable force, as the States of North Carolina and Virginia are alarmed and making great preparations and exertions. Our allies will be engaged in a very Active Campaign in the West Indies, which I hope will be successful and attended with decisive consequences. Twelve Spanish ships of the line and a large body of troops have arrived at Martinico, which reinforcement is to cooperate with the French in the reduction of the British Islands.

Your friends in the Jersies are all well. They have lately been alarmed at the incursions of the enemy, who have been laying waste the country about Elizabeth Town and Springfield; however, they have generally retreated with considerable loss, the militia having poured in upon them from all quarters. Gen[l.] Clinton after having garrisoned Charleston returned with a large Body of Troops to New York, and it is thought from his present movements has a design upon West Point; however, there is little reason to apprehend danger from that quarter, as it is well supplied with men and they are throwing in provisions daily.

An unlucky accident lately happened to Gouverneur Morris. In attempting to drive a pair of wild horses in a phaeton, he was thrown out and in the fall his left leg caught in the wheel and was greatly shattered. He was under the necessity of having it amputated below the knee and is now in a fair way of recovery.

I hope Mrs. Jay passes her time agreeably at Madrid. It will be some time, I imagine, before she will be reconciled to the etiquette of so formal a Court. Please to present my respects to her, as well as my compliments to Col. Livingston.

I am, with great regard and esteem, &c.,

Dear Sir,

Your obedient humble Servant

WILLIAM BINGHAM.

MADRID, July 5, 1780.

Mr. Jay waited on the Count de Florida Blanca agreeably to an appointment made by the latter to meet at his house at half-past eight this evening.

After the usual compliments, the bad news relative to the surrender of Charleston, just received, became the topic of conversation. The Count mentioned the channels through which he had received it, viz., by an express despatched by the Spanish Ambassador at Lisbon, in consequence of intelligence which Governor Johnson had received and published in that city, and by letters from the Count d'Aranda,[2] with the accounts printed at London of the affair. He expressed his sorrow on the occasion, but observed that the Count d'Aranda flattered him that the arrival of the Chevalier de Ternay in that part of the world would totally change the face of affairs, particularly as there would be eight vessels of the line, and more than five thousand troops instead of three thousand, and three vessels of the line, which he had been informed were demanded by General Washington.

He seemed to think it strange that the place had not been better defended, and that more vigourous measures had not been taken to impede the enemy's progress, and observed that, if the town was not in a condition to stand a siege, it would have been better to have withdrawn the troops and stores and reserved them for the defence of the country. Mr. Jay replied

---

[1] See notes to letters of May 11 and June 7, 1780.
[2] Spanish Minister at the French court.

that, probably, when all circumstances relative to this affair were known, there might be reasons which would account for the conduct of the Americans on this occasion ; to the truth of which remark the Count appeared to assent. He then mentioned the death of M. Mirales,[1] and regretted his loss at this time. He said he had recommended to his Majesty a person to succeed him, whom we knew, that spoke English, whom he expected soon, and to whom he would explain his ideas on the subject of the bills, and on other matters touching which Mr. Jay had written to him, and who would confer also with Mr. Jay on those subjects.

Mr. Jay mentioned that, if it was agreeable to his Excellency to permit M. Del Campo (a confidential secretary of the Count, who speaks English, and who translated all the letters to and from the Count) to be present, he should be able to explain his sentiments more fully and clearly. Though the Count did not object to this proposal, he appeared disinclined to it, and said that, with the assistance of Mr. Carmichael, then present, they could understand each other very well.

He then proceeded to speak of the bills of exchange in the possession of the Messrs. Joyce,[2] and seemed to be surprised that that house should be posssessed of so many of them. He advised Mr. Jay to be cautious of those gentlemen, saying that they were as much English in their hearts as the Ministry of that

---

[1] Representative of the Spanish court at Philadelphia.
[2] Mercantile house at Bilboa.

country; that he had known them long; that he thought their conduct extraordinary in being so urgent for the acceptance of these bills. Mr. Jay then informed his Excellency that he had paid those gentlemen a visit in order to obtain further time, and that they had consented to wait until Monday next. The Count mentioned a fortnight or three weeks as necessary, in order that he might have an opportunity of seeing the person he had sent for, and making some arrangements with him. He said that it would be more agreeable to his Majesty to pay those bills at Cadiz, Bilboa, or Amsterdam, than here; lamented the precipitancy with which Congress had entered into this measure, saying that, if they had previously addressed the King on the subject, ways and means might have been found, either to transport from their possessions in America specie for the service of Congress, or to have enabled them to have drawn bills of exchange at a shorter sight, which would have prevented the loss of one third of the money to which Congress had subjected themselves, by the terms on which the present bills were sold. Mr. Jay assured his Excellency that, by letters he had received from America, from members of Congress and others, he was informed that the terms were judged so unfavourable to the buyers, that the bills drawn on him sold heavily from that circumstance solely, and not from any doubt of their credit and payment.

This did not, however, appear to convince his Excellency, who spoke much of the deranged state of our finances and credit; of the advantages taken of Congress by merchants and others, who availed themselves of that circumstance, which he called cruel extortions, frequently expressing the King's wishes and his own to render America all the service in their power in this crisis of their affairs ; but observed that it was impossible to obtain much money in Europe while France, England, and Spain were making use of every resource to obtain it for the enormous expenses of the war, and while the channel through which the European merchants received supplies of specie was stopped, viz., the arrival of the usual quantity from America. This induced him to mention the arrival at Cadiz of three millions of piastres, all of which was on account of the merchants, and again to dwell on what he had before said of the possibility of transmitting specie to the States from the Spanish possessions abroad, and of the effect that this would have in re-establishing the credit of our money. Mr. Jay observed, in reply, that if a supply of specie could be sent to America, and his Excellency thought that measure more convenient and advisable than bills, the Congress would, in his opinion, readily suspend drawing on receiving that information ; to which the Count answered that, when the person he had sent for arrived, this matter might be further discussed.

Mr. Jay then proceeded to observe that, by papers which he had transmitted to his Excellency, he would see that Congress had adopted a system to redeem and destroy the former emissions, and to emit other bills to be paid in Europe with interest in a certain

term of years, and in fully establishing this system, it
would be probably in their power, not only to sustain
the credit of their money, but to contribute, in some
measure, to assist Spain in the way proposed by his
Excellency, viz., in building of frigates, etc., etc. He
added that as his Majesty's treasure was detained in
America, and as much expense would be incurred by
the armaments employed by Spain there, bills on
the Havana in favour of the United States might
be more convenient to Spain, and equally contribute
to the end proposed. The Count did not seem to
disapprove of the idea, but did not enlarge upon it.
He asked Mr. Jay if America could not furnish Spain
with masts and ship timber. Mr. Jay replied that
those articles might be obtained there. The Count
then said that he would defer further remarks on this
head till the arrival of the person whom he expected
would succeed M. Mirales, and appeared desirous of
leaving this subject, and, indeed, all other matters
relative to American affairs, to be discussed when he
came.

In the further course of conversation, he recurred
to the subject of the bills in question, and told Mr.
Jay, if an immediate acceptance of them was insisted
on, that he might accept them payable at Bilboa, but
rather seemed to wish that their acceptance might be
delayed till the coming of the above-mentioned person. Mr. Jay expatiated on the impression which
the acceptance of these bills and every other mark of
friendship would make in America at this particular
crisis, and the Count, in a very feeling and warm

manner, assured him that his desire to serve the States increased in consequence of their distresses. By his whole conversation he endeavoured to show how much he interested himself in the prosperity of our affairs, more than once desiring Mr. Jay not to be discouraged, for that with time and patience all would go well ; expatiating on the King's character, his religious observation of, and adherence to, his promises, and his own desire of having Mr. Jay's entire confidence. Mr. Jay seized this opportunity of assuring him of his full reliance on the King's justice and honour, and his particular and entire confidence in his Excellency, asserting to him that all his letters to Congress breathed these sentiments. The Count appeared much pleased with this declaration, and, seeming to speak without reserve, hinted his hopes that the combined fleets would soon be in condition to give the law to that of England in the seas of Europe, repeating that measures would be taken, on the arrival of the person expected, to provide for the payment of the bills of exchange, and that other arrangements would be made with the same person, which would contribute to relieve, as much as it was in his Majesty's power, the present distresses of America, of which he frequently spoke very feelingly in the course of this conversation.

Mr. Jay reminded his Excellency, in a delicate manner, of the supplies of clothing, etc., etc., which had been promised in a former conference, and said that if they could be sent in autumn they would be essentially useful. The Count assured him that measures would be taken for this purpose, with the person so often hinted at in the course of the conference ; that probably these goods would be embarked from Bilboa, as every thing was so dear at Cadiz. He also once more told Mr. Jay that at all events he might accept the bills presented by Messrs. Joyce, payable at Bilboa, though he appeared to wish that this measure might be delayed for a fortnight if possible. The conference ended with compliments and assurances on the one part and the other, the Count endeavouring to persuade Mr. Jay of his Majesty's desire to assist the States, and Mr. Jay assuring him of his reliance on his Excellency, and of the good effects which such proofs of his Majesty's friendship would have in America at the present juncture.

In this conference not a single nail would drive. Every thing was to be postponed till the arrival of the person intended to succeed M. Mirales.

***

JAY TO THE PRESIDENT OF CONGRESS.

SIR :   MADRID, July 10, 1780.

As a late and particular letter from me to your Excellency is now on the way to America, and as I purpose to write again very fully by the successor of M. Mirales, I decline saying much in this letter, which I shall send by a circuitous and hazardous route.[1]

---

[1] Jay's caution in transmitting official letters to America is shown in this endorsement of one of his parcels : "By Captain De Sansure, who is to sink it in case of capture, and in time of action to give such directions to the officers that, in case of his death, they may see it done."

I have accepted bills to the amount of between eleven and twelve thousand dollars. They arrive slowly, and I am very glad of it. No news of Mr. Laurens ; I regret his absence. I hope the terms for the sale of the bills on me will not be lowered. Remittances have really become necessary. Distressed American seamen cost a great deal. The house of Le Couteulx has advanced money for them at Cadiz.

I had yesterday an application from the director of a hospital at St. Andeira, desiring to be informed whether I would be responsible for the ordinary expenses of receiving and curing a New England master of a vessel, who had escaped from captivity pennyless, having one of his legs so injured by iron fetters as to be in danger of losing it. These are calls of humanity, and I entreat Congress to enable me to obey them, and to establish specific regulations for the conduct of these affairs.

The surrender of Charleston is the subject of much speculation and many unfavourable conjectures. I have received no public letters since I left America, except one from the Committee, enclosing the resolutions for drawing bills on me.

I have the honour to be, etc.,

JOHN JAY.

KITTY LIVINGSTON TO MRS. JAY.

July 10, 1780.

We have not, my dear friends, had the happiness of hearing from you for a long time. My dear sister's letter (and its the last one we have received) was dated at Cadiz, the

4th of March; thrice welcome was it, as it informed us of
your arrival once more on *terra firma*, and that we had no
longer to dread for you the dangers of the ocean. Thanks
is forever due from all your family to the Supreme Being
for his merciful interposition in the preservation of those
so dear to them. May you long continue thus favoured by
his power.

The letters you mention having written are not come to
hand, nor any letters from Mr. Jay to Congress since your
arrival at Madrid, where we now suppose you to be in
scenes very different from any thing you have been accustomed to. Do you know that I am trading on your stock
of firmness; and if you are not possessed of as much as I
suppose you to be I shall become bankrupt, having several
wagers depending that you will not paint nor go to plays
on Sundays. The Chevalier [Luzerne] is not to be convinced that he has lost his bet to me, till Mr. Carmichael
informs him you do not paint. Mr. Witherspoon informed
me that he was questioned by many at Martinique if you
did not.[1] Mr. Bingham makes very honorable mention of
you and Mr. Jay to your friends at Philadelphia. I consider myself very unfortunate in leaving town but a day or

---

[1] Mrs. Jay, writing from Madrid, December 1, 1780, replies to this letter:
"The bets depending between you and the Chevalier I hope are considerable,
since you are certainly entitled to the stake, for I have not used any false
coloring, nor have I amused myself with plays or any other diversions on
Sundays."

Mrs. Robert Morris also wrote from Philadelphia, July 12, 1781, to Mrs.
Jay: "Kitty and myself often avail ourselves of the pleasure memory affords
us, in the recollection of the many happy days spent to-gether in this city.
The Chevalier de la Luzerne, M. de Marbois, and Mr. Holker, expect great
pleasure at your remembrance of them, and request your acceptance of their
best wishes. The Chevalier acquiesces in the loss of his bet, presented Kitty
with a handsome dress cap, accompanied with a note acknowledging your firmness. Mr. Gov. Morris's friends here and, indeed, all who know him, were
exceedingly shocked at his irreparable misfortune—the loss of his leg. . . .
I never knew an individual more sympathized with."

two before that gentleman arrived.   By his return we received your journal ; the letter written to mama after it I received long before I left Philadelphia.

In our last distresses from the invasion of the British troops, Mr. and Mrs. Morris sent for me to come and reside with them.[1]   It was exceeding friendly and kind, and it is no small alleviation to our infelicities when we have such friends as can feel for us.   They have at present a delightful situation at Spingsberry.   Mr. Morris has repaired and enlarged the buildings and converted the greenhouse into a dining room which far exceeds their expectations in beauty and convenience.   I flatter myself with the pleasure of paying them a visit in the fall or in the winter ; at present I decline accepting their invitation.   .   .   .

Brother Jack has received a summons to his duty on board the *Saratoga*[2] (as senior midshipman), the ship being shortly

---

[1] Robert Morris, in a note to Jay, dated Philadelphia, July 6, 1780, writes : " Kitty stayed the winter with us, and went into the Jersies in May or beginning of June.   Mrs. Livingston about that time moved with the family to Elizabethtown, and was there when Mr. Knyphausen came out the other day. At first the family were treated politely, but after a while they found it necessary to leave that place, being threatened hard by the *Brutish*, as our soldiers now call the British."

[2] Another sister, Susan Livingston, mentioned in Jay's letter of February 27, 1779, writes to Mrs. Jay, October 21, 1780, as follows : " We have received intelligence upon which we think we may rely that Johnny is returned from a cruise as far as Chester in Delaware, and that the *Saratoga* in her last voyage has taken three prizes, all letters of marque of considerable force, and laden partly with rum and partly with sugar.   As the officers and men are entitled to one half the prizes, and a midshipman has three shares, it is supposed that Johnny's share will amount to near twenty thousand pounds.   It is the second time the *Saratoga* has sailed ; the first time she convoyed Mr. Laurens off the coast and returned with a prize of 225 puncheons of rum.   By a newspaper I see Mr. Laurens was afterwards captured, and his dispatches likewise, and both sent to England.   .   .   .   Next month I expect the favor of a visit from Nanny and Cornelia Van Horne.   I shall endeavour to persuade Nanny to desert his Majesty's banners and to turn *Rebel* and join us.   If I succeed I shall merit the united thanks of the officers of the American army for gaining so fine a girl to our party."

due on account of our salaries; we shall otherwise soon be in a very disagreeable situation. To take up money from individuals would not be eligible or reputable, and it would not be prudent to trouble government, already a little sore about the bills, with further requisitions at present. If the servants of Congress here must live awhile on the credit they may seek and find with others, I think it more decent to recur to their ally. France, I know, has already done great things for us, and is still making glorious exertions. I am also sensible of your difficulties and regret them, though I am happy in reflecting that since they must exist they have fallen into the hands of one whose abilities and influence enable him to sustain and surmount them, and at a Court which does not appear inclined to do things by halves.

It is necessary you should be informed the papers enclosed are known to Count Montmorin, and are therefore probably no secrets. I am on good terms with the Count, whom I esteem as a man of abilities and a friend to our country. As France had interested herself so deeply in our cause, and had been requested to interpose her friendly offices for us here, I could not think of withholding from him all the confidence which these considerations dictate, especially as no personal objections forbid it. To have conducted the negotiation with unnecessary secrecy and equivocating cunning was irreconcilable with my principles of action, and with every idea I have of wisdom and policy. In a word, France and America are, and I hope always will be, allies; and it is the duty of each party to cultivate mutual confidence and cordiality. For my own part, while their conduct continues fair, firm, and friendly, I shall remain strongly attached to their interest and grateful for their benefit.

Mrs. Jay is much pleased with, and thanks you for, the print you were so kind as to send her ; it is a striking likeness. I find that in France great men, like their predecessors of old, have their bards. Your strictures are very just, though a little severe. While there are young Telemachuses and fascinating Calypsos in the world, fancies and pens and hearts will sometimes run riot in spite of the Mentors now and then to be met with. . . .

I am, dear sir, with very sincere regard,

Your most obedient servant,

JOHN JAY.

JAY TO JOHN ADAMS.

MADRID, 17 July, 1780.

DEAR SIR :

On the 4th of June last I had the pleasure of writing you a letter acknowledging the receipt of yours of the 15th of May, since which none of your favours have reached me.

I have just been reading the capitulation of Charleston. I suspect they wanted provisions. The reputation of the garrison will suffer till the reasons of their conduct are explained. I wish a good one may be in their power ; they are severely censured here. What the consequences of the event may be cannot easily be conjectured. I should not be surprised if they should eventually be in our favour.[1] It is difficult, while invaded in the centre, to defend extremities which have little natural strength.

I wish Ternay's squadron may touch at Halifax. The capture of that place would reduce the English navy in American seas to extreme difficulties. The affair at Charleston has an unfavourable aspect on the expedition against New York.

After the conclusion of this campaign I think you will have something to do. In my opinion, all the powers at war wish for peace. The pride of the King of England will be the great obstacle, and it may happen that in attempting to save his dignity he may lose his crown.

> I am, dear sir,
> With great regard and esteem,
> Your most obedient servant,
> JOHN JAY.

---

[1] In regard to the fall of Charleston, William C. Houston, delegate from New Jersey in the Continental Congress, wrote as follows to Jay, under date of July 10, 1780:

"Every person who has attended to the course of our Revolution will know the meaning of what seems a paradox, 'that our misfortunes are our safety.' They are certainly, under God, the source of it. Our captive soldiers will as usual be poisoned, starved, and insulted; will be scourged into the service of the enemy; the citizens will suffer pillagings, violences, and conflagrations; a fruitful country will be desolated; but the loss of Charleston will, to all appearance, promote the general cause. It has awakened a spirit unknown since the year 1776, a spirit which is fast pervading the mass of the community, a spirit which enlivens and increases daily. I am more afraid of an unfavorable effect of this disaster on your side of the water, and hope you will take the proper means for preventing any ill impressions it might otherwise have."

JAY TO DE NEUFVILLE & SON.[1]

MADRID, July 29, 1780.

GENTLEMEN :

Your favour of the 13th instant was delivered to me last evening. I admire the generous principles, which lead you to take so decided and friendly a part in favour of America. I have too great confidence in the honour, justice, and gratitude of Congress to suspect that they will permit you to be sufferers by your exertions in their favour. On the contrary, I am persuaded they will entertain a proper sense of your disinterested attachment, and with pleasure take every opportunity of acknowledging it.

Mr. Laurens' absence is much to be regretted ; his endeavours, aided by your assistance, would probably have prevented the embarrassments which have taken place. I have not as yet received any advices of his having sailed, and your information of his not having left America in May is true. By a letter from a gentleman at Cadiz of the 21st instant I learn that a vessel from North Carolina had arrived in forty-nine days, and left Mr. Laurens there on his way to Philadelphia. I am at a loss to account for this, having no intelligence from America on the subject. Perhaps his design was to sail from Philadelphia. If so, we may still look out for him. Prudence, however, demands that every possible step be taken to alleviate the inconveniences arising from his absence. If my power extended to this case I should, without hesita-

---

[1] Further communications with this firm at Amsterdam appear in vol vii. of " Diplomatic Correspondence."

tion, authorize you in a proper manner to make a loan in Holland, and be much obliged to you for undertaking it. But my instructions do not reach so far; all I can do is to advise as an individual, and as a public servant to represent in a true light to Congress your benevolent efforts to preserve their credit. If Dr. Franklin has such instructions as you suppose, and his circumstances will admit of it, I can at present see no objections to his taking some such measures as you propose until Mr. Laurens' arrival; but of this, he alone can properly judge. I shall write to him on the subject, and you may rely on my doing every thing in my power. I assure you I feel myself, as an American, so much obliged by your generous zeal to serve my country, that I shall be happy in being instrumental to render the issue of it as agreeable and honourable to you as the principles on which you act are meritorious and noble.

I flatter myself that the unfavourable influence which the capture of Charleston has on the public will be of short duration. When they reflect that America has nobly sustained a six years' war, fought hard battles with various success, and lost and regained several of their cities, they will find it ridiculous to believe that the fate of the Thirteen States is involved in that of one or two towns. The like impressions were made when New York, Philadelphia, and Ticonderoga fell into the enemy's hands; and those impressions were again removed by the battle of Trenton, the evacuation of Philadelphia, the battle of Monmouth, the defeat and capture of General Burgoyne and his army,

and other victories on our side. Many of these great
events happened when America had no ally, and when
Britain had no other objects to divide her force. It
is not reasonable, therefore, to imagine that the power
of Britain has been augmented by the accession of
two formidable enemies, or that the· power of America has been diminished in proportion as the number
of her friends increased.

Depend upon it, that as the spirit of America has
always risen with the successes of her enemies, they
will not, on this occasion, throw away their arms and
ingloriously pass under the yoke of a nation whose
conduct towards her has been marked by injustice
and oppression in peace, and by malice and wanton
barbarity in war.

With sentiments of sincere regard and esteem, I
have the honour to be, etc.,

JOHN JAY.

ROBERT R. LIVINGSTON TO JAY.

PHILADELPHIA, 26th August, 1780.

DEAR JOHN,

I received yours of the 23d May from Madrid, with
duplicates thereof, and the letters you wrote from Cadiz
and Martinique.

Your remembrance of the pleasurable days of our youth,
and the scenes in which we mutually bore our parts, together with the attractions which this country still has for
you, afford me the most pleasing hope that neither time nor
absence will weaken a friendship which has so long stood
the test of both. This indeed I expected from the steadi-
ness of your temper; but I must confess that I had little

hopes that your early return would afford me a prospect of deriving that consolation from it in the decline of life, to which I looked even while it directed the pursuits and animated the pleasures of youth.

You mistake your own heart when you say you are unambitious; and without the assurance contained in your letter, I should have believed that the love of glory would have always kept you in the line in which you now are, more especially as the general satisfaction that your appointment and conduct since has given, renders it the wish of everybody less interested in your return than I am, to keep you abroad.

I have not been able to procure at this place the key to the cipher that you directed me to, though I believe I have it at home; besides that, it is very intricate and troublesome; I shall therefore be obliged to confine what I have to say to mere common occurrences. I enclose you a cipher which is very simple, and not to be deciphered while the key is concealed, as the same figure represents a variety of letters. In order that you may know whether it comes safely to hand, I have in this letter used the precaution mentioned in yours.

Nothing astonishes me more than the confidence with which the British ministry and their dependants assert, that America sighs to return to their government, since the fact is that we never were more determined in opposition, nor if we except the derangement of our finances (which the loan of half a million would re-establish, if remitted in specie or merchandise), were we ever so capable of resistance. Our crops are uncommonly fine, and the militia of every State north and east of Delaware, is armed, disciplined, and inured to the duties of a camp. The southern militia are now at school, and I have no doubt will improve by the lessons they receive from the enemy. Our friend Smith, who has probably contributed to this ministerial madness, uninstructed by his repeated disappointments from the beginning of the war, is said to have advised Kniphausen to erect the royal standard in the Jerseys before General Clinton returned from Charleston, persuaded that our troops, and particularly the militia, would flock to it, and thus he have the honour of reducing the country, without sharing it with Clinton. He accordingly came over with great parade, with his whole force, scattering exaggerated accounts in printed handbills of the loss of Charleston, which, instead of discouraging, only animated the militia. They were all in motion upon the first alarm, and though opposed only by them and less than a thousand continental troops, he was disgracefully driven out with the loss of 500 men killed, wounded, and taken, after having penetrated ten miles from the shore, and done us no other injury than the burning of a few houses, and the abuse and murder of some women ; since which they have been more cautious and less sanguine. Adieu ; remember my compliments to the colonel and Mr. Carmichael. I am, dear John,

Most sincerely yours,

ROBERT R. LIVINGSTON.

JAY'S ACCOUNT OF CONFERENCES WITH THE FRENCH AMBASSADOR AT MADRID.[1]

ST. ILDEFONSO, August 27, 1780.

Mr. Jay waited on the Count de Montmorin this morning at nine o'clock, agreeably to appointment the day before. The former commenced the conver-

---

[1] The vacillation and delays of the Spanish Minister prompted Jay to present his case to Count Montmorin. "It appeared to me proper," he writes, "to mention my embarrassments to the French Ambassador, who had always been friendly, and ask his advice and aid on the subject. The next day I had a conference with him, and the following are the notes of it "—as above.

sation by observing that in his first conferences with the Minister of Spain, at Aranjues, the Minister divided the subject into two parts, and spoke largely on that of the bills drawn on Mr. Jay, and on the treaty proposed to be entered into between Spain and America. Mr. Jay recapitulated the minister's assurances relative to the former, and informed the Ambassador that the result of this conference was a promise of the Minister to send him written notes on *both* points, a few days afterwards. That with respect to the notes relative to the treaty, Mr. Jay had not received them as yet. That on the other point, he had received notes, which, as well as his answer, he had shown to the Ambassador. That on the 5th of July he had another conference with the Minister at Madrid, in which he had endeavoured to turn the conversation to the several objects of his business and mission here, but that the Minister postponed the discussion of them, until a person for whom he had sent, with a view to succeed M. Mirales, should arrive, when all the necessary arrangements should be made. He indeed told Mr. Jay that if the Messrs. Joyce were pressing, he might accept their bills, payable at Bilboa, and throughout the whole conference had given Mr. Jay warm and repeated assurances, not only of the King's good faith and friendly disposition towards America, but of his own personal attachment to her interest, on both of which, as well as in his candour and promises, he desired him to place the greatest reliance.

Mr. Jay proceeded further to inform the Ambas-

sador that, being exceedingly pressed by Messrs.
Joyce and others, holders of the bills, for a decisive
answer, which they had required to have on the Monday last past, he had signified the same to the Minister by three letters, requesting his directions, to
none of which he received any answers.   .   .   .

The Ambassador told Mr. Jay that he ought to ask
an audience of the Minister. To this Mr. Jay replied that he could not hope to have an answer to
this request, as he had not been able to procure one
to the different applications he had already made.
The Ambassador said that he would willingly speak
to the Minister, but that he feared he should not be
able to enter fully into the subject with him until
Wednesday, both the Minister and himself having
their time employed on objects, which at present, and
for some time past, had engrossed much of their
attention.   He then asked Mr. Jay if he had written
to Congress to stop drawing bills on him.   Mr. Jay
replied that he could not with propriety give such information to Congress, after the general and repeated
assurances made him by the Count de Florida Blanca
ever since his arrival here, and particularly the Minister's declaration that he should be able to furnish
him with thirty or forty thousand pounds sterling,
at the end of the present or commencement of the
next year, and that in the meantime other arrangements might be taken to pay such bills as might
become due after that period.   He added that if the
Count had candidly told him that he could not furnish
him with money to pay the bills, he should then im-

mediately have informed Congress of it, who would have taken, of course, the proper measures on the occasion, but that should he now send a true account of all that had passed between the Count de Florida Blanca and himself thereon, he could not answer for the disagreeable effects such intelligence would produce. The Count seemed to think the Spanish Minister would pay the bills that had been already presented. . . .

The conference ended with a promise of the Count de Montmorin that he would endeavour to speak to the Count de Florida Blanca on the subject, but that he was afraid he should not be able to do it fully until Wednesday next. . . .

On Wednesday afternoon, 30th of August, I waited on the Ambassador, to know the result of the conversation he had promised to have with the Minister on our affairs. He did not appear very glad to see me. I asked him whether he had seen the Minister and conversed with him on our affairs. He said he had seen the Minister, but that as Count d'Estaing was present, he had only some general and cursory conversation with him, and slipping away from that topic, went on to observe that I would do well to write another letter to the Minister, mentioning the number of letters I had already written, my arrival here, and my desire of a conference with him. I told the Ambassador, that while four letters on the subject remained unanswered, it could not be necessary to write a fifth. That these letters had been written with great politeness and circumspection ; that the last was written the day of my arrival at St. Ildefonso;

that I had also gone to the Minister's house to pay my respects to him, and on being told that he was sick, had left a card; and that, notwithstanding these marks of attention and respect, I still continued un-answered and unnoticed. I observed to him further, that this conduct accorded ill with the Minister's assurances; that unless I had met with more tender-ness from the holders of the bills, they would have been returned noted for non-acceptance; that if such an event should at last take place, after the repeated promises and declarations of the Minister, there would of necessity be an end to the confidence of America in the Court of Spain.

He replied, that he hoped things would take a more favourable turn; that to his knowledge the Minister had been of late much occupied and perplexed with business; that I ought not to be affected with the inattention of his conduct; that I should continue to conduct the business smoothly, having always in view the importance of Spain, and remembering that we were as yet only rising States, not firmly established, or generally acknowledged, etc., and that he would by all means advise me to write the Minister another letter, *praying* an audience.

I answered that the object of my coming to Spain was to make *propositions* not *supplications*, and that I should forbear troubling the Minister with further letters, till he should be more disposed to attend to them. That I considered America as being, and to continue, independent in *fact*, and that her becoming so in *name* was of no further importance than as it concerned the common cause, in the success of which all the parties were interested ; and that I did not imagine Congress would agree to purchase from Spain the acknowledgment of an undeniable fact at the price she demanded for it ; that I intended to abide patiently the fate of the bills, and should transmit to Congress an account of all matters relative to them ; that I should then write the Minister another letter on the subject of the treaty, and if that should be treated with like neglect, or if I should be informed that his Catholic Majesty declined going into that measure, I should then consider my business at an end, and proceed to take the necessary measures for returning to America ; that I knew my constituents were sincerely desirous of a treaty with Spain, and that their respect for the House of Bourbon, the desire of France signified in the Secret Article, and the favourable opinion they had imbibed of the Spanish nation, were the strongest inducements they had to wish it ; that the policy of multiplying treaties with European nations was with me questionable, and might be so with others ; that for my own part, I was inclined to think it the interest of America to rest content with the treaty with France, and, by avoiding alliances with other nations, remain free from the influence of their disputes and politics ; that the situation of the United States, in my opinion, dictated this policy ; that I knew it to be their interest, and of course their disposition, to be at peace with all the world ; and that I knew, too, it would be in their power, and I hoped in their inclination, always to defend themselves.

The Ambassador was at a stand ; after a little

pause, he said he hoped my mission would have a more agreeable issue. He asked me if I was content with the conduct of France. I answered, most certainly ; for that she was spending her blood as well as treasure for us. This answer was too general for him. He renewed the question, by asking ·whether I was content with the conduct of France relative to our proposed treaty with Spain. I answered that, as far as it had come to my knowledge, I was. This required an explanation, and I gave it to him, by observing that, by the Secret Article, Spain was at liberty to accede to our treaty with France whenever she pleased, and with such alterations as both parties might agree to ; that Congress had appointed me to propose this accession now, and had authorized me to enter into the necessary discussions and arguments ; that, to give their application the better prospect of success, they had directed me to request the favourable interposition of the King of France with the King of Spain ; that I had done it by letter to Count de Vergennes, who, in answer, had assured me of the King's disposition to comply with the request of Congress ; and informed me that instructions analogous to this disposition should be given to the Ambassador at Madrid ; that it gave me pleasure to acknowledge that his conduct towards me had always been polite and friendly, but that I still remained ignorant whether any and what progress had been made in the mediation. He seemed not to have expected this ; but observed that all he could do was to be ready to do me any friendly office in his power, for that he did not see how his *mediation* could be proper, except in cases which gave occasion to mutual and complimentary professions too unimportant to repeat. I told him that the holders of the bills, after having shown me great forbearance and delicacy, were at length perfectly tired ; that the house of Casa Mayor had sent their bills after me, but that as I was not to expect the honour of a conference with the Minister until Tuesday evening, at soonest, I had requested time till Wednesday to give my answer. I therefore begged the favour of him to mention this to the Minister, and obtain his directions what I should do. He asked to what amount Congress had resolved to draw. I told him. He observed, that the Court ought previously to have been applied to. In answer to which I recapitulated the reasons before given to the Minister. He dwelt largely on the necessities of the State, and I expatiated on the extensive ideas entertained of Spanish opulence in America. He assured me they were mistaken, and spoke of the difficulties occasioned by the detention of their treasures abroad. He then remarked, that we offered no *consideration* for the money we solicited. I replied, that we offered the same consideration that other nations did who borrowed money, viz., the repayment of the principal with interest. He asked me if we had nothing further to offer, and mentioned ship timber. I said we had ship-timber, but that as it belonged to individuals, the public could not get it otherwise than by purchase, and that it could answer no purpose to borrow money with one hand and instantly repay it with the other, for that a repayment in money, or in ship timber, was the same thing in fact, and differed only in name. Besides, that if Spain wanted timber from America, it would be better, in case he went there, that he should be charged with that business, than that it should be under the direction of Congress, for that public works were always more expensive than private. He agreed in this. He again asked me whether I could think of nothing else to offer. I told him no. Whether there was nothing on the side of the Mississippi that I could offer. I told him nothing that I could think of except land, and that I did not think it would be worth the King's while to buy a hundred thousand pounds worth of land there, considering the immense territories he already possessed. He inquired whether I thought Congress would draw for the whole sum. I answered that it was in my opinion not improbable, for that they would consider the acceptance of ten or twelve thousand dollars as a prelude to further aids, naturally supposing, that if the King afforded us any supplies at all, they would be such as would correspond with his dignity, and not be limited to that little pittance. He desired me to meet him the next day at M. Del Campo's, which I promised to do.

In the evening M. Gardoqui again paid me a visit, and pointedly proposed my offering the navigation of the Mississippi as a consideration for aids. I told him that object could not come in question in a treaty for a loan of one hundred thousand pounds, and Spain should consider, that to render alliances permanent, they should be so formed as to render it the inter-

France, with whom we were allied, and who were richer than they; that the King must first take care of his own people, before he could supply us; that Spain had been brought into the war by our quarrel, but received no advantage from us; that they had been told of our readiness to assist in taking Pensacola, etc., but instead of aids, he had heard of nothing but demands from us; that our situation was represented as being deplorable, and that the enemy talked of the submission of some of the States, and of negotiations being on foot for that purpose.

Whether this style proceeded from natural arrogance, or was intended to affect my temper, I cannot say; in either case, I thought it most prudent to take no notice of it, but proceed calmly and cautiously, and the more so as this was the first time I had ever conversed with this man. I told him in substance, though more at large, that the assurances given Congress of the friendly disposition of Spain by M. Mirales and others had been confided in, and had induced Congress to expect the aids in question. That if this application could be called a demand, it was still the first they had made to my knowledge; that men in arms against the enemies of Spain were serving her as well as themselves, and therefore might without impropriety request her aid; that our separation from Britain was an object important to Spain, and that the success with which we had opposed her whole force for six years showed what the power of both, if under one direction, might be capable of; that I knew nothing of Spain's having been drawn

into the war by or for us, and that this was not to be
found among the reasons she had alleged for it; that
an attack on Pensacola could not be expected to be
made by troops actually employed in repelling the
enemy's assaults from their own doors, and that the
principles of self-defence would not permit or justify
it; that Spain had much to expect in future from our
commerce, and that we should be able as well as
willing to pay our debts; that the tales told of our
despondency and submission resulted from the policy
of the enemy, not from fact, and I believed no more
of their private negotiations between America and
Britain than I did of there being private negotiations
between Spain and Britain for a separate peace,
which the Minister assured me was not the case;
that if on the arrival of the bills I had been told
plainly that no money could be advanced, further
drafts would soon have been prevented; but that a
contrary conduct having been adopted, other expectations had been excited; that as to France, she had
done, and was still doing much for us, and that her
being our ally did not confer propriety upon every
request that we could make to her. He still pressed
this point, and complained that the greater part of
the money heretofore advanced by Spain had been
laid out in France. He saw that France was deriving great commercial advantages from us, but that
our commerce never would be an object with Spain,
because all her productions would find a better market in her own colonies. He desired a note of the bills
which had arrived, and then made some reflections on

the proposal of a treaty. We agreed perfectly well that mutual interest should be the basis of it, and I added, that the good opinion entertained of the King and nation by America was also a pleasing circumstance. He said, however that might be, America did not seem inclined to gratify Spain in the only point in which she was deeply interested. Here followed much common-place reasoning about the navigation of the Mississippi, of which your Excellency has heretofore heard too much to require a repetition. He spoke also much of the difficulties of Spain as to money matters, saying that their treasures in America could at present be of no use to them, as they had given orders that none should be sent home during the war, even if it continued these ten years ; and this was done in order, by stopping the usual current of specie into Europe, to embarrass the measures which Great Britain must take to obtain her necessary supplies. . . .

On the 13th of September, M. Gardoqui delivered me the following verbal message from Count de Florida Blanca : " That the exigencies of the State would not permit his Majesty to provide for the payment of more of the bills drawn upon me than had been already accepted." I expressed my regret that this had not been told me at first, and told him it appeared a little extraordinary that the Minister should employ himself and me three months in making and answering propositions relative to a loan, which it was not in his power to make. . . .

As the Count's message was a verbal one, and

might hereafter be denied or explained away as convenience might dictate, I thought it important to establish it, and for that and other reasons which need no explanation, I wrote the Count the following letter.

Sir :   St. Ildefonso, September 14, 1780.

The information I received yesterday from your Excellency by M. Gardoqui, has drawn the affair of the bills of exchange to a conclusion. He told me, that the exigencies of the State would not permit his Majesty to provide for the payment of more of those bills than were already accepted, amounting to about fourteen thousand dollars.

As it is important that every nation at war should know exactly the state of their resources, and as America has been induced to consider the friendship of his Catholic Majesty as among the number of hers, I must request the favour of your Excellency, to tell me frankly whether the United States may expect any, and what aids from Spain. The general assurances of amity, which that country has received from this, together with what has passed between your Excellency and myself relative to clothing for our troops, and supplies of specie in America, will I hope be considered as authorizing this question ; and the more so, as M. Gardoqui, to whose arrival your Excellency postponed the discussion of these matters, informs me he is not instructed to say any thing to me on these, or indeed any other subjects.

I have the honour to be, etc.,

John Jay.

The next day, the 15th of September, M. Gardoqui delivered to me a paper by way of answer to my letter of yesterday to the Minister. It is in these words:

ST. ILDEFONSO, September 15, 1780.

The following answer has been dictated to me in his Excellency's name by Don Bernardo del Campo, to be delivered to the honorable John Jay.

That it is not his Majesty's intention to stop assisting the States, whenever means can be found to do it, but that it will be impossible to supply them with money in Europe, there being none to spare, for that which ought to have come this year from America, has neither come, nor is it known when it will, and that which would have facilitated a far advanced negotiation is likely to produce no effect, in a great measure, *through the undermining of some persons of rank in France.*

The States not giving timely advice, nor having taken his Majesty's previous consent, he could not arrange his affairs beforehand, in order to assure the acceptance and payment of the bills they have drawn, for which reasons, and that Congress has not to this day given any tokens of a recompense, his Majesty might have just cause of disgust, but notwithstanding he does not, nor will change his ideas, and will always retain those of humanity, friendship, and compassion, that he has had towards the colonies. That consequently, if Mr. Jay or his constituents should find money upon credit, to the sum of one hundred or one hundred and fifty thousand dollars, that his Majesty will be answerable for the said sum, payable in the space of three years; that his Majesty will besides exert all that is possible to assist them with clothing and other things, and, finally, in order that his Majesty may extend his further dispositions, it is precisely necessary that they should give sure and effective tokens of a good correspondence, proposing reciprocal measures of a compensation that may establish a solid friendship and confidence, without reducing it to words and protests of mere compliment.

This being the substance, I would futher suggest to Mr. Jay's consideration, that the continuance of assisting the States by answering the sum expressed in a manner much more public than that of paying the money privately, shows plainly the sincerity of his Majesty, although the States have not to this day proposed any equivalent to the assistance already given, and to the expenses occasioned by a war, which had its true origin from them, to all which must be added, (though by the way no credit is given to it,) that there are hints of some understanding between the colonies and England.

JAMES GARDOQUI.

It is to be observed, that this paper when first delivered was not signed, and suspecting that this omission might not be accidental, I mentioned it to M. Gardoqui a day or two afterwards. After some hesitation, and doubts of its being necessary, he signed it. I made no remarks at all to M. Gardoqui on any part of this paper except the last article, which I treated with great indignation. . . .

Three days afterwards, I had a long and satisfactory conversation with the French Ambassador, in which he was very unreserved, candid, and confidential. He read to me part of a letter he intended to send to Count de Vergennes on our affairs, and justice calls upon me to say that we are obliged to him for it.[1]

---

[1] See Jay's letter to Vergennes, dated September 22, 1780, in which he reviews the situation at the Spanish Court, and appeals to France for financial aid.

MRS. GENERAL MONTGOMERY TO MRS. JAY.

NEW JERSEY, September 6, 1780.

DEAR COUSIN :

The singular satisfaction I hoped for in a correspondance with you is almost lost, since at the splendid Court of Madrid you have forgot the promise made. I however take too much pleasure in the idea to give it up without having by a line reminded you of it, and at the same time of a very sincere friend who loves you with affection, & who will continue to do so whether you write or not.

As every thing from you will be new so any thing from your own Country will be interesting tho' never so trivial in itself. I write to you from the battery (?) where I have found the whole family as happy as the Birth of a fine girl can make them—my Sister well and the Chancellor blessed. As this girl is designed for your Boy, whom I admire extremely, I can only pray that she may live to cement our familys in a still closer union. I saw your father well and very fat a few days since ; your mama is gone to live at Elizabeth Town with her Family.

Yesterday when informed from Camp of the Death of your Cozin William Alexander Livingston who received his Death from a Mr. Steeks in a Duel, there was buried at the same time in like circumstances a Mr. Peyton from Virginia. You may judge how fashionable dueling is grown when we have had five in one week and one of them so singular that I cannot forbear mentioning it. It happened between two Frenchmen who were to stand at a certain Distance and march up and fire when they pleas'd. One fired and missed ; the other reserving fire till he had placed his Pistol on his antagonist's forehead, who had just time to say, *Oh mon Dieu, pardonna moy*, at the same time bowing whilst the Pistol went off with no other mischief but singeing a few of his hairs.

Tell Harry to beware of engaging in a quarrel with the Dons in Spain—this dueling is a very foolish way of putting ones self out of the world. Mr. Jay at Fishkill is not as well as he has been I am told, tho all with him are so. Sir James is at Philadelphia and I hear solicitous to go to France.

Pray are you very distant from Lisbon and do you never see any one from that place? I have a Brother at the English ——— I feel the utmost tenderness for each individual of my lost Soldier's Family; and whilst life and memory are left me his loved Idea must ever retain my whole heart and fill it with regret that my every hope of happiness is no more. This is a subject that always obtrudes itself let me begin with what I will and unfits me for every other Duty. Then I am lost to all but this; but as I am not fond of appearing like a memento to my friends I generally have the strength of mind to quit my imployment before I have given them a turn of thought, that might perhaps throw them into the vapors. You have a Soul superior I know to this; you look forward doubtless to events like my misfortune with the eye of a Philosopher, and the mind of a Christian. May you never have occasion to exert either & for such a loss till age has blunted those fine feelings which when it happens in early life drives the sensible Soul to despair. Make my Compliments to M^r. Jay, Col. Livingston, and M^r. Morris. M^rs. Livingston sends her love to you & bids me tell you a hundred fine things of her daughter—but at present I can only say that I am

With much Esteem

Yours

J. MONTGOMERY.[1]

---

[1] Mrs. Janet Montgomery was the daughter of Judge Robert R. Livingston. In 1773 she married General Richard Montgomery, who fell in the assault upon Quebec, December 31, 1775.

JAY TO BENJAMIN FRANKLIN.

St. Ildefonso, 8th September, 1780.

Dear Sir :

.   .   .   .

I have received but one, and that an unimportant public letter, since I left Philadelphia. You cannot conceive how little information and how few letters reach me from our country. Whenever you write to me, send your letters either to the French embassador or under cover to Marquis D'Yranda. The post is the most precarious of all conveyances. No letters suspected to be for or from me pass safe by it ; many are suppressed and the remainder suspected.

Our affairs here go on heavily. The treaty is impeded by the affair of the Mississippi and the fate of my bills is not yet decided. I have been permitted indeed to accept to the amount of about $11,000, and this circumstance gives me more hopes for the rest than any thing else. The fact is there is little corn in Egypt—this *entre nous*.

Cumberland is here still. His hopes and fears (?) are secret. He went from here a few days ago and is soon expected back again. To what policy are we to ascribe this ? I am told we have nothing to fear ; it may be so, but my faith is seldom very extensive. If we have nothing else to fear we have always danger to apprehend from such a spy—so situated, so surrounded by inquisitive, communicative, and, some say, friendly Irishmen. In short, I wish you could hear me think. I must leave time to inform you of many things which at present must not be written.

Be so kind as to deliver the enclosed letters, and believe me to be with sincere regard and esteem,

Dear sir,

Your most obedient servant,

JOHN JAY.

JAY TO THE PRESIDENT OF CONGRESS.

ST. ILDEFONSO, September 16, 1780.

Sir :

This letter and several copies of it are to be sent by the next post to Bilboa, Cadiz, Nantes, etc. The object of it is to inform you that it is necessary immediately to cease drawing bills upon me for the present.

Your Excellency may soon expect a full detail of particulars, you will then receive an answer to every question that may be raised upon this letter.

His Catholic Majesty has been pleased to offer his responsibility to facilitate a loan of one hundred and fifty thousand dollars for us, payable in three years, and to promise us some clothing. This need not be kept secret. I have written several letters to your Excellency, but have received only one from the Committee since I left America. It covered the resolutions respecting these bills.

The Philadelphia bank, the ladies' subscriptions, and other indications of union and public spirit have a fine effect here.

I have the honour to be, etc.,

JOHN JAY.

JAY TO EGBERT BENSON.

St. Ildefonso, 17th September, 1780.

Dear Benson :

I have written many letters to my friends in the State of New York since I left America, but have not yet received a single line from any of them. Is not this a little hard ? Am I to suppose that all your letters have miscarried, or that your attention has been too much engaged by affairs at home to extend to an old friend abroad ? Whatever is the cause I assure you I regret it. While America continues the theatre of the war, it is natural to desire intelligence of what may be passing on it. This satisfaction I seldom enjoy though I often ought.

As few private opportunities offer of conveying letters to the other side, I frequently write by the post. This letter will go that way. It must therefore be proportionately reserved. Indeed I make it a rule to write on the subject of politics only to Congress, and though various other subjects present themselves, yet as it is not the fashion in this country either to let one's tongue or pen run very freely, I think it best not to be singular. Your government ought by this time to have received many of my letters and, I may add, have answered some of them. Has your legislature thought of their western country ? I incline to think it time. By no means sleep over Vermont. Our people would not apply the maxim, *obsta principiis*, at first ; further delays will be equally unwise especially considering the resolutions of Congress on that subject. I am told you have made R. Morris, Chief-Justice ; this is well. I had my apprehensions about this matter. In my opinion Duer should not be forgotten ; he is capable of serving the State, and it would be bad policy to let any useful man leave it who can be retained with advantage in it.

The State of New York is never out of my mind nor heart, and I am often disposed to write much respecting its affairs, but I have so little information respecting its present political objects and operations that I am afraid to attempt it. An excellent law might be made out of the Pennsylvania one for the gradual abolition of slavery. Till America comes into this measure, her prayers to Heaven for liberty will be impious. This is a strong expression, but it is just. Were I in your legislature, I would prepare a bill for the purpose with great care, and I would never leave moving it till it became a law or I ceased to be a member. I believe God governs this world, and I believe it to be a maxim in his as in our court, that those who ask for equity ought to do it. Remember me to my old friends.

I am very much yours,

JOHN JAY.

JAY TO T. MATLACK.

ST. ILDEFONSO, 17th September, 1780.

SIR :

Accept my thanks for your favour of the 21st April, which was delivered to me the 27th August. Knowledge is essential to the duration of liberty, and Pennsylvania is wise in making them both the objects of public care. I have read your oration with pleasure. The subject is a fine one, the field large, and you have interspersed it with useful remarks and entertaining reflections. I put it into the hands of the Count D'Estaing and the French ambassador. They both said civil things of it.

The society [1] have done me much honour by placing me on the list of their members. I shall endeavour to evince the sense I have of it, by now and then sending them whatever I may find here worth their attention.

I congratulate you on the glorious spirit spreading from your city through America. Your bank is the subject of much conversation and encomium, and the patriotism of the ladies renders them very celebrated. Such marks of union and public spirit are worth a victory. To be respectable abroad we must be respectable at home, and the best way to gain friends is to be formidable to our enemies. But you know these things as well as I do, and I am persuaded your endeavours will not be wanting to place our country in both these points of light. Dr. Foulke may rely on my omitting no opportunity of being useful to him; we must take care of young Americans. Much depends on the rising generation, and no pains should be spared to render them equal to the task that devolves upon them.

Be assured that it will give me pleasure to continue this correspondence, and that I am, sir,

Your most obedient and humble servant,

JOHN JAY.

[1] The American Philosophical Society, Philadelphia.

JAY TO KITTY LIVINGSTON.

ST. ILDEFONSO, 18th September, 1780.

You are really a charming correspondent as well as a charming every thing else. We have had more letters from you than from all our other friends in America put together. I need not tell you, therefore, that I am proportionately the more obliged to you, and you will easily conceive how much pleasure it gives me to be obliged by one who has so great a share in my esteem and regard.

Sally is at Madrid. She intended to write you a long letter, and I dare say has done so. I won't repeat what I am sure she must have told you. I often wish you were with us for our sake, and as often am content that you are not for yours. We go on tolerably well, flattering ourselves that we shall not long be absent, and anticipating the pleasures we are to enjoy on our return. . . .

How does my dear little boy do? I hope he goes on well. Tell me a good deal of those matters which you may readily suppose I have a curiosity to know, and the more you say of yourself the better I shall like your letters. I expected Judy would have written us a wedding letter, but I presume she has been too much engaged by a nearer correspondent to think of those on this side the ocean. Present my congratulations and best wishes to the doves. Billy, I suppose, continues as *unusual* as ever. How does Susan do? Give us the history of your late retreat from Elizabethtown. I fancy you began to think there was some weight in my objections to your being there. I am a little afraid that you had given up the house at Persippany ; if so, you have been puzzled.

Do you hear from Fishkill ? I have not since I have been here. I wish you would endeavour to get and send me some news of the family there ; they are either too lazy or their letters very unfortunate. My love to the whole household of Liberty Hall.

JAY TO COUNT DE VERGENNES.

St. Ildefonso, September 22, 1780.

Sir :

I have never taken up my pen with so much reluctance as I now do, although my design is to write a letter to your Excellency. But, Sir, there are few sensations more painful than those which they experience who, already covered with benefits, are impelled by cruel necessity to ask for more. Such is my present situation, and hence proceeds my regret.

My uniform and unreserved communications to the Count Montmorin, who has my fullest confidence, precludes the necessity and consequently the propriety of a minute detail of American affairs here.

Your Excellency will recollect the resolution of Congress for drawing bills on me, as well as the reasons assigned for that measure. In my first conference with the Minister on that subject, he enlarged on the necessities of the State, but nevertheless told me he should be able, at the end of the present or beginning of the next year, to advance thirty or forty thousand pounds sterling, and that further arrangements respecting the residue should then be made.

I afterwards received and answered propositions for the reimbursement of this money ; and from time to time was permitted to accept such of the bills as were most pressing.

Things remained in this state till the 5th of July, when, after many warm assurances of friendship and good-will, the further discussion of these matters was postponed by the Minister until the arrival of a person intended to succeed M. Mirales, the late Spanish agent at Philadelphia, and I was told that they should then be arranged and adjusted.

Several weeks elapsed after the time assigned for his arrival had expired. The holders of the bills became importunate, and insisting on my accepting or refusing them.

I wrote several letters to the Minister, requesting his directions, but was not favoured with an answer to any of them.

On the 3d instant, after fruitless endeavours to see the Minister, I received the following note from him by the hands of M. Gardoqui :

"The Count de Florida Blanca sends his compliments to Mr. Jay, and advises him to become acquainted with the bearer of this letter, who is the person that has been expected from day to day."

This gentleman made many remarks tending to show the propriety of America's offering some specific consideration for this money, and hinted at the navigation of the Mississippi, ship timber, vessels, tobacco, etc., etc. I replied that the only consideration Congress could offer was that which all other nations at war, who borrowed money, offered, viz., to repay the principal with a reasonable interest after the war; that I should deceive him, were I to enter into contracts to pay it sooner; that the proposition of paying it during the war, in ship timber, tobacco, or other articles, did not lessen the difficulty, for that these things were worth and cost money in America as well as in Europe; and that as to the Mississippi, it could not come in question as a consideration for one hundred thousand pounds. The conversation was concluded by his desiring me to meet him at M. Del Campo's the next morning. M. Gardoqui then, and since, behaved with temper, candour, and politeness.

The next day we saw M. Del Campo. He was liberal in his censures on the measure of drawing the bills in question on Spain. He informed me that the King must first take care of his own people before he gave supplies to others; that Spain, instead of deriving advantage from America, heard of nothing but demands. That if Congress wanted money, they should have drawn on France, with whom they were in alliance, and who had all the profit of their trade; that we ought to have distinguished between our allies and those who only wished us well, and that applications for aid might be proper to the one, which were not so to the other; that our affairs were in a ruinous condition, and that it was even said some of the States were holding secret negotiations for peace with the enemy, etc., etc., etc. My replies were such as the subject naturally suggested, and as prudence dictated ; there are seasons when men mean not to be convinced, and when argument becomes mere matter of form. On such occasions, we have little more in our power than moderation and temper. I gave M. Del Campo credit for his frankness, and wish I could with propriety have extended it to his delicacy.

A day or two afterwards, viz., the 6th instant, I was permitted to accept bills to the amount of one thousand one hundred and ten dollars.

On the 13th, M. Gardoqui, by order of the Minister, told me that the exigencies of the State would not permit the King to provide for the payment of more of the bills than had been already accepted, amounting to about fourteen thousand dollars. This gave occasion to my letter to the Minister of the 14th, and to his answer of the 15th, which was dictated by him to M. Del Campo, and by M. Del Campo to M. Gardoqui, copies of both of which your Excellency will receive from Count Montmorin. The Minister's answer made a conference between us expedient. I requested that favour the 15th instant, and have been informed that the Count de Florida Blanca will endeavour to see me on Saturday evening next.

I forbear remarks on this singular conduct. I wish it could be explained in a manner compatible with the reputation Spain enjoys in North America. I much fear partial resentments, which ought not to affect America, have been permitted to have an undue degree of influence, and that the Minister forgot, in his zeal for a certain scheme of finance, that it was unjust to wound opponents through the sides of their friends. But whatever may have been the cause, the effect, unless removed, will be destructive, and France only can at present afford the means of doing it.

When I consider, on the one hand, that France was our first, and is still our best, and almost only friend; that she became our ally on terms of equality, neither taking, nor attempting to take ungenerous advantages of our situation; that she has clothed and armed our troops, and is at this moment assisting us with her fleets, her armies, her treasure, and her blood; gratitude and generosity forbid me to solicit a further tax on her magnanimity. But, on the other hand, when I reflect that the loss of American credit would be a loss to the common cause, and an eventual injury to France; that such an event would be a matter of triumph to our common enemy, and of pain to our friends; that the honour of Congress, suspended on the fate of these bills, now hangs as it were by a hair, and that our enemies here and elsewhere are doing all in their power to cut it; when I consider, that America would feel more sensibly the loss of reputation in this instance, than the loss of battles in many others; I say, Sir, when I consider these things, I find it to be my duty to request your Excellency to interpose the amity of France, and that his Majesty will be pleased to add this strong link to the chain of benefits, by which he has already bound the affections of America to his family and people.

I ought to inform your Excellency, that bills for about fifty thousand dollars remain unaccepted. The greater part of these are in the hands of merchants, who waited my answer with a degree of patience, I could not have expected ; some of them ever since the month of June last. Further delays, therefore, were not to be asked or obtained, and I was reduced to the necessity, either of promising to accept them, or permit the credit of Congress to perish with them. I could not long hesitate. I promised to accept them. Fortunately, these bills have hitherto come on slowly, though, it is probable, that the assurances of Spain, which I have communicated to Congress, may quicken their pace. A period, however, will soon be put to their drawing, as I have written to them by several conveyances immediately to stop.

I ought also to inform your Excellency, that a promise made me in June last of some clothing for our troops has been renewed, and that his Majesty has been pleased to offer us his responsibility to facilitate a loan of one hundred and fifty thousand dollars. I shall endeavour to make the most of this offer, and your Excellency may rest assured that I shall gladly embrace every measure, which may be calculated to lessen the weight with which the American cause presses on the finances of France.

I have the honour to be, etc.,

JOHN JAY.

NOTES OF CONFERENCE BETWEEN JAY AND FLORIDA BLANCA.[1]

St. Ildefonso, September 23, 1780.

After the usual civilities, the Count began the conference by informing Mr. Jay that the Court had

[1] Respecting previous conferences, see notes to letters of May 11 and June 7, 1780, *ante*.

received intelligence from the Havana, of Congress having so far complied with the request made to them to permit the exportation of provisions for the use of his Majesty's fleets and armies there, as to give license for shipping three thousand barrels of flour, circumstances not admitting of further supplies at that time ; that this business was conducted by Mr. Robert Morris in a manner with which he was well pleased ; that Congress had also, in order to promote the success of the Spanish operations against Pensacola, etc., agreed to make a diversion to the southward, to detach a considerable body of regular troops and militia to South Carolina under General Gates ; that his Majesty was well pleased with, and highly sensible of, these marks of their friendly disposition, and had directed him to desire Mr. Jay to convey his thanks to them on the occasion.

Mr. Jay expressed his satisfaction at this intelligence, and promised to take the earliest opportunity of conveying to Congress the sense his Majesty entertained of their friendship, manifested by these measures. He told the Count it gave him pleasure to hear the business of the Spanish supplies was committed to Mr. Robert Morris, and assured him that the fullest confidence might be reposed in that gentleman's abilities and integrity. He requested his Excellency again to assure his Majesty that he might rely on the good disposition of Congress, and of their evincing it in every way, which the situation of their affairs and the interests of the common cause might render practicable and expedient. The Count told

Mr. Jay that he had proposed to the French Ambassador to send to Congress, for the use of their army, clothing for ten regiments lately taken in the convoy bound from Britain to Jamaica, and in which the two Crowns were equally interested ; that the Ambassador approved the proposition, but had not yet given his final answer. He then observed that a negotiation for peace between Britain and Spain appeared at present more distant than ever ; that the former had offered his Majesty every thing he could desire to induce him to a separate peace ; but that the King, adhering to the same resolutions in favour of America, which had influenced his conduct in his mediation for a general peace and since, had rejected them, and that Congress might rely on his Majesty's determination never to give up or forsake America, but on the contrary continue affording her all the aids in his power.

He told Mr. Jay that the Court of London, disappointed in their expectations of detaching Spain, had it in contemplation again to send Commissioners to America to treat with Congress on the subject of an accommodation with them ; that this measure was at present under the consideration of the Privy Council, and that there was reason to suppose it would be adopted. He observed that the English had hitherto discovered much finesse and little true policy ; that first they endeavoured by their intrigues in France, to separate that kingdom and America, but not succeeding there, they sent Commissioners to America ; that the last year they attempted to detach France, and this year Spain, and that being unsuccessful in both they would again attempt America; that the best way of defeating their designs was mutual confidence in each other. He remarked that America could not rely on any promise of Britain, and asked, if she was once detached from France and Spain, who could compel an observance of them? Mr. Jay thanked the Count for this communication, and assured him that Congress would not only adhere to their engagements from motives of interest, but from a regard to their honour, and the faith of treaties; that the opinion of Congress on this subject corresponded with that of his Excellency, and that their conduct, with respect to the former English Commissioners, gave conclusive evidence of their sentiments on the subject. Mr. Jay promised in case he received any intelligence relative to this matter, his Excellency might depend on its being communicated immediately to him.

The Count appeared satisfied with this, and again repeated his former assurances of the King's good disposition towards America, etc., etc.

Mr. Jay informed his Excellency that the subject on which he was desirous of conversing with him, arose from the paper he had received from M. Gardoqui the 15th instant, containing his Excellency's answer to Mr. Jay's letter of the 14th.

Mr. Jay then requested the Count to communicate to his Majesty his thanks for the offer he had been pleased to make, of his responsibility in order to facilitate a loan of one hundred and fifty thousand dollars, and also for the promise of clothing, etc., etc., and to assure him that the gratitude of the States would always be proportionate to the obligations conferred upon them ; he observed to the Count that he intended to attempt this loan in Spain, France, and Holland, and begged to be informed in what manner he should evidence the responsibility of his Majesty to the persons who might be disposed to lend the money, for that in this and other similar cases he meant to be guided by his Excellency's directions. The Count replied that as this matter fell within the department of M. Musquir, the Minister of Finance, he would consult him upon it on Tuesday evening next, and immediately thereafter inform Mr. Jay of the result.   He then apologized and expressed his regret for not being able to furnish the money he had expected to supply (alluding evidently to the *thirty or forty thousand pounds* which, in the conference at Aranjues, the 11th day of May last, he said he expected to be able to supply by the end of this or beginning of next year).   He said he had been disappointed in the remittances expected from America, for he was advised that two ships which he had expected would arrive from thence with treasure in December or January next would not come, and that this and other circumstances rendered it impossible for him to advance us any money in Europe.   But that he would, nevertheless, agreeably to the King's intentions, give us all the assistance in his power.

. Mr. Jay desired to be informed whether any steps were necessary for him to take for forwarding the clothing at Cadiz to America. The Count answered that he waited the French Ambassador's answer on the subject, and that he had as yet no inventory of them, but that he would again speak to the Ambassador, and make arrangements for sending them on to America as soon as possible.

Mr. Jay then proceeded to regret that the pleasure he derived from these instances of his Majesty's friendship to the United States was mingled with pain from being informed by the above-mentioned paper, that the King conceived he might have just cause to be disgusted with them.

Because, 1st, they had drawn the bills of exchange without his previous consent; and, 2dly, because they had not given any tokens of a recompense. Mr. Jay reminded his Excellency that these bills were drawn upon himself, and not on Spain, and although that Congress might have hoped, for reasons already assigned, to have been enabled to pay them by a loan from his Majesty, yet that every other usual measure was left open for that purpose. That an application to Spain for such a loan could give no just cause of offence, for that if it had not been convenient to her to make it, all that she had to do was to have told him so, and he was then at liberty to take such measures for procuring it elsewhere as he might think proper. The Count replied that what Mr. Jay observed was true, but that certainly the bills were drawn with an expectation of their being paid by Spain, and that this might probably have been done if previous notice of the measure had been given.

That he always intended to have done something towards their payment, but had been prevented by disappointments, and the exigencies of the State. Mr. Jay continued to observe that the second cause assigned for this disgust, viz., that Congress had given no tokens of a recompense must have arisen from a mistake. He reminded his Excellency that he had never requested a donation from Spain, but that, on the contrary, he had repeatedly offered to pledge the faith of the United States for the repayment with interest, within a reasonable time after the war, of whatever sum his Majesty might be so kind as to lend them. To these remarks the Count said only that interest for the money would have been no object with them ; that they would gladly have lent it to us without interest, and repeated his regret at the disappointment which had prevented them. He appeared rather uneasy and desirous of waiving the subject.

Mr. Jay next called the Count's attention to a part of the paper in question, which informed him " that there were hints (though no credit was given to it) of some understanding between America and the Court of London." He observed that this subject was both delicate and important ; that so far as this understanding related to Congress, or the governments of either of the States, he was sure that this insinuation was entirely groundless ; that there might possibly be intriguing individuals who might have given cause to such suspicions ; that if there were such men or bodies of men it would be for the good of the common cause that they should be detected and their designs frustrated. He therefore requested that if his Excellency had any evidence on this subject he would be pleased to communicate it, and thereby enable him to give Congress an opportunity of taking such measures as circumstances might render proper. The Count said he had nothing specific or particular as yet to communicate ; that he was pursuing measures for further discoveries, and that he would mention to Mr. Jay whatever information might result from them.

Mr. Jay resumed his animadversions on the paper in question by observing that it assured him it was necessary " that Congress should give sure and effective tokens of a good correspondence, proposing reciprocal measures of a compensation, etc., in order that his Majesty might extend his further dispositions towards them." That for his part he could conceive of no higher tokens, which one nation could give to another of friendship and good-will, than their commissioning and sending a person for the express purpose of requesting his Majesty to enter into treaties of amity and alliance with them, and that on terms of reciprocity of interest and mutual advantage. To this the Count replied that to this day he was ignorant of these terms, and that no particular propositions had been made him. Mr. Jay then reminded him of his letters from Cadiz, and of the conference on the subject at Aranjues on the 2d day of June last, in the latter of which, after conferring on the subject of aids, and of the treaty, his Excellency had promised to reduce his sentiments on both to writing, and send him notes on each ; that as to the first, Mr. Jay had received the notes, but not on the last ; that he had been in constant expectation of receiving them, and that delicacy forbade pressing his Excellency on that matter, or offering any thing further till he should have leisure to complete them.

He said he thought he had given them to Mr. Jay or Mr. Carmichael, which both of them assured him he had not. Of this the Count appeared after a little time satisfied, when Mr. Jay resumed the subject by remarking that the order of conducting that business appeared to him to be this : that as a right was reserved by the Secret Article to his Majesty to accede to the treaty between France and America whenever he thought proper, and that the latter would go into a discussion of any alteration the King might propose that should be founded on reciprocity of interest, the first question was, whether his Majesty would accede to it as it was, or whether he would propose any and what alterations.

The Count here interrupted Mr. Jay by saying that the interest of France and Spain with respect to America were so distinct as necessarily to render different treaties necessary. Mr. Jay answered, that admitting this to be the case, the treaty with France might be made the basis, and then go on *mutatis mutandis*. The Count proceeded to say that it would not conduce to the general pacification to hurry on the treaty ; that finding Congress were not disposed to cessions, without which the King would not make a treaty, he thought it best, by mutual services and acts of friendship, to continue making way for more condescensions on both sides, and not excite animosities and warmth by discussing points which the King would never yield. That, therefore, Mr. Jay might take time to write to Congress on the subject, and obtain their instructions.

He said that previous to Mr. Jay's or M. Gerard's arrival at Madrid, M. Mirales had informed him that Congress would yield the navigation of the Mississippi, but that M. Gerard informed him that Congress had changed their resolution on that subject ; that he had mentioned these obstacles to Mr. Jay and Mr. Carmichael, and it was probable that having done this, he had neglected or forgotten to give Mr. Jay the notes in question. Mr. Jay here reminded his Excellency that the conference between them of the 2d day of June last turned among other points on these obstacles, and that they had then mutually expressed hopes that regulations calculated to remove them in a manner satisfactory to both parties might be adopted, and that the conferences respecting them were concluded by his Excellency's promising to give Mr. Jay notes of his sentiments on the proposed treaty. The Count admitted this, and made several observations tending to show the importance of this object to Spain, and its determination to adhere to it, saying, with some degree of warmth, that unless Spain could exclude all nations from the Gulf of Mexico, they might as well admit all ; that the King would never relinquish it ; that the Minister regarded it as the principal object to be obtained by the war, and *that obtained*, he should be perfectly easy whether or no Spain procured any other cession ; that he considered it far more important than the acquisition of Gibraltar, and that if they did not get it, it was a matter of indifference to him whether the English possessed Mobile or not ; that he chose always to speak his sentiments plainly and candidly on those occasions, for which reason he generally acted differently from other politicians, in always choosing to commit himself to paper, and appealing to the knowledge of the French Ambassador and others, who had done business with him, for the proofs of this being the principle of his conduct. He concluded by saying he would give his sentiments in writing on this subject to Mr. Jay.

Mr. Jay made no reply to the Count's remarks on the navigation, but observed that, being little acquainted with the practice of politicians, he was happy in having to treat with a Minister of his Excellency's principles. He added that there were many points necessary to be adjusted in order to a treaty ; that they might proceed to agree upon as many as they could, and with respect to the others he should state them clearly to Congress, and attend their further instructions.

Mr. Jay then again turned the conference to the paper before-mentioned, by observing to the Count that it appeared from it that the King also expected from Congress equivalents to the supplies formerly afforded, and also the expenses of the war, which it alleged had its origin from them ; that as to the first he could only repeat what he had before said, that a general account of them was necessary ; that he neither knew the amount of them, nor the terms on which they were granted ; that it was a transaction previous to his appointment ; that on being furnished with the necessary information he would transmit it to Congress, and wait their instructions ; that an expectation of an equivalent to the expenses sustained by Spain in the war was inadmissible on every principle. He read the passage in question, and remarked that America could no more be justly chargeable with the expenses of the war sustained by Spain, than Spain could be justly chargeable with the expenses of the war sustained by America. The Count replied, that Mr. Jay had mistaken his meaning, and that he urged it merely to show that as the States were deriving considerable advantages from very expensive operations on the part of Spain, that consideration should incline them to more condescension towards the latter.

Mr. Jay assured his Excellency that he knew it to be the disposition of Congress to contribute all in their power to the success of the common cause, and that they would on every occasion give proofs of it, and among others that he was confident they would permit his Majesty to export from thence, *during the war*, ship-timber and masts for the royal navy, and would readily consent to such measures as might be proper and necessary for facilitating it. He further observed that, having been informed by M. Gardoqui

that his Majesty would like to take and finish a
seventy-four gun ship now on the stocks in one of
the eastern ports, on which it was said no work was
doing, he would with pleasure write to Congress and
propose their transferring her to his Majesty's at
prime cost ; that this previous step was necessary,
as Congress might perhaps intend that vessel for particular services, but he was confident they would otherwise be happy in indulging his Majesty's inclinations.
The Count appeared pleased with this. He said that
with respect to timber they stood most in need at
present of yards, and should be glad to obtain a
supply of them from Congress ; that as to the ship,
he wished to be informed exactly of her present state,
and the materials wanted to complete and equip her,
which he observed might be sent from the Havana,
and whether a crew of Americans could be had to
navigate her there. Mr. Jay replied, that though he
was sure that Congress would readily give their aid
in these and other matters interesting to Spain, yet
he could not forbear reminding his Excellency, as a
friend, that public business done under the direction
of public bodies was always more expensive than when
done by individuals. That, therefore, he would submit it to his consideration whether it would not
be more advisable to commit the management of
these affairs to the agent intended to succeed M.
Mirales, who, by being on the spot, would have opportunities of acting on exact information, and in a
manner more consistent with the views of his Excellency. The Count agreed in this opinion, and prom-

ised to communicate to Mr. Jay his further intentions on this subject.

Mr. Jay informed the Minister that as his further stay there would now be unnecessary, and business called him to Madrid, he purposed to return there on Monday next. The Count concurred and the conference ended.

Congress will permit me to observe that many things in this conference are important, and demand instructions. I forbear to point them out, because they are obvious; and I take the liberty of giving this hint from a knowledge of the delays attending the proceedings of large bodies.[1]

I returned to Madrid on the day appointed; and whether to accept or not to accept the bills became a very serious question. After reviewing all the reasons for and against it, which are numerous, and which Congress will readily perceive without a particular enumeration, I determined to put a good face on the business, and accept all that should be presented, which I have accordingly done, and am daily doing. What the event will be I cannot pretend to decide. All that I can say is, that my endeavours shall not be wanting to render it successful. The responsibility of the King will not produce much, and the difficulty of borrowing money has been increased, by the number of agents sent to Europe for that purpose by

[1] As previously stated, the account of this conference and Jay's criticisms form a part of his second report to Congress, dated November 6, 1780.

several of the different States, who I am told have imprudently bidden on each other.

M. Gardoqui returned to Madrid a few days after I did, and brought me word from the Minister, that instructions should be sent to their Ambassadors in Holland and France, to assure in due form the responsibility of the King to such persons as might there incline to lend us money on the credit of it, and that the Minister would do the same here. He told me further that the Minister hoped I would not be discouraged, nor consider things only on the dark side, for that it was still his intention to afford America every aid in his power. All this I ascribe to the exertions of America, and I am confident that it will always be necessary for the United States to be formidable at home, if they expect to be respectable anywhere.

For my own part, I shall be disappointed if I find Courts moving on any other principle than political ones, and, indeed, not always on those. Caprice, whim, the interests and passions of individuals, must and will always have greater or less degrees of influence. America stands very high here, at present. I rejoice at it, though I must confess I much fear that such violent exertions may be followed by languor and relaxation. What the plan of this Court is with respect to us, or whether they have any, is with me very doubtful. If they have rejected all the overtures of Britain, why is Mr. Cumberland still here? And why are expresses passing between Madrid and London through Portugal? If Spain is determined that we shall be independent, why not openly declare us so, and thereby diminish the hopes and endeavours of Britain to prevent it? She seems to be desirous of holding the balance, of being in some sort a mediatrix, and of courting the offers of each by her supposed importance to both. The drawing of bills on me was considered as a desperate measure, prompted by our imbecility, and was a bad card to play at a time we were endeavouring to form a treaty, and when prudence demanded that the importance of Spain to us should not have been brought forward, or placed in such a glaring point of view.

One good consequence, however, has resulted from it. The cordiality of Spain has been tried by it. For I know of a certainty, that it was in her power easily to have made the loan we asked. Indeed, we shall always be deceived, if we believe that any nation in the world has, or will have, a disinterested regard for us, especially absolute monarchies, where the temporary views or passions of the Prince, his Ministers, his women, or his favourites, not the voice of the people, direct the helm of State. Besides, from the manner in which the war is carrying on, it would seem as if it was the design of France and Spain that the longest *purse*, not the longest *sword*, should decide it. Whether such be really their intention, or how far it may be politic, I cannot pretend to determine. This, however, is certain, that it would be putting the affair on a hard issue for us. It is also certain, that some respect is due to appearances and probable events, and we should be cautious how we spend our money, our men, or our public spirit, uselessly.

In my opinion, we should endeavour to be as indedent on the charity of our friends, as on the mercy of our enemies. Jacob took advantage even of his brother's hunger, and extorted from him a higher price than the value of the Mississippi even for a single dinner. The way not to be in *Esau's* condition, is to be prepared to meet with *Jacob's*.

From what I can learn of the King's character, I am persuaded that a present from Congress of a handsome fast-sailing packet-boat would be very acceptable, and consequently very useful.

I am informed, and believe, that a loan from individuals in France is impracticable. Here nothing can be done in that way. What may be expected from the like attempts in Holland, I am unable to say.

I have received no answer to my letter to Count de Vergennes; the Ambassador informs me that the Count has written him on the subject, and the following is an extract from his letter.

[Translation.]

" I doubt whether I shall be able to render Mr. Jay the service he requests of me, independently of what the Ministry has furnished the Americans in the course of the year. Dr. Franklin is urgent for a million extra, to meet the drafts of Congress to the 31st of December. I am sensible how important it is to prevent them from being returned protested, but the difficulty is to find the means. I shall do my best in this exigency, but am not sure of success; beyond this, it would be impossible for me to go."

BENJAMIN FRANKLIN TO JAY.

DEAR SIR :   PASSY, October 2, 1780.

I received duly and in good order the several letters you have written to me of August 16th, 19th, September 8th, and 22d. The papers that accompanied them of your writing gave me the pleasure of seeing the affairs of our country in such good hands, and the prospect, from your youth, of its having the service of so able a minister for a great number of years. But the little success that has attended your late applications for money mortified me exceedingly ; and the storm of bills which I found coming upon us both, has terrified and vexed me to such a degree that I have been deprived of sleep, and so much indisposed by continual anxiety, as to be rendered almost incapable of writing.

At length I got over a reluctance that was almost invincible, and made another application to the government here for more money. I drew up and presented a state of debts and newly-expected demands, and requested its aid to extricate me. Judging from your letters that you were not likely to obtain any thing considerable from your court, I put down in my estimate the 25,000 dollars drawn upon you, with the same sum drawn upon me, as what would probably come to me for payment. I have now the pleasure to acquaint you that my memorial was received in the kindest and most friendly manner, and though the court here is not without its embarrassments on account of money, I was told to make myself easy, for that I should be assisted with what was necessary. Mr. Searle arriving about this time, and assuring me there had been a plentiful harvest, and great crops of all kinds ; that the Congress had demanded of the several States contributions in produce, which would be cheerfully given ; that they would therefore have plenty of provisions to dispose of ; and I being much pleased with the generous behaviour just experienced, presented another paper, proposing, in order to ease the government here, which had been so willing to ease us, that the Congress might furnish their army in America with provisions in part of payment for the services lent us. This proposition, I was told, was well taken ; but it being considered that the States having the enemy in their country, and obliged to make great expenses for the present campaign, the furnishing so much provisions as the French army might need, might straiten and be inconvenient to the Congress, his majesty did not at this time think it right to accept the offer. You will not wonder at my loving this good prince: he will win the hearts of all America.

If you are not so fortunate in Spain, continue however the even good temper you have hitherto manifested. Spain owes us nothing ; therefore, whatever friendship she shows us in lending money or furnishing clothes, etc., though not equal to our wants and wishes, is however *tant de gagne ;* those who have begun to assist us, are more likely to continue than to decline, and we are still so much obliged as their aids amount to. But I hope and am confident, that court will be wiser than to take advantage of our distress, and insist on our making sacrifices by an agreement, which the circumstances of such distress would hereafter weaken, and the very proposition can only give disgust at present. Poor as we are, yet as I know we shall be rich, I would rather agree with them to buy at a great price the whole of their right on the Mississippi, than sell a drop of its waters. A neighbour might as well ask me to sell my street door.

I wish you could obtain an account of what they have supplied us with already in money and goods.

Mr. Grand, informing me that one of the bills drawn on you having been sent from hence to Madrid, was come back unaccepted, I have directed him to pay it ; and he has at my request, undertaken to write to the Marquis D'Yranda, to assist you with money to answer such bills as you are not otherwise enabled to pay, and to draw on him for the amount, which drafts I shall answer here as far as 25,000 dollars. If you expect more, acquaint me. But pray write to Congress as I do, to forbear this practice, which is so extremely hazardous, and may, some time or other, prove very mischievous to their credit and affairs. I have undertaken, too, for all the bills drawn on Mr. Laurens, that have yet appeared. He was to have sailed three days after Mr. Searle, that is, the 18th July. Mr. Searle begins to be in pain for him, having no good opinion of the little vessel he was to embark in.

We have letters from America to the 7th August. The spirit of our people was never higher. Vast exertions making preparatory for some important action. Great harmony and affection between the troops of the two nations. The new money in good credit, etc.

I will write to you again shortly, and to Mr. Carmichael. I shall now be able to pay up your salaries complete for the year; but as demands unforeseen are continually coming upon me, I still retain the expectations you have given me of being reimbursed out of the first remittances you receive.

If you find any inclination to hug me for the good news of this letter, I constitute and appoint Mrs. Jay my attorney, to receive in my behalf your embraces. With great and sincere esteem,

I have the honour to be, dear sir,

Your most obedient and most humble servant,

BENJAMIN FRANKLIN.

INSTRUCTIONS FROM CONGRESS TO JAY.

In CONGRESS, October 4th, 1780.

On the report of a committee to whom were referred certain instructions to the delegates of Virginia by their constituents, and a letter of the 26th of May, from the

Honorable John Jay, Congress unanimously agreed to the following instructions to the Honorable John Jay, Minister Plenipotentiary of the United States of America, at the Court of Madrid.

That the said Minister adhere to his former instructions, respecting the right of the United States of America to the free navigation of the river Mississippi into and from the sea; which right, if an express acknowledgment of it cannot be obtained from Spain, is not by any stipulation on the part of America to be relinquished. To render the treaty to be concluded between the two nations permanent, nothing can more effectually contribute, than a proper attention, not only to the present but the future reciprocal interests of the contracting powers.

The river Mississippi being the boundary of several States in the union, and their citizens, while connected with Great Britain, and since the revolution, having been accustomed to the free use thereof, in common with the subjects of Spain, and no instance of complaint or dispute having resulted from it, there is no reason to fear, that the future mutual use of the river by the subjects of the two nations, actuated by friendly dispositions, will occasion any interruption of that harmony which it is the desire of America, as well as of Spain, should be perpetual. That if the unlimited freedom of the navigation of the river Mississippi, with a free port or ports below the 31st degree of north latitude, accessible to merchant ships, cannot be obtained from Spain, the said Minister in that case be at liberty to enter into such equitable regulations as may appear a necessary security against contraband; provided the right of the United States to the free navigation of the river be not relinquished, and a free port or ports as above described be stipulated to them.

That with respect to the boundary alluded to in his letter of the 26th of May last, the said Minister be, and hereby is instructed, to adhere strictly to the boundaries of the United States as already fixed by Congress. Spain having by the treaty of Paris ceded to Great Britain all the country to the northeastward of the Mississippi, the people inhabiting these States, while connected with Great Britain, and also since the revolution, have settled themselves at divers places to the westward near the Mississippi, are friendly to the revolution, and being citizens of these United States, and subject to the laws of those to which they respectively belong, Congress cannot assign them over as subjects to any other power.

That the said Minister be further informed that in case Spain shall eventually be in possession of East and West Florida, at the termination of the war, it is of the greatest importance to these United States to have the use of the waters running out of Georgia through West Florida into the Bay of Mexico, for the purpose of navigation; and that he be instructed to endeavor to obtain the same, subject to such regulations as may be agreed on between the contracting parties; and that as a compensation for this, he be and hereby is empowered to guarantee the possession of the said Floridas to the Crown of Spain.

THE PRESIDENT OF CONGRESS TO JAY.

PHILADELPHIA, Oct. 6, 1780.

DEAR SIR:

I am honoured with your kind favour of the 28th of May with the prints which your lady has been pleased to present to Mrs. Huntington.

Be assured, Sir, it gave me much pleasure to find yourself and family safe arrived at Madrid after a dangerous and tedious passage; and that it is peculiarly acceptable to Mrs. Huntington to receive those prints from so amiable a personage as was pleased to bestow them.

Congress have been pleased to signify their desire that I should continue in the Chair another year, but the burden and fatigue of the business, to which you are no stranger, makes me doubtful whether I can endure it much longer.

Mrs. Huntington joins with me in compliments to yourself and lady. Wishing health and happiness may attend your person and family, and your embassy be crowned with honour and desired success.

> I am most sincerely yours,
> SAM^L. HUNTINGTON.

JAY TO LE COULTEUX & CO.[1]

MADRID, October 15, 1780.

GENTLEMEN :

I have been honoured with your favour of the 3d instant, and am much obliged by your attention to the letter it enclosed. You were not mistaken in supposing that the handwriting was mine. That letter was enclosed in one for Mr. Harrison, and sent under cover to you.

It gives me concern to find that you have so much trouble with American seamen, and I much lament that it is not in my power to comply with the terms on which alone you incline to continue it. I have written more than once to Congress on the subject, and submitted to their consideration the propriety of establishing proper regulations for the conduct of that business, but as yet I have received none. I presume that their attention has been so

---

[1] A mercantile firm at Cadiz which had agreed to return destitute American seamen to their country.

engaged by other matters of higher and more pressing importance, as not to have had leisure for making these arrangements. The refusal of American captains to give passages to their unfortunate countrymen is certainly unkind. I shall communicate to Congress, and I hope proper measures will be taken to remove that obstacle. At any rate, however, I cannot leave these unhappy captives friendless, in a strange country. The unfeeling treatment of the captains rather stimulates than represses my commiseration, and, therefore, gentlemen, as it is not convenient to you to proceed in your care of them, but on terms not in my power to comply with, I find myself reduced to the necessity of requesting that favour from others. For this purpose I have written to Mr. Harrison of your city, and proposed his undertaking it, and have desired him, in case he consented, to mention it to you. On that event I must beg the favour of you to give him such information and advice as may be useful to him in the management of those affairs. Be pleased also to liquidate your accounts with him ; they shall be paid without further delay.

The attention and kind offices you have regularly paid to Americans, and the personal civilities that myself and family experienced from you, while at Cadiz, will always continue to excite my warmest acknowledgments, and lead me to omit no opportunity of convincing you of the esteem and regard with which I am, gentlemen, etc.

JOHN JAY.

JAY TO BENJAMIN FRANKLIN.[1]

MADRID, 25th October, 1780.

DEAR SIR:

Your very agreeable and friendly letters I have received, and shall take an early opportunity of answering fully. I have no reason as yet to think a loan here will be practicable. Bills on me arrive daily. Be pleased to send me a credit for residue of our salaries. America rises in the general estimation here.

Tell Mr. Deane I have received four of his letters and written three to him. He may expect to hear from me again soon.

Prince Masserano sets out for France early in the morning. I had intended to devote this afternoon and evening to writing by him, but have been prevented by company. It is now late at night, and I can say little. I am much indebted to the politeness of this nobleman, and except at his table, have eaten no Spanish bread that I have not paid for since my arrival in this city. This circumstance will, I flatter myself, recommend him to your particular attention, which I have reason to think would be very acceptable, for the respect and esteem which he frequently expresses for you. The Duke of Crillon who accompanies the Prince has also been polite to us, and I fancy they will both receive pleasure from finding me sensible of their attentions. The Princess appears to me to have much merit. I regret her absence, and

---

[1] From Hale's "Franklin in France," Part I., p. 416.

the more so, perhaps, as it will not be supplied. She is a lady of much observation and discernment. God bless you, my dear sir.

JAY TO JAMES LOVELL.

MADRID, 27th October, 1780.

DEAR SIR:

Your letter of the 11th July gave me much pleasure ; there is a degree of ease and cordiality in it which, as a mere letter of business, it did not require. I am the more obliged to you for it.

It is true that I might write to Congress very often, indeed by every vessel, and there are many of them, but how are my letters to get to the seaside ? By the post ? They would be all inspected, and many suppressed. There is scarce a man in any of the ports, except Mr. Harrison, at Cadiz, with whom I would trust them ; so that if under different covers I could get them there, the danger would not end. To write often, and write nothing material, would be useless ; and when you see my public letter by this opportunity, you will perceive that to be well understood I must write a great deal. I would throw stones, too, with all my heart, if I thought they would hit only the committee without injuring the members of it. Till now I have received but one letter from them, and that not worth a farthing, though it conveyed a draft for one hundred thousand pounds sterling on the bank of hope. One good private correspondent would be worth twenty standing committees, made of the wisest heads in America, for the purpose of intelligence. What with clever wives, or pleasant walks, or too tired, or too busy, or do *you* do it, very little is done, much postponed, and more neglected.

If you, who are naturally industrious and love your country, would frequently take up your pen and your ciphers, and tell me how the wheel of politics runs, and what measures it is from time to time turning out, I should be better informed, and Congress better served. I now get more intelligence of your affairs from the French Ambassador than from all the members of Congress put together.

I had written thus far when I received a letter from Mr. Le Coulteux, at Cadiz, enclosing a letter of the 16th of September, written at St. Ildefonso from me to Congress. It had been enclosed in one to Mr. Harrison, and that again put under cover to Mr. Le Coulteux, and under these two covers was put into the post-office. Now mark its fate. The director of the post-office at Cadiz showed it to Mr. Le Coulteux, naked and stripped of its two covers, of which he made no mention. He said it came from Bayonne, but Le Coulteux, knowing my handwriting, paid the postage and returned it to me.

This is only one among the many instances of the fate to which my letters are subjected. To avoid it I must now be at the expense of sending Colonel Livingston to the seaside with my despatches.

I am, dear sir,

Your most obedient servant,

JOHN JAY.

JAY TO BENJAMIN FRANKLIN.

MADRID, 30th October, 1780.

DEAR SIR:

The pleasure given me by your letter of the 2d instant may more easily be conceived than expressed. I am greatly obliged by your attention to my embarrassments. In my last on that subject which you received, was a copy of my letter to Count de Vergennes, from which it appeared that the sum I should have occasion for would probably be considerable, and far exceeding 25,000 dollars. Bills to the amount of 100,000 dollars have arrived. A loan cannot be effected here. What the Court will do is as yet uncertain, and will long continue so. I should have replied to your letter before, but as I daily expected to hear from Count de Vergennes, I waited, with a view of mentioning the import to you. The enclosed copy of a note I received from Count Montmorin contains all the advices I have on that head. My situation continues unpleasant, and though my endeavours are not wanting to better it, future events are too uncertain to be relied upon. To be active, prudent, and patient is in my power; but whether I shall reap as well as sow and water, God only knows.

I have often been told of the former supplies, and asked how they were to be reimbursed. My answer has uniformly been, that I knew neither their amount nor terms, and that I wished to be furnished with an account of both, etc., etc. As yet I have not been able to obtain it.

Some mistake must have given occasion to any of

the bills drawn on me being returned without acceptance. The fact is, that though I often delayed (with
the consent of the holders), yet I never refused to
accept any of them.

I have written several letters to Congress, requesting them to forbear drawing further bills till proper
funds should be established for their payment. Mere
contingent assurances, or flattering inferences drawn
from flattering expressions, ought never to be considered as a sufficient foundation for serious measures.

Cornwallis, it seems, has cropped some of Gates'
laurels ; and Mr. Laurens is in the Tower. European
politicians will, I suppose, though often deceived in
the same way, again think America on her knees in
the dust. Had Ternay been supported, the campaign
would have had a different termination. Much money
and spirit has been wasted by this disappointment Of
the latter, indeed, we shall never be in want, and I
should be happy if the like could be said of the former.
The conduct of France towards us has been friendly ;
and though I cannot forbear to think she has been
too inattentive to this object, my gratitude towards
her is not impaired by it. I regret it as a misfortune,
not blame it as a designed omission.

I wrote to you last week, and now enclose a dupli-
cate of another letter. You may rely on my reim-
bursing you the advances on account of our salaries,
out of the first remittances I receive.

I have often congratulated my country and myself
on your being at present in France. I once expected
to have seen you there, and to have profited by the

lessons which time and much experience have taught you. Miracles have ceased, and my constitution does not promise length of days, or I should probably desire you, when you ascend, to drop me your mantle. That you may long retain it is one of the prayers of

Your friend and servant,

JOHN JAY.

JAY TO GOUVERNEUR MORRIS.

MADRID, 5th November, 1780.

DEAR MORRIS :

Three of your letters have reached me ; the last was of the 12th July. Some of mine to you were worth little, and their miscarriage was of no consequence ; there was one from Madrid, which I wish may come to your hands ; it was interesting.

Where are you ?—what are you doing ? Achilles made no figure at the spinning-wheel. The State of New York I take to be your field ; if prudently cultivated, it will yield much. Letters, though the best, are poor substitutes for conversation ; but we must be content. I wish to hear many things of and from you.

Mrs. Jay is in tolerable health ; she has had a fine little daughter, but she is gone home, and I am resigned. I have it in charge from Mrs. Jay to say many friendly things to you. Drawing bills on me was impolitic in many respects. The navigation, etc., is strongly insisted on. Many fair promises of aids, delays unavoidable or designed, the Court undecided and waiting events; the British courting them. Why was not Ternay supported? Depend on yourselves principally. The French Ambassador here has excellent intelligence from your city. I know but little of what passes among you, and shall be obliged to you for such traits of public and private matters as you may think interesting. I have had some letters from Deane; he is much displeased with what he thinks the duplicity of certain persons, who in particular I don't know; he is endeavouring to establish here a bargain with Mirales about masts, and talks of coming here;—how did you and he part?

Should this find you at Philadelphia, remember me to my friends there. I know you, and therefore am, and will be cordially,

Your friend,

JOHN JAY.

JAY TO ROBERT MORRIS.

MADRID, 19th November, 1780.

DEAR SIR:

I have lately received a letter from Francis Child, a lad whom I had taken by the hand after his father's death, and put apprentice to Mr. Dunlap, your printer. He complains that Dunlap refuses to give him the clothes stipulated in the indentures, and requests that I will save him from nakedness. You will oblige me by giving him twenty-five hard dollars, or the amount of it in paper. If you can conveniently discover how he behaves and is likely to turn out, I beg you will inform me ; for, as his father had a warm and steady attachment to me, I feel myself interested in the welfare of the son, who it seems was his favourite.

My friend, you are not a little indebted to me on the score of letters. Only one has reached me. I am content to go on writing two or three for one, but really you must let us hear sometimes of you and Mrs. Morris. There are some hearts which, like feathers, stick to every thing they touch, and quit each with equal ease. Mine is not one of this kind ; it adheres to few, but it takes strong hold ; you must, therefore, write to me ; and if you would make your letter very agreeable, dwell on the objects you will find at or near the hills, and within your own walls. Mrs. Jay writes by this opportunity to Mrs. Morris, whom she loves and esteems for many reasons unnecessary to repeat to you.

Should the following cipher reach you safe, we may afterward write with less reserve. Entick's Spelling Dictionary, printed in 1777, paged backwards. The last page in the book is numbered 468. Let this be page the first, and mark the first page (which is the title-page) 468. Count the words from the top, distinguishing the columns by a [.] over the first figure for the first column, and a [.] over the second figure for the second column. For instance, the word *absent* is the fifth word in the *first* column of the 434th page, and is to be thus written : 5.434.

Remember me to your friends, Mr. and Mrs. Mease,

and your other usual guests near the hills. I wish I had a few such honest, open-hearted companions here. God bless you.

I am, dear sir, very sincerely, your friend, etc.,

JOHN JAY.

JAY TO EGBERT BENSON, ESQ.

MADRID, November, 1780.

DEAR BENSON :

There seems to be a spell in the pens of my friends in New York. Except Livingston, I have not had a line from either of them since I left America ; not even from either of my brothers, nor from you, who also are several letters in my debt. I have a favour to ask of you ; it is that you would make a visit to my father, and send me a minute account of his health, and that of the family. Make a half dozen copies of your letter, and send them either to some friend at Boston, or to Mr. Robert Morris, at Philadelphia, to be forwarded in different vessels. Don't neglect to do me this friendly office. You can easily conceive how painful it is to be so long in ignorance and suspense about the situation and welfare of persons so near and dear to me as many of those are to whom I allude. Tell me also how your mother and brothers do ; and believe me to be, as I have long been, your

Affectionate friend,

JOHN JAY.

JAY TO GENERAL SCHUYLER.

MADRID, November 25, 1780.

DEAR GENERAL :

As there is reason to believe that you are still in Congress, I refer you for the political state of affairs here to my public letters, which you will find long and particular.

I am a little apprehensive, as the great exertions of America during the last campaign have not produced correspondent events, that either relaxation or divisions may succeed. They are both to be dreaded, and therefore, if possible, to be avoided. The defensive part which Mr. d'Ternay was obliged to act for want of reinforcements may have made impressions to the disadvantage of our allies. On this subject I have good authority to assure you that the commanding officer of the French fleet in the Islands had orders to afford him aid on his application. Whether such application was made, or, if made, why not complied with, I am uninformed. I have also good reason to believe that plans in favour of America are now under consideration at Versailles. What they will be, or whether they will ever be adopted, I cannot pretend to say. At any rate, it appears to me of great importance that no distrust of our allies appear ; and though prudence may teach us to rely chiefly on ourselves, yet it ought to be remembered that one of the most certain methods of destroying friendship is to entertain suspicions of its sincerity. The greatest attention is doubtless paid to the Marquis de Lafayette and other French officers ;

their representations will have great weight in France.

I was happy to find your name among those of the committee sent to camp. This was a wise measure. The most severe economy in the expenditure of public money will, I hope, be observed. The credit of the United States has, both at home and abroad, been so heavily and perhaps imprudently laden that care should be taken lest the strength should become inadequate to its burdens.

The loss of Charleston had a wonderful effect here, and the ill consequences resulting from it had no sooner been removed by the subsequent glorious efforts of America, than the defeat of General Gates again turned the tide against us; and the more so as the small and unequal number of troops by whom that victory is said to have been achieved gave occasion to remarks much to our disadvantage. I am impatient to see the Congress account of that disaster; it has not yet made its appearance, and Cornwallis' letter still remains uncontradicted, except by ship news, which, in such cases, is seldom greatly regarded.

Gibraltar continues closely besieged, and unless soon relieved (which is not very improbable), will be greatly straitened. This is an expensive expedition, and the object of it may, in my opinion, be more easily and speedily gained in America than in Spain.

I received a letter this morning from Holland informing me that Mr. Laurens was still closely confined, but that his health was much mended. I hope you

are looking out for a proper object of retaliation.
The honour as well as the interest of the States demand it, and I am persuaded such a proper and
spirited step would have a favourable influence on our
affairs in Europe, especially if done in a manner
consistent with the dignity and justice of Congress.
There is reason to fear that all his papers fell into
the enemy's hands. Copies of letters (found among
them) from Mr. d'Neufville to Congress were sent
to the Stadtholder, and occasioned much noise, but
that gentleman and his party avowing them firmly, it
soon subsided.

The Dutch, I believe, will remain pacific. They
have too much in the funds to risk; and some of
them seem surprised that Congress should be at a
loss for money while the produce of the country
continues greatly to exceed the consumption of its
inhabitants.

Adieu—I am, dear sir, very sincerely yours, etc.,

JOHN JAY.

JAY TO THE PRESIDENT OF CONGRESS.

MADRID, November 30, 1780.

Your Excellency will receive herewith enclosed
certain papers from Morocco, viz. : . . .

These papers ought to have been sent with my
letters of May last, but recollecting, as I was about
to put them up, that if the originals should be lost
on the passage it might be difficult to obtain others,
I thought it most prudent to detain them to be cop-

ied, and wait for some other opportunity of getting them to the sea; none has, however, since occurred, and I did not think them of sufficient importance to render it necessary that either Mr. Carmichael or Colonel Livingston should carry them to one of the seaports.

It is proper that your Excellency should be informed that on the 8th instant I had a conference with the Minister at the Escurial, in which I received many good *words* and friendly assurances, but time only can decide how they will terminate. I received a letter yesterday from Mr. Harrison, of the 24th instant, and then no orders had arrived about the clothing. These delays may seem singular, but they are not uncommon. Mr. Cumberland [1] is still here. The French and English fleets are at sea.

Although appearances are not very flattering at present, I hope they will in time become more so. Patience, prudence, and perseverance sometimes effect much. It is in my opinion very important that no dissatisfaction be expressed in America at the conduct of Spain. Complaint and disgust can answer no good purpose, but may be productive of many disagreeable consequences. A cautious silence is the more necessary, as I am confident that there are persons in America who would make a merit of collecting and transmitting the sentiments of Congress, or *members* of Congress, on subjects interesting to the views and objects of persons in power here.

Colonel Livingston would have returned this fall at

---

[1] One of Lord Germaine's secretaries.

the expiration of the term expressed in his leave of absence, had I not taken the liberty of advising him to remain, and taken upon myself to adjust this matter with Congress. As he is employed and industrious in obtaining knowledge which may enable him to be useful in future to his country, I must join with him in requesting that Congress will be so kind as to extend his leave of absence to such further period as may be agreeable to them.

The enclosed paper, marked No. 6, is a copy of a state of the revenues and expenditures of Spain, in the year 1778. It was formed by a secretary to one of the embassies, and a copy of it was given to Mr. Carmichael. I received it the last day of July, and had no safe opportunity of sending it before. What credit may be due to this account I cannot determine, and I have reason to think that there are few men in the kingdom who can. This government, disposed to concealment and mystery in most matters, will not probably permit an accurate knowledge of their revenues to be easily attained. This account is perhaps as near the truth as any other. The gentleman, it is said, took much pains in forming it, and it also met with the approbation of some foreign Ministers; but how far those Ministers were judges of the subject I am uninformed. The remarks subjoined to this account are Mr. Carmichael's, and were added to the copy I received from him.

I send copies of several letters which passed between Messrs. de Neufville and Son, of Amsterdam, and myself, relative to the bills drawn on Mr. Laurens. The conduct of that House has been so friendly and disinterested that I think Congress should be particularly informed of it, and by taking proper notice of it induce others to follow the example.

I have the honour to be, etc.,

JOHN JAY.

JAY TO THE COMMITTEE OF FOREIGN AFFAIRS.

MADRID, November 30, 1780.

GENTLEMEN :

I have had the honour of receiving from you a letter of the 16th of June, and another the 12th of July, 1780, with the several papers mentioned in them. With respect to the subjects of the first, you will find them fully discussed in my letter to the President of Congress, which will accompany this. The description of the bills will, I hope, answer good purposes.

How far the resolution, which immediately follows the one respecting Mr. Dohrman, can be fully executed, is hard to determine. Had I funds necessary for the purpose, I should meet with few difficulties. The measure is a wise one, and my attention to it shall be unremitted. In a future letter I shall say more on this subject ; as yet nothing has had time to ripen.

I must request your attention to the necessity of putting your correspondence with the public servants in Europe on a better footing. I am now at the expense of sending Colonel Livingston to the seaside with my despatches, with orders to wait for American vessels, and deliver them to the captain with his own hands. I receive no letters by the post, but with marks of inspection, and after much delay. Some that I write never come to hand, and I know of letters having arrived from America for me, which I have never seen, and never expect to see. I know of but one man at the seaports whom I can confide in, viz., Mr. Harrison, at Cadiz. I cannot even find a courier that I can depend on. Is it not time for America, like other nations, to provide against these inconveniences by proper regulations and establishments? Would it not be well to have American agents or consuls in one or more of the ports of France and Spain? Public despatches might be sent by packet-boats, or other vessels, to these agents, and should on no account be delivered to any other person; the agents might be ordered to send them to the Courts to which they may be directed by a trusty American—one of the officers of the ship, for example; and he should be ordered to wait for, and return with, the despatches of the Minister.

Would it not also be proper to provide for the safe-conduct of letters to Congress after their arrival in America? I have reason not only to suspect, but to believe, that certain persons in America are attentive to these matters, and care should be taken to keep American letters out of their way.

This is an important subject and merits attention. For my own part I find several persons here who have more intelligence from America than myself; and it is the more mortifying when considered that they are probably often indebted for their information to the contents of letters directed to me.

I have the honour to be, etc.,

JOHN JAY.

JAY TO SILAS DEANE.

MADRID, 26th December, 1780.

DEAR SIR:

At length your first letter, contrary to my expectations, has arrived, and my attention to it shall not be wanting. I have also received your favour of the 18th September; since which more of my letters than one have, I hope, reached you, this being the fourth.

I have read, considered, and reconsidered the facts and reflections you communicate, and am persuaded that the consequences you draw, though in a certain degree just, are not quite so extensive as you seem to suppose. I am not free from similar apprehensions, but they are not so strong as yours. But however well founded they may be, they ought only to increase our prudence. If I had leisure, it would give me pleasure to go largely into this subject; at present I cannot, because matters of more immediate importance engage me.

That you have been hardly treated I know, and shall never hesitate to say; but I cannot think the cases of the gentlemen are similar, or prove the points to which you apply them. You was blamed, not for omitting finally to settle your accounts in France, but for not being in *capacity* to show (when in America) what those accounts were; and I don't know that those gentlemen were or will be chargeable with the like incapacity. I mention this only to show the distinction between the cases.

How far the distinction is important, or how far that incapacity could justify the treatment it occasioned, are other questions. For my own part I think it could not justify it. It will also remain a question how far your measures were prudent. I think some of them were, and some not; but this inquiry requires many considerations, and combinations, and circumstances, which I must defer for the present. The discoveries you allude to respecting secret practices surprise me exceedingly; I have no such suspicions: perhaps you may give more weight to circumstances than they may merit. The inquiry nevertheless is very important, and while any doubts remain, the pursuit should be continued. Justice demands that we should not even in our opinions injure men who may be innocent; and prudence also demands that we permit not a good heart to impose on a good head, —a case by no means uncommon.

I wish there were twenty other motives than those you mention for your passing to Spain, exclusive of the satisfaction it will give me to see you. The matters you mention are highly interesting in a public and a private view. They cannot be so well handled in letters as conversation. Whether it will be in my power to meet you I cannot predict, and therefore cannot promise. It would be agreeable, but I have hitherto found so many matters not to be neglected constantly demanding my attention, that I cannot flatter myself with being more disengaged till the greater objects of my coming here shall be either attained or become unattainable. If I should nevertheless be able, I will ; if not, I hope you will come on.

The attachment you express for your country, notwithstanding your complaints of her ingratitude, does you much honour. The injustice of resenting on a whole people the mistakes or transgressions of a few is obvious ; but there are comparatively not many who, under similar circumstances, either think right or act so. Truth is seldom so immersed in darkness as not to be capable of being brought to light if attempted in season ; and as the mass of the people mean well, they will finally do justice, though their mistakes and passions sometimes delay it. Persevere therefore, do good to your country, and evince the rectitude of your conduct while in her service. I believe you honest, and I think you injured. The considerations will always prompt me to every friendly office in my power to render. I must again advise you to collect, review, and ascertain precisely the evidence you may have or can obtain of the duplicity of the persons you allude to, whoever they may be. I see this business in many important lights, and the time may come when you may rejoice in all the trouble you may now be at about it. Nay, all this evidence, provided it should appear material, ought to be committed to paper, and not permitted to diminish or die in or with your memory ; put it in the power of your friends to vindicate your reputation when you may be no more. It will be of particular importance to your son, to whom you cannot leave a better inheritance than a good, nor a worse one than a bad or doubtful, reputation. Remember too that time is spending, men forgetting or dying, papers wasting, etc., and therefore the sooner you reduce these matters to a certainty the better.

Mrs. Jay and the Colonel desire to be particularly remembered to you. This will go under cover to Dr. Franklin. Be pleased to assure him of my regard and esteem, of which also believe you have no little share.

I am, dear sir, very sincerely yours, etc.,

JOHN JAY.

JAY TO ELBRIDGE GERRY.

MADRID, 9th January, 1781.

DEAR SIR :

I should have much wondered what could have detained my letter, mentioned in yours of September last, so long from you, had not my correspondence been strangely interrupted ever since my arrival.

Your Constitution gives me much satisfaction. It appears to me to be, upon the whole, wisely formed and well digested. I find that it describes your State as being in New England, as well as in America. Perhaps it would be better if these distinctions were permitted to die away.

Your predictions respecting the fate of Lord Cornwallis have, thank God! been verified. It is a
glorious, joyful, and important event. Britain feels
the force of that stroke, and other nations begin to
doubt less of the continuance of our independence.
Further successes must prepare the way for peace ;
and I hope that victory will stimulate instead of re-
laxing our exertions.

Although myself and family have most severely
suffered by the Continental money, I am resigned to
its fate. Provided we preserve our liberty and independence, I shall be content. Under their auspices,
in a fruitful country, and by patient industry, a com-
petence may always be acquired, and I shall never
cease to prefer a little with freedom, to opulence
without it.

Your account of the plenty which abounds in our
country is very flattering, and ought to excite our
gratitude to the Hand that gives it. While our governments tax wisely, reward merit, and punish offen-
ders, we shall have little to fear. The public has
been too much a prey to peculation. Economy and
strict accounts ought to be, and continue, among the
first objects of our attention.

I have not heard any thing for a long time respecting our disputed lines. In my opinion, few things demand more immediate care than this subject ; and I
differ from those who think that such matters had
better be postponed till after the war. At present, a
sense of common danger guarantees our union. We
have neither time nor inclination to dispute among

ourselves. Peace will give us leisure, and leisure often finds improper occasions for employment. I most sincerely wish that no disputes may survive the war ; and that, on the return of peace, we may congratulate each other on our deliverance and prospects of uninterrupted felicity, without finding ourselves exposed to differences and litigations, which never fail to make impressions injurious to that cordiality and confidence which both our interest and our duty call upon us to cultivate and cherish.

Mrs. Jay charges me to present her compliments to you. I am, dear sir, with great and sincere esteem, your most obedient and very humble servant,

JOHN JAY.

INSTRUCTIONS FROM CONGRESS TO JAY.

IN CONGRESS, February 15th, 1781.

SIR :

Congress having since their instructions to you of the 29th of September, 1779, and 4th of October, 1780, relative to the claim of the United States to the free navigation of the river Mississippi, and to a free port or ports below the thirty-first degree of north latitude, resumed the consideration of that subject, and being desirous to manifest to all the world, and particularly to his Catholic Majesty, the moderation of their views, the high value they place on the friendship of his Catholic Majesty, and their disposition to remove every reasonable obstacle to his accession to the alliance subsisting between his Most Christian Majesty and these United States, in order to unite the more closely in their measures and operations three powers who have so great a unity of interests, and thereby to compel the common enemy to a speedy, just, and honorable peace ; have resolved, and you are hereby instructed to recede from the instructions above referred to, so far as they insist on the free navigation of that part of the river Mississippi, which lies below the thirtyfirst degree of north latitude, and on a free port or ports below the same; provided such cession shall be unalterably insisted upon by Spain; and provided the free navigation of the said river, above the said degree of north latitude, shall be acknowledged and guarantied by his Catholic Majesty to the citizens of the United States in common with his own subjects. It is the order of Congress, at the same time, that you exert every possible effort to obtain from his Catholic Majesty the use of the river aforesaid, with a free port or ports below the said thirtyfirst degree of north latitude for the citizens of the United States, under such regulations and restrictions only, as may be a necessary safeguard against illicit commerce.

I am, etc.

SAMUEL HUNTINGTON, *President.*

END OF VOLUME I.